Elections and Democracy after Communism?

ELECTIONS AND DEMOCRACY
AFTER COMMUNISM?

Erik S. Herron

palgrave
macmillan

ELECTIONS AND DEMOCRACY AFTER COMMUNISM?
Copyright © Erik Herron, 2009.

First published in 2009 by PALGRAVE MACMILLAN® in the United States—a division of St. Martin's Press LLC, 175 Fifth Avenue, New York, NY 10010.

Where this book is distributed in the UK, Europe and the rest of the world, this is by Palgrave Macmillan, a division of Macmillan Publishers Limited, registered in England, company number 785998, of Houndmills, Basingstoke, Hampshire RG21 6XS.

Palgrave Macmillan is the global academic imprint of the above companies and has companies and representatives throughout the world.

Palgrave® and Macmillan® are registered trademarks in the United States, the United Kingdom, Europe and other countries.

ISBN: 978-0-230-60095-9

Library of Congress Cataloging-in-Publication Data is available from the Library of Congress.

A catalogue record of the book is available from the British Library.

Design by Scribe Inc.

First edition: June 2009

10 9 8 7 6 5 4 3 2 1

Printed in the United States of America.

To Lea and Carter.

Contents

ILLUSTRATIONS

FIGURES

TABLES

PREFACE

Several events that occurred in late 2007 illustrate the contradictory trajectories of the post-Soviet states in the development of functional democracy and meaningful elections. As Ukrainian officials were counting the ballots cast in the second consecutive free and fair parliamentary election, Russian President Vladimir Putin announced his intention to lead the United Russia party's candidate list in the December 2007 election. Putin's announcement was accompanied by speculation about how he would maintain power in Russia: through the Prime Minister's seat after constitutional changes rendering that position more powerful; after a staged abdication by his newly selected Prime Minister, Viktor Zubkov; or through some other political machinations. The contrast was stark. Whereas the results of the Ukrainian election were uncertain and destined to impact the country's political course, the upcoming election results in Russia were preordained, and their impact on policymaking would be minimal.

The elections and their aftermath continued to illustrate the sharp differences in governance between Russia and Ukraine. After Ukraine's late September election, the parliament slowly, deliberately, and controversially moved toward government formation. Political developments in the capital were punctuated by rumors about party defections, charges of attempted bribery, assertions that parliament's work would be blocked by a dissatisfied minority, and accusations of improper conduct during the selection of the speaker and prime minister. The political theater in Kyiv prompted some observers to characterize Ukraine's politics as anarchic, and this perception extended to Russia, where a Levada Center poll indicated that 27 percent of Russians considered Ukraine to be chaotic and disorderly.[1]

Instead of chaos, Russian voters were rewarded with order. The parliamentary election-cum-referendum on Putin as "national leader" yielded a constitutional majority for the president's United Russia party. While three other parties entered parliament, only one could be considered a true opposition group. After the 2007 parliamentary election, the sole voice in Russia's parliament challenging the sitting government was the successor to the Communist Party of the Soviet Union.

Russia and Ukraine's contradictory trajectories were further illustrated by events a few weeks later. At the same time that Yuliya Tymoshenko was being vigorously questioned by members of Ukraine's parliament over her nomination as a candidate for the post of prime minister, Putin's chosen successor for the presidential office, Dmitriy Medvedev,[2] called for Putin to become prime minister of Russia following the March 2008 presidential election. After Medvedev's victory, Putin took the helm of the United Russia party and accepted the post of prime minister with overwhelming parliamentary support. In Ukraine, Tymoshenko's initial bid to be prime minister fell short in a vote that was marred by allegations of falsification, but she eventually claimed the post. However, her tenure was marked by discord and disunity among the ruling coalition and challenges from opponents.

Trajectories change in post-Soviet politics. But, as the twentieth anniversary of communism's fall in Eastern Europe approached—an event presaging the collapse of the Soviet Union—Russia moved toward a new form of authoritarianism while Ukraine stumbled down the path toward democracy. The question mark in the title of this book—*Elections and Democracy after Communism?*—reflects the contradictions of the post-Soviet era illustrated by the stories of Russia, Ukraine, and their fellow successor states.

At the collapse of communism in the Soviet Union at the end of 1991, hope was high for democracy's introduction to Eastern Europe and Eurasia. While the initial euphoria was tempered by the region's internal and sometimes bloody conflict, economic chaos, and the continued prominence of "old guard" elites, optimists continued to find positive signs that the democratization process was accelerating across the postcommunist world throughout the 1990s. By the end of the twentieth century, the dialogue had changed. Instead of discussing an inevitable democratic triumph, scholars began dissecting variation in postcommunist political outcomes: how authoritarian and semiauthoritarian regimes became entrenched in many post-Soviet states.

Research for this book began when the democratization paradigm dominated the comparative politics literature. Dual training in (Soviet) area studies and comparative politics prompted me to explore developments in institutional design and its consequences across post-Soviet space, emphasizing elections. This book reflects the broadly comparative focus fostered by my education and professional experiences. I do not deeply describe all countries and elections but rather attempt to assess trends across the region.

Despite the fact that over a decade and a half has transpired since the USSR's demise, the post-Soviet states still provide an ideal setting for comparison. The people and institutions of all fifteen countries were significantly affected by the Soviet Union, although the duration of their membership in the "brotherhood of socialist republics" varied, with some spending over seven decades under communist rule, others only five. All were swept up in the rhetoric of democratization, and all have been judged by citizens, international organizations, the media, and scholars based on their progress toward fair, functioning institutions and the rule of law. Elections are key components of this evaluation.

In democratic states, elections determine who rules. Election rules outline the basic parameters of the game: who can compete, how voters may be courted and counted, how votes are translated into seats, and who is responsible for overseeing and adjudicating the process. If all goes as planned, after engaging in direct competition for voters' support, politicians accept the results; serve as members of government, the loyal opposition, or private citizens; and begin planning for the next election cycle.

While elections are a necessary condition for democracy, the practice of elections is not sufficient to qualify a state as democratic. Authoritarian rulers often engage in electoral exercises to legitimize their rule, and liberalizing autocrats have used elections to increase legitimacy and build support for reform efforts. But, dictators sometimes find that elections they believe are controlled in fact are unpredictable and yield unwanted outcomes.

The collapse of communist rule from 1989 to 1991 created a conducive environment for the extension of electoral democracy eastward. However, with the exception of the Baltic states, the region had little practical experience with real multiparty elections.[3] Mikhail Gorbachev's reforms generated semicompetitive elections in the late 1980s, but they fell short of the criteria for free and fair contests. As the USSR dissolved, its former constituent parts lacked developed civil societies and party systems as well as tested democratic electoral institutions.

Into the void descended teams of Western experts, academics, and democracy-assistance practitioners invited by influential political entrepreneurs or seeking audiences with them. Local political actors also studied international practices to inform their design of new rules. The task before them was monumental. Politicians with no formal experience in democratic governance had to craft a set of laws and ancillary provisions that would determine who could compete and how they would compete. Uncertainty often reigned, generating disputes among political allies over the optimal set of election rules. Despite the challenges, founding elections were held over the first half of the 1990s.

Election "events" have occurred in every post-Soviet state. Some elections have been farcical exercises serving as a façade over continued authoritarian rule, others have been competitive races marred by fraud and manipulation, and a few have been free and fair contests. This book assesses the evolution of elections, their rules, and their consequences since the collapse of the Soviet Union. It is driven by an overarching puzzle: to what extent do post-Soviet elections exemplify or defy general theory and findings in the electoral studies literature? Over the next ten chapters, I introduce questions about elections and assess them using data from post-Soviet cases:

- How are election rules chosen, and how do they affect outcomes?
- How do citizens decide if and for whom they should vote?
- How do political parties function?
- How do officials manipulate the campaign environment and commit fraud, and what are the consequences of these actions?

The first two chapters set the context for the book's analytical chapters. Chapter 1 focuses on defining concepts used throughout the book by addressing several questions: What are elections? What is democracy? How do elections differ in democratic and authoritarian systems? How have post-Soviet states progressed in the democratization process? What schools of thought help to explain observable outcomes? Chapter 2 is a primer on the institutional and behavioral features associated with the Soviet electoral experience, and outlines the sources for legacies that may affect post-Soviet politics.

The next five chapters cover major questions in the electoral studies literature and present analyses drawing upon data from parliamentary, presidential, and referendum votes. Chapter 3 covers the dynamics of electoral system design. The chapter begins with a review of founding elections rules and an assessment of election rule change across the region. It concludes with analytic narratives dissecting the abandonment of mixed electoral systems in Russia and Ukraine. The inter- and intraregional analyses featured in Chapter 4 assess how election rules and contextual features determine the size and shape of party systems. Chapter 5 focuses on individual citizens, addressing what motivates them to participate in elections. The chapter includes individual- and aggregate-level analyses of the determinants of turnout in post-Soviet elections. Chapter 6 turns to political parties, assessing their organizational forms and activities. The chapter investigates party turnover from election to election and how citizens identify their preferred parties. Direct democracy is the subject of Chapter 7, and it features an assessment of referendums that have been held in the region.

The final three analytical chapters cover topics that have received less attention in the electoral studies literature. Chapter 8 outlines the architecture of elections, addressing the functions of electoral commissions, courts, and election observers. The quality of elections is the focus of Chapter 9, and the chapter highlights methods to detect election fraud and manipulation. The analysis in Chapter 10 evaluates the connection between elections and political protest, identifying features of successful and unsuccessful protest movements sparked by allegations of election fraud. The book concludes with an evaluation of findings and an agenda for future research. Additional information is available at http://vse-na-vybory.blogspot.com.

ACKNOWLEDGMENTS

This book is the result of more than a decade of interest in and research on elections in the former Soviet states. I have been the fortunate recipient of outstanding mentorship and extensive help over the years at home and abroad. At the University of Kansas, Ron Francisco and Paul Johnson deserve special thanks. Ron provided extensive comments on the manuscript and collaborated with me on a conference paper that evolved into Chapter 10. Paul Johnson's skills were instrumental in acquiring precinct-level data in Ukraine, and he collaborated with me on research that inspired Chapter 9. Through their hard work and professionalism, the staff of the Center for Russian, East European, and Eurasian Studies at the University of Kansas (Ray Finch, Kyle King, Bill London, and Tatyana Wilds) helped me find time to work on research while I served as director. I also received research assistance and helpful comments from KU undergraduate and graduate students, including Lauren Buckner, Cristian Cantir, Laura Lucas, and Irakli Mirzashvili.

Colleagues outside of the University of Kansas helped me on all aspects of the manuscript. Brian Silver particularly deserves my gratitude; he has continued to be a mentor and helpful critic long after his responsibilities as my dissertation advisor ended. Federico Ferrara provided invaluable assistance on data analysis, as well as ideas and feedback in several areas. While the following list is not complete, I extend my thanks for help with data acquisition and management, reviews of papers that developed into chapters, and valuable comments and criticism to Sarah Birch, Terry Clark, Paul D'Anieri, Timothy Frye, Brian Gaines, Batbold Ganhuu, Reuel Hanks, Ryan Kennedy, Tatiana Kostadinova, Christopher Marsh, Valentin Mikhailov, Burt Monroe, Robert Moser, Misa Nishikawa, Dennis Patterson, Timothy Power, Thomas Remington, Elchin Rizayev, Anatoliy Romanyuk, Yuriy Shveda, Frank Thames, Alex Tsiovkh, and Joshua Tucker. While conducting research abroad, I was helped tremendously by some individuals listed above, as well as Yarema Bachynsky, Olga Gulikova, Volodymyr (Walter) and Lyuda Hrytsiutenko, Viktor Krevs, and Volodymyr Kyrylych. I am also grateful to the editorial staff at Palgrave who helped move the manuscript from start to finish: Anthony Wahl, Emily Hue, Farideh Koohi-Kamali, and Asa Johnson.

Many nongovernmental organizations in the United States, Europe, and Eurasia helped me collect data, acquire copies of election legislation, gain access to members of parliament and election commissions, and function during my fieldwork efforts. I especially thank the International Foundation for Election Systems (IFES), International Republican Institute, National Democratic Institute, Organization for Security and Cooperation in Europe, and USAID's Elections and Political Processes Project and Strengthening Election Administration in Ukraine Project. Several organizations provided financial and material support for my research, including the University of Kansas College of Liberal Arts and Sciences (research and sabbatical support) and Center for Research (New Faculty General Research Fund); Fulbright Scholar Program; Ivan Franko National University in L'viv, Ukraine; and American Councils for International Education (Research Scholar Exchange Program). None of the individuals or organizations listed above is responsible for any errors, omissions, or faulty interpretations in the book.

Finally, I thank my loving family for constant help and support. My parents, Thomas and Yvonne, and my wife, Lea, read and edited the entire manuscript. Lea and our son Carter endured the challenges of fieldwork abroad, exaggerated responses to occasional mishaps and lost files, and the annoyances of dealing with an author under deadline with patience, kindness, and just the right amount of humor.

CHAPTER 1

UNDERSTANDING ELECTIONS AND DEMOCRACY IN POST-SOVIET SPACE

The complicated relationship between elections and democracy is exemplified by the experience of the states that emerged from Soviet-style authoritarianism in Eastern Europe and Eurasia in the twentieth century's waning years. In the early part of the twentieth century, the Soviet Union developed into the quintessential totalitarian state,[1] experienced decline and change in leadership, and finally died a quiet death at the end of 1991. Fifteen newly independent states carved up the USSR's corpse, and embarked on efforts to create political and economic institutions, construct functioning state apparatuses, and develop a sense of national identity associated not with the old union, but with the symbols, borders, and ideals of these new countries. In this process of birth, growth, and development, each post-Soviet country has held elections. In some cases, the election process has matured to the point where it meets international norms and standards. In most corners of the old empire, however, elections suffer from significant shortcomings.

This chapter addresses several theoretical issues in the study of post-Soviet elections: what is the role of elections in democratic and nondemocratic politics, how have elections been linked to the democratization literature, and how do expectations about the relationship between elections and political outcomes translate to post-Soviet space? The first section addresses the question of elections, defining their forms and functions in democratic and authoritarian societies. The second section presents definitions of democracy and outlines challenges of applying them in post-Soviet space. The third section reviews how post-Soviet states have fared in implementing democratic practices, including free and fair elections. The chapter concludes with a discussion of competing theoretical orientations in the study of East European and Eurasian politics.

ELECTIONS AND THEIR ROLE IN POLITICS

Democratic Elections

Elections in democratic societies are generally viewed as the primary tool[2] to solicit and evaluate citizen preferences over policy matters and to hold representatives accountable.[3] By indirectly and directly engaging citizens in the policy-making process, elections can engender feelings of efficacy and encourage other forms of political participation. Public involvement in the selection of leaders and policies also confers legitimacy on government, and by extension, on the policies it promulgates.

Elections also induce behavioral responses from political actors. To muster the support needed to win office, politicians may organize themselves by creating political parties that contest for public support. Citizens use these group labels as shortcuts to select the candidate or party that most closely represents their positions on policy matters. Based on election results, rulers can gauge citizens' views on government performance and adjust their course of action if the public demonstrates dissatisfaction. By regularly testing politicians, elections allow citizens to hold officials accountable by removing from office poorly performing, unresponsive, or corrupt representatives.

Citizens in democratic societies often assume that their elections are free and fair, although they may not fully understand what criteria should be met to earn that label. Several international agreements identify the norms and expectations for free and fair elections. These agreements typically include characteristics such as those summarized below from an Inter-Parliamentary Council declaration (Inter-Parliamentary Union 1994):

- Citizens should have the right to contest office, form political parties, access alternative sources of information, express their opinions, and enjoy universal adult suffrage.
- Voters should have the right to register for the polls and cast secure, private ballots.
- Candidates should have the right to contest seats freely, access the media, maintain security of property and person, and appeal decisions in the election process.
- Government officials should create a legislative framework supporting free and fair elections, maintain a transparent process of voter and candidate registration, support a political environment conducive to the open expression of ideas and preferences, conduct appropriate civic education, create a level playing field by appropriately training impartial election administrators, maintain order and security without infringing upon the ability of contestants to campaign, and ensure that the casting, counting,

and compiling of votes reflects the intended actions of the voting public at the polls.

To summarize, in ideal elections, *citizens freely express informed views through their vote, any eligible citizen may run for office, parties and candidates offer clear alternatives for voters, elections serve as the primary vehicle to policy-making power*, and *elections evidence minimal distortion between citizens' expressed preferences and reported outcomes*. This notion of ideal elections may be applied to either a populist or liberal interpretation of the role of elections in democracy. The former suggests that policies should reflect the people's collective preferences, while the latter requires only that elections facilitate accountability by allowing voters to reject politicians who do not adequately perform. While this definition may be flexible, several impediments undermine its practical application:

- The choice set provided to voters by the political system—the candidates and parties that successfully register and gain ballot access, or the wording on a referendum[4]—may constrain the free expression of preferences
- Voters do not always have fully developed preferences on the issues that differentiate parties.[5]
- Voter choices may be subject to manipulation by agents of government or other political interests.

While all of these impediments are relevant in the study of post-Soviet elections, manipulation of the electoral process is particularly notable. Elections produce vote totals and seat allocations that reflect the *observed* support expressed by the voters for a set of parties, candidates, or initiatives. *Observed* support consists of the results reported by government officials and the press and determines who wins and loses. However, *observed* support may differ from the voters' real intentions, or *true* support.[6]

In the process of determining the vote choice and physically casting a ballot, the connection between a voter's intentions and the outcome expressed on the ballot may be severed in several ways. Confusion arising from ballot structure, as well as outright vote theft through invalidation or destruction of properly cast ballots, intentional misreporting of the vote by election officials, or voter intimidation, could create dissonance between a voter's intended behavior and the result that is recorded. Moreover, voters sometimes make mistakes that are not systematic; they may simply record their votes incorrectly. The *true vote* diverges from the *observed vote* when it is affected by this systematic and random error. For elections to approximate their ideal functions noted above, systematic distortions of the vote should be as close to zero as possible.

Elections are thus *an expression of voters' preferences, conditioned by the clarity of views held by voters and parties, and the choice set presented on the ballot. To the extent that systematic error and manipulation in the process can be reduced, the results will better reflect expressed preferences.*

Authoritarian Elections

Authoritarian elections are not designed or implemented as analogs to democratic elections, except through their rituals. In authoritarian elections, candidates are nominated, campaigns are held, voters go to the polls, ballots are counted, and results are formally announced. But, authoritarian elections generally lack a critical element common in democratic elections: uncertain outcomes.

Authoritarian elections serve several functions internally and externally. For government, elections provide a veneer of legitimacy covering leaders and their policies,[7] although in the Soviet case the effectiveness of elections as a tool for legitimacy changed over time.[8] Authoritarian elections also facilitate the selection process for officials who administer policies; success in "electoral" politics could yield promotions to positions with more responsibility. In addition, service to the Soviet state on electoral commissions, or as civic organizers to "get out the vote," could benefit career advancement. Authoritarian societies also use elections to provide citizens an outlet for participation, to train them in the "proper" ways to be politically active,[9] to practice government-sanctioned mobilization,[10] and to facilitate the identification and monitoring of potential malcontents.[11]

The Soviet Union regularly held elections and promoted them as a more democratic alternative to elections in the West. Mid-twentieth century Soviet propaganda claimed that

> Bourgeois electoral systems are not democratic because they are not representative. Capital controls the elections, the workers and farmers don't influence the legislatures, and the will of the people is thwarted by monopolists behind the scenes who manipulate the reactionary national, state, and local bodies. The majority of voting allows minority candidates, those with less than 50% of the total vote to be elected (such a practice is forbidden by the Soviet statute), and this is undemocratic. The voters have no voice in the nomination of candidates! Terror, bribery, swindling, and cheating are component parts of all Western elections. Various kinds of voting qualifications, e.g., literacy, residence, property, race and education, prevent a large proportion of the electorate, especially Negroes, from ever getting to the polls. These qualifications are set up by monopolists as a means of strengthening their hold on the country. Really progressive forces such as Communists are, for all practical purposes, disenfranchised. (Mote 1965, 55–56)

While some of the criticisms leveled by Soviet propagandists reflect intentional misinterpretations of electoral practices in the West, many points echo critiques about election quality within democratic societies: access for minority voters, concerns about the influence of lobbyists and big business, the monopoly of parties over the selection of candidates, and concerns about improper influences on the vote.[12] Moreover, citizens of the USSR enjoyed a kind of universal suffrage[13] and were active participants in the electoral process as candidates and as voters.

Prior to Mikhail Gorbachev's tenure as General Secretary of the Communist Party of the Soviet Union, Soviet elections featured little drama, save the rare cases in which the sole nominated candidate was rejected by the voters. While the rejection rate of nominated candidates was low, the process of vetting potential candidates could produce vigorous competition. The goal of nominating candidates to run—and win—an election was to choose an appropriate representative of the Soviet people and simultaneously reward citizens who behaved in an exemplary manner. Rather than interpreting the function of an "elected" representative as an advocate or agent, as in democratic politics, the Soviet deputy's main role was largely symbolic. Elected politicians showcased the diversity, character, and commitment of the Soviet people (Fainsod 1965; Jacobs 1970)[14] although they would occasionally intervene in politics to assist local constituents in resolving problems with Soviet bureaucracies (Swearer 1961; Mote 1965; Zaslavsky and Brym 1978). Elected representatives did not make policy but rather showed solidarity across professions and peoples in support of Communist Party decisions (Carson 1955; Mote 1965). With the advent of the Gorbachev era in the mid-1980s, this role began to change, as elections became increasingly competitive and open to candidates who challenged the regime. Just as the role of representatives changed during the waning years of the Soviet Union, so too did the functions of elections.

Defining Democracy

Since the advent of the "third wave" of democratization in the early 1970s,[15] and accelerating with the collapse of communism in Eastern Europe and the Soviet Union by the early 1990s, scholars in comparative politics have analyzed many questions about the democratization process: What is democracy, and what are the necessary features of a democratic society? What are the causes and patterns of authoritarian collapse and democratic transition? How does variation in political institutions affect the quality of democracy? How can democracy be measured and compared cross-nationally and temporally? What factors contribute to democracy's short-term survival and long-term success?

While political theorists have debated the notion of democracy for centuries, definitions intended to facilitate empirical research are predominantly a twentieth-century phenomenon. An early, and prominent, definition of democracy directly connects elections to the democratic process. In the 1940s, Joseph Schumpeter noted that "the democratic method is that institutional arrangement for arriving at political decisions in which individuals acquire the power to decide by means of a competitive struggle for the people's vote" (Schumpeter 1942, 269). While subsequent scholarship has not seriously challenged the inclusion of free and fair elections as a necessary condition for democracy, researchers have acknowledged that the existence of elections alone cannot guarantee citizens a full set of rights to express themselves, compete for office, and cast ballots meaningfully.

Schumpeter's definition of democracy spawned a vast literature to classify democratic regimes, differentiating them along several dimensions.[16] The diversity in conceptualizations of democracy is so great that scholars have identified over five hundred subtypes of democracy (Collier and Levitsky 1997). Further refined definitions better capture cross-national and temporal variation in the forms and quality of democratic practices and political institutions, but they complicate classification for empirical analysis. As definitions become more nuanced, they carry greater data demands, generate the possibility that existing data will be incompatible across countries or that necessary data will be unavailable, and potentially increase the ambiguity of the democracy measures themselves.

If states are measured dichotomously (democracy versus nondemocracy) and the sole criterion is the regular practice of free and fair elections to select national-level officials who have policy-making authority, classification seems relatively straightforward. The only data required is a measure of free and fair elections and information about elections that have occurred. States that meet the criteria for free and fair elections are deemed to be democratic, those that fall short are deemed nondemocratic. Yet, the only way to assess free and fair elections is to use a variety of sources—election assessments from nongovernmental or international organizations, media reports, or political party press releases—or to rely upon an existing index that has compiled these sources into its own assessment of democracy. This seemingly simple dichotomous assessment is not so simple; collecting and evaluating data on the quality of elections is a significant task. As the number of factors comprising democracy rises and the number of potential classification categories increases beyond two, classification becomes even more challenging.

Despite these challenges, researchers have established various metrics to measure the quality of democracy. At least nine major datasets assess variation in democratic quality cross-nationally, and each has advantages and flaws (Munck and Verkuilen 2002). While its limitations have been explored in detail (Bollen 1980; 1993; Bollen and Paxton 2000; Munck and Verkuilen 2002), Freedom House's dual measures of political rights and civil liberties, with ordinal scores based on expert assessments, are perhaps the most commonly used data in the press and in political science research. I use these data throughout the book to compare and assess post-Soviet progress in democratization.

Based on the extensive democratization literature, it is reasonable to include four key factors in a definition of democracy. First, *adults enjoy universal suffrage*. Second, *free and fair elections determine who governs, and there exist mechanisms for holding government officials accountable*. Third, *standard civil liberties are recognized, including freedom of speech, the press, and assembly*. Fourth, *the rule of law prevails*. These four components combine most of the critical elements in procedural and substantive definitions of democracy. Moreover, these four elements are encompassed by the coding rules of Freedom House, with the first two features covered by political rights scores, and the latter two covered by civil liberties scores.

Interpretations of Democracy in Post-Soviet Space

While the debates over democracy measures among Western academics focus on validity and reliability, political elites in many parts of the globe—including Eastern Europe and Eurasia—have challenged the very construct of democracy. In the early 1990s, the seductiveness of the argument that liberal democracy would inevitably triumph over authoritarianism, coupled with the simplicity of Schumpeter's minimalist definition of democracy, influenced the behavior of domestic and international actors in post-Soviet space. International actors' apparent obsession with the quick implementation of elections raised concerns about the rise of the "fallacy of electoralism" (Schmitter and Karl 1991; Zakaria 2003), the notion that holding elections is equivalent to introducing democratic rule, even when other political rights and civil liberties are not extended to the public or the rule of law is weak.

As founding elections were being planned or held, elites engaged in political and economic reforms in many parts of the former USSR that displaced workers, cost many citizens their life savings, and helped to impoverish senior citizens and other vulnerable populations. Moreover, elections in the newly independent states often did not generate democratic outcomes, instead producing leaders who were minimally accountable to citizens and fully willing to manipulate electoral processes to legitimize authoritarian or semiauthoritarian rule (Levitsky and Way 2002). For many people in Eastern Europe and Eurasia, the term democracy became equated not with a system of government providing citizen sovereignty, but a kleptocracy that benefited a small number of wealthy, corrupt elites.

The sustained focus of the international community, particularly the United States, on democracy promotion and elections, coupled with the ouster of regimes in Georgia, Kyrgyzstan, and Ukraine following election-related protests in the early to mid 2000s, prompted a harsh response from many regional leaders with authoritarian tendencies. They argued that Western forms of democracy do not apply universally; some societies are not "ready" for this form of government.[17] In Russia, for example, politicians have advocated the concepts of "managed democracy" and "sovereign democracy" (Okara 2007) as alternatives. *Managed democracy* is an oxymoron, suggesting centralized control with a façade of democratic institutions and some accommodations for carefully controlled citizen input. *Sovereign democracy* rejects the interference of international actors in the natural development of domestic political regimes. Defenders of the sovereign democracy approach, for example, portray election observation missions as foreign policy tools designed not to assess election quality, but to undermine regimes that challenge the West while ignoring antidemocratic behaviors of pro-Western countries (Frolov 2005). Russian President Vladimir Putin weighed in on this issue, noting that "attempts are being made to turn the OSCE [Organization for Security and Cooperation in Europe] into a vulgar instrument of protecting the political interests of one country or a group of countries in relation to other countries" (RFE/RL 2007a). Russian officials acted on their suspicions that observation missions are politically motivated by inviting a small number of

OSCE observers to the 2007 parliamentary election and delaying their visas. These actions prompted the OSCE to cancel its observation mission a few weeks before the election. Russia has also spearheaded efforts to modify the terms under which election observation missions operate.

The notion that post-Soviet states are not yet ready for "Western-style democracy," or that democracy does not match local conditions, has been echoed by current and former leaders such as Askar Akayev (Kyrgyzstan), Heydar Aliyev (Azerbaijan), Gurbanguly Berdymukhammedov (Turkmenistan), Islam Karimov (Uzbekistan), Nursultan Nazarbayev (Kazakhstan), and Saparmurat Niyazov (Turkmenistan).[18] In Tajikistan, the director of the president's political think tank noted, "In the countries of Central Asia they have their own democracy and mentality and every election in this region differs from what is happening in European countries. Therefore, the election in Tajikistan will be held according to Tajik standards" (Pannier 2006).

Carefully controlled democracy is antithetical to a system more typically characterized as "organized uncertainty" (Przeworski 1991), in which political actors know the parameters of possible action but do not know which of the many potential outcomes will prevail. Under authoritarianism, by contrast, a single ruler or small group ultimately determines policy by fiat; there is little uncertainty in leadership selection and policy-making. Because elections give insight into the level of "uncertainty" that guides politics, they are a key to understanding the nature of transition from communist to postcommunist rule.

Elections and Democracy in the Post-Soviet Context

The disintegration of communist power in the Soviet Union's East and Central European client states in the late 1980s and the formal dissolution of the USSR at the end of 1991 prompted many to proclaim triumphantly that democracy had prevailed over other competing regime types. The most widely publicized representative of this argument was Francis Fukuyama, whose essay and book noted that human civilization may be witnessing a final stage of institutional evolution, represented by the universal spread of liberal democracy (Fukuyama 1989; 1992). While the pace of democratization might vary, and some societies might experience awkward ebbs and flows of democratic progress, authoritarian systems were waning.

The scholarly literature on democratization may not have overtly adopted Fukuyama's tone, but an underlying assumption permeating much of the literature was that democracy would be the outcome of most regime transitions. In the wake of communism's collapse, these spoken and unspoken expectations about democratization were extended to the post-Soviet region. Freedom House even dubbed the twentieth century "democracy's century," in light of the tremendous advances made by democratic regimes. By the end of the twentieth century, however, it became clear that some assumptions about democratization were problematic, and that some postcommunist societies had established seemingly stable semiauthoritarian or authoritarian regimes (Carothers 2002; Levitsky and Way 2002).

The trajectory of democratization in post-Soviet states is complicated, with few countries evidencing a clear, consistent progression from autocracy to democracy. Freedom House rankings illustrate the ebbs and flows of change.[19]

As Freedom House scores on Table 1.1 illustrate, linear development patterns toward democracy characterize few post-Soviet states, although five improved their ratings in the postcommunist period. In 1992, the founding year of postcommunism in the post-Soviet territories, only one newly independent state was labeled "free": Lithuania. Estonia and Latvia followed closely behind, with a "partially free" label and scores in political rights slightly below Lithuania's. These scores are not surprising as the Baltic states led the secessionist charge from the USSR and made efforts to restore the symbols of their early twentieth-century independence. Gorbachev's reforms unintentionally restarted the public conversation about the illegal occupation of the Baltic region as a result of the Stalin-era Molotov–Ribbentrop Pact, and Baltic activists capitalized on opportunities presented by glasnost to build a case for secession.[20] Independence movements in the Baltic states were the most progressive and active in the USSR, better preparing them for responsibilities of political and economic transition, as well as state- and nation-building after the USSR's collapse. Scores in the Baltic states gradually improved, especially as Estonia and Latvia addressed issues of the Russian-speaking minority (Barrington 1995) and all three Baltic states prepared for accession to the European Union.[21]

Over the fifteen years following these initial assessments, progress in democratic development has been mixed. Estonia, Latvia, and Lithuania received "perfect" scores on political rights and civil liberties in 2007, and all were labeled free. Six of the fifteen states recorded improvements in their scores. Ukraine improved only one point in civil liberties, but its overall assessment moved from "partly free" to "free." Ukraine's scores vacillated as the regime of President Leonid Kuchma chipped away at free expression in the 1990s and early 2000s. The Orange Revolution in 2004 produced contentious political maneuvering between the remnants of the Kuchma regime and its opponents. While post-Orange Revolution politics have been hotly contested, they have exhibited more democratic tendencies than politics in the Kuchma-era.

Moldova improved two points in political rights and one in civil liberties. The enduring conflict in Transnistria particularly inhibited further improvements in its ratings. But, even with contentious ethnic and language issues, and the accession to power of Communist President Vladimir Voronin amid terrible economic conditions, Moldova has witnessed modest progress in democratization.

After a period of decline and improvement, Georgia's rating in 2007 was almost identical to its 1992 score; it improved one point in political rights and two in civil liberties. Democratic quality suffered during the civil war

Table 1.1 Freedom House Scores for Post-Soviet States, 1992–2007

	1992	1993	1994	1995	1996	1997	1998	1999	2000	2001	2002	2003	2004	2005	2006	2007	
Armenia	4/3 PF	3/4 PF	3/4 PF	4/4 PF	5/4 PF	5/4 PF	4/4 PF	4/4 PF	4/4 PF	4/4 PF	4/4 PF	4/4 PF	5/4 PF	5/4 PF	5/4 PF	5/4 PF	→
Azerbaijan	5/5 PF	6/6 NF	6/6 NF	6/6 NF	6/5 NF	6/4 PF	6/4 PF	6/4 PF	6/5 PF	6/5 PF	6/5 PF	6/5 NF	6/5 NF	6/5 NF	6/5 NF	6/5 NF	→
Belarus	4/3 PF	5/4 PF	4/4 PF	5/5 PF	6/6 NF	6/6 NF	6/6 NF	6/6 NF	6/6 NF	6/6 NF	6/6 NF	6/6 NF	7/6 NF	7/6 NF	7/6 NF	7/6 NF	→
Estonia	3/3 PF	3/2 PF	3/2 F	2/2 F	1/2 F	1/2 F	1/2 F	1/2 F	1/2 F	1/2 F	1/2 F	1/2 F	1/1 F	1/1 F	1/1 F	1/1 F	←
Georgia	4/5 PF	5/5 PF	5/5 PF	4/5 PF	4/4 PF	3/4 PF	3/4 PF	3/4 PF	4/4 PF	4/4 PF	4/4 PF	4/4 PF	3/4 PF	3/3 PF	3/3 PF	4/4 PF	=
Kazakhstan	5/5 PF	6/4 PF	6/5 NF	6/5 NF	6/5 NF	6/5 NF	6/5 NF	6/5 NF	6/5 NF	6/5 NF	6/5 NF	6/5 NF	6/5 NF	6/5 NF	6/5 NF	6/5 NF	→
Kyrgyzstan	4/2 PF	5/3 PF	4/3 PF	4/4 PF	4/4 PF	4/4 PF	5/5 PF	5/5 PF	6/5 PF	5/5 PF	6/5 PF	6/5 PF	6/5 NF	5/4 PF	5/4 PF	5/4 PF	→
Latvia	3/3 PF	3/3 PF	3/2 F	2/2 F	2/2 F	1/2 F	1/2 F	1/2 F	1/2 F	1/2 F	1/2 F	1/2 F	1/2 F	1/1 F	1/1 F	2/1 F	←
Lithuania	2/3 F	1/3 F	1/3 F	1/2 F	1/2 F	1/2 F	1/2 F	1/2 F	1/2 F	1/2 F	1/2 F	1/2 F	2/2 F	1/1 F	1/1 F	1/1 F	←
Moldova	5/5 PF	5/5 PF	4/4 PF	4/4 PF	3/4 PF	3/4 PF	2/4 PF	2/4 PF	2/4 PF	2/4 PF	3/4 PF	3/4 PF	3/4 PF	3/4 PF	3/4 PF	3/4 PF	←
Russia	3/4 PF	3/4 PF	3/4 PF	3/4 PF	3/4 PF	3/4 PF	4/4 PF	4/5 PF	5/5 PF	5/5 PF	5/5 PF	5/5 PF	6/5 NF	6/5 NF	6/5 NF	6/5 NF	→
Tajikistan	6/6 NF	7/7 NF	7/7 NF	7/7 NF	7/7 NF	6/6 NF	6/6 NF	6/6 NF	6/6 NF	6/6 NF	6/5 NF	6/5 NF	6/5 NF	6/5 NF	6/5 NF	6/5 NF	=
Turkmenistan	7/6 NF	7/7 NF	7/7 NF	7/7 NF	7/7 NF	7/7 NF	7/7 NF	7/7 NF	7/7 NF	7/7 NF	7/7 NF	7/7 NF	7/7 NF	7/7 NF	7/7 NF	7/7 NF	=
Ukraine	3/3 PF	4/4 PF	3/4 PF	3/4 PF	3/4 PF	3/4 PF	3/4 PF	3/4 PF	4/4 PF	4/4 PF	4/4 PF	4/4 PF	4/3 PF	3/2 F	3/2 F	3/2 F	←
Uzbekistan	6/6 NF	7/7 NF	7/7 NF	7/7 NF	7/6 NF	7/6 NF	7/6 NF	7/6 NF	7/6 NF	7/6 NF	7/6 NF	7/6 NF	7/6 NF	7/7 NF	7/7 NF	7/7 NF	→

Note: The trajectory is labeled up if scores on both measures improved from the initial score in 1992 to the final score in 2007 or if the classification of F, PF, NF changed. The trajectory is labeled down if scores on both measures declined or if the classification of F, PF, NF changed. The trajectory is labeled the same if one or both measures remained the same (if one measure changed, it only changed by one point) and the classification of F, PF, NF did not change.

Source: Freedom House, http://www.freedomhouse.org (accessed 4/30/07 and 1/17/08).

in the early 1990s. Georgia's scores improved after Eduard Shevardnadze's accession to the presidency, despite the failure to resolve the civil war's "frozen conflicts" in Abkhazia and South Ossetia. But, as Shevardnadze increasingly exhibited authoritarian tendencies, Freedom House scores deteriorated until the Rose Revolution in 2003 rehabilitated Georgia's "partly free" status. President Mikheil Saakashvili's decreased tolerance for political dissent prompted Georgia's ratings to once again decline in 2007.

Assessments of democratic quality declined in seven post-Soviet states and remained constant in two. Conditions in Armenia and Azerbaijan varied over time as the Karabakh conflict intensified and then reached stalemate in the early to mid 1990s, and leadership changed in both states. Armenia's scores declined in both political rights and civil liberties; Azerbaijan slipped in political rights, but its overall assessment also dropped to "not free." Belarus experienced a steady decline in political rights and civil liberties after Alyaksandr Lukashenka's accession to the presidency and relentless efforts to strip away the limited democratic gains Belarus witnessed in the aftermath of Soviet collapse. Russia also witnessed steady decline, with the uncertainty of the Boris Yeltsin era followed by President Vladimir Putin's creeping authoritarianism.

Across Central Asia, democratic quality is the lowest among post-Soviet states. After a brief period as the "Switzerland of Central Asia," Kyrgyzstan's scores declined. The ouster of Askar Akayev in 2005 did little to improve democratic quality, as President Kurmanbek Bakiyev's regime proved to be similarly oriented toward cronyism and authoritarianism. Tajikistan's brutal civil war and weak state and the actions of authoritarian President Emomali Rahmon produced some variation over time in raw scores but no change in Tajikistan's overall status as "not free." Personalistic authoritarian regimes in Turkmenistan and Uzbekistan yielded consistent scores of "not free" over the entire post-Soviet period. Despite a decade and a half of postcommunism, only four post-Soviet states were deemed free in 2007, a modest improvement from one in 1992.

Overall assessments of democracy track closely with the quality of elections, largely because assessments of elections are an integral component of democracy measures. The most extensive source for election observation data is the Organization for Security and Cooperation in Europe (OSCE). While the OSCE is not the only international organization that has dispatched observation missions to monitor post-Soviet elections,[22] it has produced publicly accessible reports for more elections than any other organization. Moreover, it has developed a relatively consistent lexicon to describe election quality, facilitating comparison cross-nationally and over time.

Of the fifty-four national-level elections monitored by the OSCE from 1995 to 2008,[23] only eight have been assessed as meeting international standards:[24] all elections in the Baltic states, Moldova's 2001 parliamentary election, and Ukraine's 2006 and 2007 parliamentary elections. Twenty elections were rated as significantly flawed and below international standards. Twenty-six elections were assessed in a broadly defined grey area: they did not fully meet international standards but showed significant positive elements or progress from previous contests.

This middle category is diverse and includes elections held under widely different circumstances. Tajikistan's 2000 parliamentary election, involving competitors from both sides of the brutal civil war, was deemed to be demonstrating progress, although the administrative process fell short of several important benchmarks (OSCE 2000e). Less dramatic improvements could also produce a report that focused on achievements, such as notable efforts to develop election legislation in Armenia's 1999 parliamentary election (OSCE 1999a), "political will" expressed by officials to increase election quality in Azerbaijan's 1998 presidential election (OSCE 1998a), expanded access for candidates to contest seats and better civic education in Kazakhstan's 2007 parliamentary election (OSCE 2007b), or improved transparency in more representative electoral commissions in Ukraine's 2002 parliamentary election (OSCE 2002b).

One must exercise caution in creating an overall picture of election quality based solely on OSCE reports, however. Since the OSCE does not send large observation missions to countries with strong democratic standards or extremely weak standards, the dataset is censored both at the bottom and top. That is, the countries likely to produce the "best" and "worst" elections are generally not monitored, and few reports are available for them. In addition to the fifty-four monitored presidential and parliamentary elections, the countries under study held an additional forty-eight presidential and parliamentary elections, three European parliamentary elections, and forty-two referendums (although some of these elections were concurrent) that did not receive full scrutiny. Table 1.2 lists all elections and referendums held in post-Soviet space at the national level from 1992 to 2008.

Competing Theories of Behavior

As I have noted, post-Soviet states have fared quite well in terms of the *quantity* of elections held, but the *quality* of these events has often been poor. It is precisely because election quality and regime type has varied that the former USSR is a particularly useful region for comparative study. All of the states experienced Soviet rule, although the Baltic countries, Moldova, and parts of Ukraine had more limited experience, as they were not incorporated into the USSR until World War II. This common baseline of Soviet-style political socialization, institutional practices, and the system's basic incentive structure provides a fertile environment in which to assess how and why elections and their consequences vary.[25]

The significant variation in post-Soviet regime type and election quality, however, also raises important methodological issues about the equivalence of cases under analysis. As a general rule, election studies exclude cases that fail to pass international tests of open contestation, free participation, and accurate translation of votes into reported outcomes. Poor-quality elections are omitted because the production mechanisms for election data differ substantially from

Table 1.2 Dates of National Elections in Post-Soviet States, 1992–2008[1]

	Parliamentary	Presidential	Referendum
Armenia	Jul. 5, 1995 May 30, 1999 May 25, 2003 May 12, 2007	Sept. 22, 1996 Mar. 16/30, 1998 Feb. 19/Mar. 5, 2003 Feb. 19, 2008	Jul. 5, 1995 May 25, 2003 Nov. 27, 2005
Azerbaijan	Nov. 12/26, 1995 Nov. 5, 2000/Jan. 7, 2001 Nov. 6, 2005	Jun. 7, 1992 Oct. 3, 1993 Oct. 11, 1998 Oct. 15, 2003 Oct. 15, 2008[2]	Aug. 29, 1993 Nov. 12, 1995 Aug. 24, 2002
Belarus[3]	May 14/29, 1995 Oct. 15/29, 2000 Oct. 17/27, 2004 Sept. 28, 2008[4]	Jun. 23/Jul. 10, 1994 Sept. 9, 2001 Mar. 19, 2006	May 14, 1995 Nov. 24, 1996 Oct. 17, 2004
Estonia	Sep. 20, 1992 Mar. 5, 1995 Mar. 7, 1999 Mar. 2, 2003 Jun. 13, 2004 (EU) Mar. 4, 2007	Sep. 20, 1992	Jun. 28, 1992 Sep. 14, 2003
Georgia	Oct. 11, 1992 Nov. 5/19/Dec. 3, 1995 Oct. 31/Nov. 14, 1999 Nov. 2, 2003 Mar. 28, 2004 May 21, 2008	Nov. 5, 1995 April 9, 2000 Jan. 4, 2004 Jan 5, 2008	Nov. 2, 2003 Jan. 5, 2008
Kazakhstan[5]	Mar. 7, 1994 Dec. 9, 1995 Oct. 10/24, 1999 Sep. 19/Oct. 3, 2004 Aug. 18, 2007	Jan. 10, 1999 Dec. 4, 2005	Apr. 29, 1995 Aug. 30, 1995
Kyrgyzstan	Feb. 5/19, 1995 Feb. 20/Mar. 12, 2000 Feb. 27/Mar. 13, 2005 Dec. 16, 2007	Dec. 24, 1995 Oct. 29, 2000 Jul. 10, 2005	Jan. 30, 1994 Oct. 22, 1994 Feb. 10, 1996 Oct. 17, 1998 Feb. 2, 2003 Oct. 21, 2007
Latvia	Jun. 5/6, 1993 Sep. 30/Oct. 1, 1995 Oct. 3, 1998 Oct. 5, 2002 Jun 12, 2004 (EU) Oct. 7, 2006		Oct. 3, 1998 Nov. 13, 1999 Sep. 20, 2003 July 7, 2007
Lithuania	Oct. 25/Nov. 15, 1992 Oct. 20/Nov. 10, 1996 Oct. 8, 2000 Jun. 13, 2004 (EU) Oct. 10/24, 2004 Oct. 12, 2008[6]	Feb 15, 1993 Dec. 21, 1997/ Jan 4, 1998 Dec. 22, 2002/Jan. 5, 2003 Jun. 13, 2004	May 23, 1992 June 14, 1992 Oct. 25, 1992 Aug. 27, 1994 Oct. 20, 1996 Nov. 10, 1996 May 10/11, 2003 Oct. 12, 2008[7]

Table 1.2   Dates of National Elections in Post-Soviet States, 1992–2008[1] *(continued)*

	Parliamentary	Presidential	Referendum
Moldova	Feb. 27, 1994 Mar. 22, 1998 Feb. 25, 2001 Mar. 6, 2005	Nov. 17/Dec. 1. 1996	Mar. 6, 1994
Russia	Dec. 12, 1993 Dec. 17, 1995 Dec. 19, 1999 Dec. 7, 2003 Dec. 2, 2007	Jun. 16/Jul. 3, 1996 Mar. 26, 2000 Mar. 14, 2004 Mar. 2, 2008	Apr. 25, 1993 Dec. 12, 1993
Tajikistan	Feb. 26/Mar. 12, 1995 Feb. 27/Mar. 12, 2000 Feb. 27/Mar. 13, 2005	Nov. 6, 1994 Nov. 6, 1999 Nov. 6, 2006	Nov. 6, 1994 Sep. 26, 1999 Jun. 22, 2003
Turkmenistan	Dec. 6, 1992 (Khalk Maslikhaty) Dec. 11, 1994/ Jan. 8, 1995 Dec. 12, 1999 Apr. 6, 2003 (Khalk Maslikhaty) Dec. 19, 2004 Dec. 9, 2007 (Khalk Maslikhaty) Dec. 14, 2008[8]	Jun. 21, 1992 Feb. 11, 2007	Jan. 15, 1994
Ukraine	Nov. 20, 1994 Mar. 29, 1998 Mar. 31, 2002 Mar. 26, 2006 Sep. 30, 2007	Jul. 10, 1994 Oct. 31/Nov. 14, 1999 Oct. 31/Nov. 21/Dec. 26, 2004	April 16, 2000
Uzbekistan	Dec. 25, 1994/Jan. 8/22,1995 Dec. 5/19, 1999 Dec. 26, 2004/Jan. 9, 2005	Jan. 9, 2000 Dec. 23, 2007	Mar. 26, 1995 Jan. 27, 2002

Sources: OSCE, International IDEA, Shvetsova (1999), Election Results Archive (http://cdp .binghamton.edu/), Central Electoral Commission of Armenia Web site (http://www .elections.am), Central Election Commission of Azerbaijan Web site (http://www.cec.gov .az), Central Commission of Belarus for Elections and Referenda (http://www.rec.gov.by), Estonian National Electoral Committee (http://www.vvk.ee), Central Electoral Commission of Georgia (http://www.cec.gov.ge/), Central Electoral Commission of Kazakhstan (http:// www.election.kz/), Central Commission on Elections and the Conduct of Referenda (http:// www.shailoo.gov.kg), Central Electoral Commission of Latvia (http://web.cvk.lv), Central Electoral Committee of Lithuania (http://www.vrl.lt), Central Electoral Commission of Russia (http://www.cikrf.ru/), Central Electoral Commission of Ukraine (http://www.cvk .gov.ua/).

their democratic counterparts. Indeed, the underlying processes generating election data—for example, in Estonia and Turkmenistan—reflect democratic standards in the former and authoritarian manipulation in the latter. In grey-zone states like Armenia, where elections are regularly tainted by accusations of manipulation, the quality of election data production is more difficult to discern.

Post-Soviet states are equivalent on at least one critical dimension: their joint participation in the Soviet enterprise for at least the latter half of the twentieth century. To assess how this inheritance may have affected political outcomes, no countries or elections are excluded a priori. However, data from all regime types are assessed and interpreted in the context of the processes that generated them.

The theoretical expectations of this research are situated within a broader debate about how to study and evaluate politics. The advent of postcommunism in the final decade of the twentieth century coincided with the "third wave" of democratization (Huntington 1991). A contentious question arose as political scientists not familiar with the region, but possessing powerful analytical tools, eyed the newly independent states as potential targets for research: are these cases equivalent to other transitional societies passing through the process of democratization, or did the experience of totalitarian rule under the Soviet Union create a unique postauthoritarian political environment that defies interregional comparison? Layered upon this issue was another vexing question for scholars of comparative politics: to what degree do inherited norms, values, beliefs, and expectations—the legacy of prior social and political arrangements—affect behavior, and to what degree do political actors respond to stimuli in a similar manner to their counterparts outside the postcommunist region?

The question of how to study this "new" region occupied significant scholarly attention and was debated in an especially vigorous manner in the early to mid 1990s, exemplified by an exchange among scholars in several editions of the journal *Slavic Review*.[26] While the specific controversy focused on the application of the democratic transition literature's lessons from Latin and South America to postcommunist East Europe and Eurasia, it spoke to a deeper divide in the scholarly community.

One side of the debate focused on the unique features of the Soviet system and the transition process, as well as the challenges of cross-regional research, to argue against research designs that would apply general theories of politics to the region.[27] Instead, this side advocated a continuation of the area studies approach, focusing on the region's unique conditions and the need to have deep linguistic, cultural, and historic context woven into research.

The alternative approach advocated broader cross-national comparisons in the context of a literature predicting the presence of certain elite-driven processes at the core of democratization. Its proponents suggested that incorporating postcommunist states into cross-regional research would facilitate a test of the region's inherent uniqueness and was preferable to asserting uniqueness a priori. If the process of democratization in the postcommunist world differed systematically from other postauthoritarian regions, such as Latin and South America, a cross-regional research design would uncover this phenomenon, whereas analysis of the region on its own would not. Moreover, others argued that by insisting that the features of the Soviet system undermined interregional comparison, and that this uniqueness precluded the use of emerging methods, area studies became disengaged from the social sciences.[28] This epistemological debate has continued in comparative politics generally and in postcommunist studies specifically.[29] But, recent research has worked to bridge this divide and synthesize approaches (Clark 2002; Jones Luong 2002).

Research on elections directly confronts this debate. Do voters, politicians, and officials behave in ways that cannot be explained outside of the cultural context and political socialization endemic to the region? Or, do they behave as rational actors, responding to institutional incentives and assessing the costs and benefits of particular actions?

The former approach implies that the legacy of preexisting political and social arrangements influences contemporary behavior, even when the mechanisms reinforcing those arrangements have disappeared. At least two possible "legacies" may affect the conduct of post-Soviet elections. The first is an *institutional legacy*, characterized by the inheritance of institutional rules. The formal institutional legacy is the easiest to identify because it requires the retention of rules from the past. For example, in the early 1990s, many post-Soviet states did not adopt new constitutions as their first order of business but retained their Soviet-era constitutions. In Russia, the inherited constitution was accompanied by the continued tenure of parliament members selected in the Soviet period. This gave rise to the constitutional crisis of 1993, culminating in President Boris Yeltsin's decree dissolving parliament and the Constitutional Court, his decision to violently oust protesters from the parliament building, and the introduction of a new, post-Soviet Russian constitution.

The second legacy, the *behavioral legacy*, is more difficult to identify and distinguish. If individuals are responding to a behavioral legacy, they are acting *as if* incentives have not changed, even when the political environment has changed. This behavior may be prompted by the continued relevance of informal norms or the successful inculcation of the lessons from early socialization. The Soviet Union's messianic efforts to remake society included an introduction to critical Soviet values, proper and improper conduct, and a sense of identity as a Soviet citizen. As the Soviet Union matured, another layer of norms emerged underneath the official expectations, as citizens recognized that the official ideology was hollow but that it must be paid at least "lip service" in public activities.[30] Individual behavior thus confronted the incentives promoted by the official version of the system, and the incentives promoted by a more realistic understanding of how the system functioned. Individuals developed a keen sense of how to behave publicly and how to behave privately, and these systems of behavior sometimes came into conflict with one another (Carnaghan 2007). The challenge of assessing a legacy's effect is to disentangle outcomes associated with incentives that predominated in the past[31] from those that predominate in the present.

In politics and elections, what should we expect from post-Soviet man and woman? One often finds reference to common attitudes such as the desire for order and a "strong leader," an emphasis on collective benefits and distrust of those who advance individual benefits, and participation in public rituals; while private behavior diverges from public actions. In terms of elections, if institutional and behavioral legacies persist, one might find evidence of path dependence in election rule choice, voters participating in elections out of practice and duty, centralized decision making on the part of party leaders and elected officials, politicians officially supporting egalitarian policies, and a tendency to hold public rituals but behave differently behind the scenes.

An alternative view of behavior suggests that instead of responding to incentives that no longer pertain, citizens and politicians recognize the costs and benefits associated with particular actions and make decisions accordingly. Individuals have goals and are confronted with alternative mechanisms that can lead to the achievement of those goals. They assess available options according to their preferences, evaluate the outcomes that are likely to be associated with those choices, and attempt to maximize the benefits that accrue from their decisions. The focus of this approach is not on the origins of the preferences but rather on the decision-making process. In short, the underlying assumption is that actors in the political process—voters and politicians—have similar motivations and respond similarly to stimuli across the globe. Thus, if researchers understand the parameters of behavior allowed by the rules, the tools available to participants in the political process, and the identity and motivations of actors, they should be able to assess likely outcomes.

This book explicitly and implicitly incorporates questions about the mechanisms of decision making into the analysis. The major issues addressed in this book—how election rules are selected, how variation in rules affects outcomes, how citizens make decisions about voting, how politicians form and organize parties and their platforms, how election administrators implement rules, how political actors test the limits of the rules in their attempts to manipulate elections, and how citizens mobilize to protest fraud—are assessed using qualitative and quantitative techniques. The analysis in each chapter employs research methods that best match the demands of the questions and strives to disentangle behaviors associated with instrumental rationality from those colored by the Soviet legacy. While the analysis in this book does not resolve the ongoing debate about epistemology and methods, it should contribute to a more nuanced and balanced interpretation of politics in post-Soviet space.

Chapter 2

Elections under Soviet Authoritarianism

Although more than fifteen years have passed since the Soviet Union's collapse, its imprint is still visible. In Eastern Europe and Eurasia, some formal institutions bear similarities to their Soviet-era counterparts, some voters seem to be habituated to casting ballots even when their votes are not meaningful, and some politicians rhetorically recall the power of the Soviet era. This chapter describes the common starting point for all of the countries in this book, setting the stage for subsequent analytical chapters by identifying three distinct eras of Soviet elections and describing how formal and informal practices developed over time. The story of Soviet elections also provides insight into the potential institutional and behavioral inheritances that could influence post-Soviet behavior, a point addressed in the chapter's concluding section.

DEVELOPMENTAL STAGES OF SOVIET ELECTIONS

Elections in the communist era evolved through at least three stages,[1] characterized by the level of centralization in decision making, the stability of institutional rules and procedures, the extent of suffrage, the competitiveness of the electoral enterprise, and the overall purpose of elections in the Soviet political game. During most of the Soviet period, elections were analogous to elaborately staged theater. Soviet electoral practices required political actors to find appropriate candidates, ensure voter turnout, manage activities at polling stations, and troubleshoot problems. Moreover, these activities demanded substantial personnel, financial, material, and technical resources. Not only were citizens expected to vote, but millions of citizens served in a formal capacity during local and national campaigns as commission members, voter mobilizers, or candidates. Why would the Soviet Union direct so much effort to an enterprise with preordained outcomes?

As noted in Chapter 1, Soviet elections were designed for consumption by internal and external audiences. For the domestic audience, holding elections for local councils (soviets) continued the practices of limited enfranchisement that began in the tsarist period.[2] By controlling suffrage and nomination, the Bolsheviks could eliminate challenges to their rule while offering the people what appeared to be a voice in public affairs. For the international audience, Soviet elections could showcase the state's "democratic" credentials and facilitate propaganda efforts aimed to discredit the democratic credentials of the West. Soviet propagandists asserted that electoral practices in the West, and especially the United States, were dominated by entrenched economic interests, discriminated against minority candidates and voters, and were plagued by bribery and fraud. In Soviet rubric, elections engaged the people directly in governance and were not compromised by the shortcomings commonly found in bourgeois societies.

In addition to legitimization, elections served several additional functions to strengthen the Soviet state. The election process allowed the leadership at the national, regional, and local levels to evaluate the performance of functionaries. The selection of "appropriate" candidates whose record of accomplishments reflected Soviet ideals, success in engaging voters and limiting expressions of dissent, and the overall management of large-scale mobilization conveyed information to higher-level officials who would make decisions about promotion (Carson 1955). While direct elections were not used to select major policymakers, the expansion of contestation rights and the reconfiguration of responsibilities for officials, particularly characteristic of the late Soviet period, could provide political actors access to positions where real policy decisions were made (Roeder 1993). Elections also habituated the population to participation in the Soviet system: casting a vote for a candidate was equivalent to supporting the regime (Gilison 1968; Roeder 1989).

The intellectual forefathers of the Soviet system, Karl Marx, Friedrich Engels, and Vladimir Lenin, identified bourgeois institutions as oppressive mechanisms designed to provide the illusion of freedom and efficacy while continuing class divisions and the exploitation of the proletariat.[3] A goal of revolution, according to Lenin, would be to crush those very institutions and create a new order. Elections that emerged in the Soviet Union, consequently, were supposed to be a different kind of political institution that served the working class and not its oppressors.

The First Era of Soviet Elections, 1917–1936

The first phase of Soviet elections corresponds to the formative years of the Soviet Union, prior to the codification of the Stalin Constitution in 1936. Electoral practices in this period reflected the chaotic conditions that challenged the Bolsheviks, a small revolutionary movement unprepared to govern a vast territory. Centralized command and control of political, economic, and social conditions, stereotyped as a quintessential feature of the Soviet Union,[4] was absent at this time.[5] Rather, substantial variation in governance practices existed on the ground, bolstered by the civil war and foreign intervention, weak Bolshevik control over many areas, policy changes from War Communism to the New Economic Policy and then to superindustrialization, and patron-client entanglements (Easter 2000).

The Bolsheviks' skepticism about open electoral processes was not solely based on ideology. After Tsar Nicholas II's abdication in February 1917, local and national elections were held. In the spring and summer, Moscow, St. Petersburg,[6] and smaller cities held council elections. While socialist parties performed well, the Bolsheviks often ran in competition with more moderate socialist groups. The Bolsheviks showed strength in the largest cities and in garrison cities but were weaker in small towns. As the summer progressed, however, the Bolsheviks improved their electoral performance (Rosenberg 1969). Soon after the Bolshevik seizure of power, an election for the national-level Constituent Assembly was held. The Social Revolutionaries, a peasant-based party, outperformed the Bolsheviks, who received only 24 percent of the vote. Once again, the Bolsheviks garnered the most support in the largest cities and garrison towns; the Social Revolutionaries excelled in the Urals, Siberia, the Volga basin, Ukraine, Crimea, and cities housing the Black Sea Fleet and soldiers on the southwest front; and the Mensheviks showed strength in Georgia (Dando 1966). These elections also featured efforts to commit electoral fraud using techniques that would return after the collapse of communism (Rosenberg 1969).

After Vladimir Lenin disbanded the Constituent Assembly in early 1918, combat between the Bolsheviks and their rivals intensified. After the Soviet Union was officially founded in 1922, elections reemerged, albeit in a less competitive form. The founding documents of the Soviet Union were silent on election procedures; republics that constituted the new state had the authority to design their own rules. While decisions from Moscow could influence the timing or conduct of campaigns, early elections were characterized by great local variation.[7] This "delightful irregularity" (Carson 1955, 9) across the territory of the USSR was particularly evident in apportionment. In some urban areas, one deputy represented fifty workers or one hundred soldiers. But, in other areas, individual deputies were associated with perhaps twenty times that number of constituents.[8] This phenomenon reflected in part urban areas' preferred status and in part the disorganization of early Soviet state management.

At this time, voters selected representatives to local councils who, in turn, chose representatives to legislative bodies higher up the chain of command. Non-Bolsheviks were excluded from participating in the system, paving the way for a one-party state (Brunner 1990). The multitiered electoral commission framework was also established in this era, with committees at all levels of governance. The committees typically included politicians from the appropriate organizational level (e.g., representatives from the oblast executive committee on an oblast electoral committee), individuals representing the region's ethnic and class diversity (e.g., a member of a national minority, trade union representative, or peasant representative), and party organizations (e.g., members of the Komsomol and Communist Party). Electoral commission duties were similar to those in contemporary democracies: developing and confirming lists of eligible voters, hearing complaints about the electoral process, conducting civic education, setting up precincts, and organizing election-day activities (Carson 1955).

Candidate nomination processes also varied, largely based on the local party organization's strength (Carson 1955). The voting procedure was like a caucus, with voters gathering together, discussing candidates, and showing their support for a particular nominee (Borders 1929). In 1931, Communist Party and Komsomol members dominated the All-Union Congress of Soviets, with 75 percent of members. Nonparty representatives accounted for the remaining 25 percent (Teper 1932). Although election results increasingly favored Communist Party candidates, nonparty members were also elected throughout the Soviet period (though their nomination was vetted through party channels).

Suffrage requirements were applied more consistently across the country, although these rules also varied in implementation and permitted exceptions. The primary criterion for suffrage was class-based. Citizenship did not constitute a barrier to voting, as even visiting American observers were granted the opportunity to participate in early village elections (Borders 1929). But, many categories of potential voters were excluded from the polls, particularly those in suspect occupations or social positions. Individuals who owned industrial enterprises, earned income through others' labor, worked in trade, or were otherwise entrepreneurs were excluded from voting. In the agricultural sector, landowners who hired workers or rented machinery or livestock were denied suffrage. Voting rights were not extended to clergy or many civil servants from the tsarist era (especially in branches like law enforcement) (Borders 1929; Carson 1955; Figes 1988). The proportion of formally disenfranchised voters was generally low; it was 5 percent in 1929 and 4 percent in 1931 (Teper 1932). The low level of disenfranchisement was due to citizens changing their employment status to conform with Soviet regulations (e.g., moving out of retail trade) and to the many exceptions commissions granted. As the Soviet economy diversified, the implementation of suffrage rules became increasingly complex because of the ambiguity of excluded categories (Carson 1955).

Soviet officials' concerns about restricting suffrage highlight a characteristic of early elections that was later abandoned: limiting citizen participation (Carson 1955; Figes 1988). While the stereotypical description of a Soviet election includes an emphasis on mass participation and near complete turnout, these features were notably absent in early contests. In 1924 and 1925, less than half of the population participated in 89 percent of urban districts and 91 percent of rural districts; the average urban participation rate was 31 percent. Turnout even among Party and Komsomol members was relatively low (65 percent), given traditional expectations about iron-clad discipline in the ranks. Efforts to increase turnout by modifying the tasks of electoral commissions and instructions for voters successfully bolstered numbers in 1926. From 1927 to 1934, turnout increased from 48 percent to 83 percent in rural districts and from 59 percent to 92 percent in urban districts, yielding a nationwide increase from 51 percent to 85 percent (Carson 1955). While turnout increased, voting levels still fell below the full participation that would later become a standard feature of Soviet elections.

By 1935, Soviet officials had begun preparing for extensive institutional restructuring, ultimately codifying changes in a new constitution (often called the Stalin Constitution). Vyacheslav Molotov proposed revolutionary modifications to electoral practices, notably suggesting the implementation of direct popular elections for congresses and executive committees, equal representation for rural and urban areas, and secret ballots. Only some of these changes were put in place (Carson 1955). In addition to changing the formal rules for elections, the ratification of the Stalin Constitution led to a dramatic change in how the Soviet leadership used elections.

The Second Era of Soviet Elections, 1937–1984

Joseph Stalin substantially reorganized the Soviet system, formalizing existing election procedures and making them consistent across Soviet territory, modifying the principle of suffrage to emphasize mass participation rather than the exclusion of suspect voters, and instituting geographically based single-candidate elections with "secret" ballots (Swearer 1961).

Prior to the 1937 election, Stalin hinted that he might introduce real multicandidate competition. In a famous interview with the American journalist Roy Howard, Stalin suggested that multicandidate elections were possible, stating, "Evidently candidates will be put forward not only by the Communist Party, but by all sorts of public, non-Party organizations [sic]. And we have hundreds of these."[9] But, the tantalizing possibility of competitive elections was not realized until long after Stalin's death. Instead, elections evolved into ritualized celebrations of the Soviet system to enhance its legitimacy, train citizens, discover dissenters, and identify promising candidates for promotion into decision-making positions.

New formal rules underscored a change in philosophy about elections and their role in Soviet society. The underlying assumption of restrictive suffrage rules in the Soviet Union's first two decades was that some residents of the USSR could not be trusted to support the system (Figes 1988). Active antirevolutionary elements would undermine the USSR's progress if they were permitted to participate. By extending voting rights to all citizens, Soviet leaders conveyed a different message: the Soviet people supported the Communist Party and its objectives (Carson 1955). Political leaders coupled the underlying message of universal support for the Soviet system with the expectation that citizens would demonstrate their fealty by participating in elections and approving nominated candidates.

Turnout in second-era Soviet elections reflected the new emphasis on participation. By 1939, officially reported voter participation was nearly 100 percent, a level it would maintain during this period (Carson 1955; Swearer 1961). Several scholars have challenged the accuracy of official turnout results, suggesting that higher levels of nonparticipation were obscured by various techniques. Soviet officials did not report, nor did Western scholars have access to, reliable data on the number of citizens who did not register to vote, who obtained absentee certificates and did not use them, or the magnitude of data falsification (Zaslavsky and Brym 1978; Roeder 1989). All of these factors could explain the impressive turnout figures in Soviet elections, but coordinated mobilization efforts also encouraged citizens to cast ballots.

Electoral precincts were established to maximize participation. As one scholar noted:

> There is virtually no escape from the all-embracing organisation of the precincts. They are established on board ships with 20 or more voters, in hospitals, rest homes and sanatoria, in railroad stations, airports and on board long-distance trains—in fact, wherever human life is to be found within the borders of the U.S.S.R. The invalid is visited in his home by a representative of the local electoral commission, accompanied by a portable ballot box; the isolated weather-observation team sends its votes from the northern frozen wastelands by radio. The network is so all-inclusive and so carefully articulated that it is virtually impossible to avoid voting. (Gilison 1968, 817)

Voters scheduled to be out-of-town obtained an absentee certificate allowing them to cast their ballots outside of their home precincts (Zaslavsky and Brym 1978). A public campaign praising candidates, and the direct intervention of agitators who visited voters and pressed citizens to come to the polls, also encouraged high levels of participation (Mote 1965; Gilison 1968; Hill 1976; Zaslavsky and Brym 1978).

Each district featured a single nominated candidate, and voters cast ballots requiring "negative" votes. Voters supporting the candidate would simply submit their unmarked ballots. If a voter opposed the sole candidate, the voter was required to use the voting booth, mark the ballot, and drop it in the box. Despite strong disincentives for voters to show dissatisfaction, nominated candidates were not always successful. In 1955, 133 candidates were rejected by voters, in 1957, 167, in 1959, 182, and in 1961, 249. To put the frequency of candidate rejection in context, more than 1.5 million deputies were elected in 1955 and more than 1.8 million were elected in 1961 (Swearer 1961). Nominated candidates were not guaranteed election, but failure at the polls was rare.

Soviet officials developed a massive election infrastructure that further encouraged public participation. In the initial 1937 election, around seven million people served on commissions to help select 1.2 million representatives at all levels (Carson 1955). By the 1959 elections, personnel requirements had grown to include more than eight million citizens in electoral commissions (Swearer 1961).[10]

Elections after 1937 focused on geographic districts with representation carefully defined (one representative per 300,000 citizens for the Supreme Soviet; one per 150,000 for the Russian Republic's Soviet). At lower levels, representation was not as consistently delineated, but this inconsistency changed in 1947 and officials established a standard ratio of delegates to population (Carson 1955).

Candidates could be nominated for office through several channels: the Communist Party, public organizations such as trade unions, and groups of voters associated with their place of employment (e.g., factories, collective farms). The source of nominations varied over time, with workplace voter groups increasingly becoming the most common method of nomination. The Communist Party generally influenced nomination through the intervention of local party organizations, even when nominations were technically put forward by other groups (Carson 1955; Swearer 1961; Hill 1976). Candidate nomination could be contentious and was the only real source of competition in Soviet elections (Carson 1955; Swearer 1961; Mote 1965).

In addition to changes in the typical sources of nomination, some of the institutional rules changed during the second era. For example, Nikita Khrushchev introduced term limits in 1961, but they were subsequently eliminated after he fell from power (Gill 1991). The 1977 Soviet Constitution also codified the Communist Party as the "leading and guiding force of Soviet society" (Hill 1994), formalizing the vanguard role that it had fulfilled for decades.

While the second era of Soviet elections indeed showcased some variation in participation (Roeder 1989), government oversight, and institutional rules, the primary function of elections and their results remained the same. With the accession of Mikhail Gorbachev to the helm of the Communist Party, however, a new wave of reforms would transform elections' purpose, function, and outcomes.

The Third Era of Soviet Elections, 1985–1991

Beginning in 1985, the newly appointed General Secretary of the Communist Party, Mikhail Gorbachev, initiated another era of liberalization by promoting the policies of glasnost, perestroika, and demokratiya. The third policy, "demokratiya," introduced competitive elections for party and administrative positions. While Gorbachev instituted multicandidate elections, he remained committed to the continuation of the Communist Party's vanguard role and maintained this position until the waning days of the Soviet Union.

Although Gorbachev planned to reform the system while maintaining the dominance of the Communist Party, he faced significant opposition from conservative forces. Despite challenges from inside the Communist Party, several events encouraged his actions. Increased ethnic tensions and a faltering economy led Gorbachev to utilize the Nineteenth Conference of the

Communist Party as a forum to accelerate liberalization. Conference documents indicated that the Communist Party would retain its dominant role but change its leadership style to emphasize pluralism and a limited degree of dissent within its ranks. The reforms would increase local government's authority, create a new parliament, reestablish term limits, and institute for the first time multicandidate elections with truly secret ballots (Materialy Vsyesoyuznoi Konferentsii 1988).

While some multicandidate voting was permitted as early as 1987 (White, Wyman, and Oates 1997), the real breakthrough came with the new legislature's creation. It featured two houses: the 2,250-member Congress of People's Deputies and a 542-member Supreme Soviet. The Congress of People's Deputies would convene once annually and would choose delegates to the Supreme Soviet. The Supreme Soviet would act as a standing legislature, meeting throughout the year (Materialy Vsyesoyuznoi Konferentsii 1988).

In 1988, the Supreme Soviet accepted the changes proposed by the Nineteenth Communist Party Conference and approved new electoral laws. Based on the new laws, organizations would choose one-third of the Congress's representatives; voters would select two-thirds of the delegates in geographic districts. Of the deputies to be chosen from organizations, 525 were allocated to specific groups, and the remaining 225 were divided into three groups of 75 for election by designated national-level organizations. The remaining 1,500 deputies were divided into two groups of 750. One set would be elected through voting districts of 257,300 voters each. The second set of deputies would be affiliated with regions (with 32 deputies elected from each union republic, 11 from each autonomous republic, 5 from each autonomous region, and 1 from each autonomous district) (Chiesa 1993). Although districts were divided among organizations, political units, and geographically defined electoral districts, representatives would continue to be chosen by a majority system in single-member districts using negative ballots (Brunner 1990; Kiernan and Aistrup 1991).

The 1989 Congress of People's Deputies election was generally considered to be a triumph for proponents of political liberalization: multiple candidates contested 73 percent of the districts. More than one-half of the multicandidate districts required a runoff because no single candidate received a majority in the first round (Chiesa 1993). But, competitive districts were not uniformly distributed across Soviet space. Campaigns were most intense in Moscow and the Baltic states, with tighter controls especially evident in parts of Russia, Ukraine, and Central Asia. In addition, many organizations avoided nominating controversial candidates, forcing some prominent figures to contest territorial seats.[11]

The election featured only one political party, as the Communist Party retained its legal status as the sole political party. Nevertheless, the election campaign included candidates with diverse views. This feature of the elections was later demonstrated in televised sessions of the Congress, with prominent dissidents like Andrei Sakharov seated in the assembly and spirited debates broadcast over Soviet airwaves.

Under increasing pressure to relinquish its monopoly on power and alter the 1977 Soviet Constitution, the Central Committee of the Communist Party agreed to change the party's constitutionally defined role in February 1990. In March of the same year, articles 6 and 7 of the Soviet Constitution were rewritten to reflect the acceptance of "political parties" and the elimination of the Communist Party's vanguard role (Hill 1994). In practice, the Communist Party's privileged status remained until after the August 1991 coup attempt.

Local Supreme Soviet elections, held at the same time that the Communist Party surrendered its monopoly on political life, bolstered proreform and independence forces. In 1991, the republics turned to presidential elections, and many selected leaders who would continue in office long after the USSR's collapse (notably Boris Yeltsin in Russia, Nursultan Nazarbayev in Kazakhstan, Saparmurat Niyazov in Turkmenistan, and Islam Karimov in Uzbekistan). The presidential elections were an important milestone, further decentralizing power and accelerating the momentum leading to Soviet collapse at the end of 1991 (White, McAllister, and Kryshtanovskaya 1994).

CONCLUSION

As the discussion in this chapter has noted, electoral institutions varied over time, although they were characterized by a common set of electoral rules and administrative practices throughout most of the Soviet era. These formal institutions—candidate nomination via the party-of-power and groups of voters, negative ballots, single-member districts with majority voting requirements, and a multitiered election administration—could influence the choice of post-Soviet electoral practices and constitute one form of Soviet legacy.

The underlying social expectations about participation in the electoral enterprise, as well as the role given to elections in the political process, could influence individual decisions and constitute a behavioral inheritance. The system's focus on maximizing turnout, using elections as a mechanism to reward appropriate behavior, and training citizens in acceptable methods of civic action, as well as the deputy's place as role model and occasional advocate for small improvements in conditions, could influence the behavior of voters, candidates, parties, contributors, and other political actors.

CHAPTER 3

ELECTORAL SYSTEM
DESIGN AND REDESIGN

Following the Soviet Union's dissolution at the end of 1991, institutional designers, international organizations, and politicians directed considerable attention to the development and conduct of elections. As Chapters 1 and 2 revealed, even though elections in the USSR did not function like those in democratic societies, Soviet leaders created an elaborate elections infrastructure that performed many of the same functions as its democratic counterparts. After the USSR's collapse, politicians in the newly independent states were able to adopt or modify these institutions, or create new election rules that departed from Soviet practices. This chapter addresses the selection of initial election rules and assesses why politicians modify the rules over time.

Some scholars of institutional design emphasize the durability of initial choices following regime change (Lijphart 1984; Shugart and Carey 1992; Jones 1995). At first glance, election rules in the Soviet successor states seem to be relatively stable: nine of the fifteen countries emerging from the USSR had the same basic legislative electoral system in 2008 that they had in place for their first postcommunist election, and countries that popularly elect presidents have not substantially modified their election rules. In the early 2000s, some scholars concluded that postcommunist election systems were nearly institutionalized and experienced only minor changes over time (Bielasiak 2001; Dawisha 2000). But, a deeper examination reveals a substantial amount of change flying "under the radar," demonstrating that post-Soviet political actors have not accepted the status quo, and instead have tinkered extensively with election rules.

To address the dynamics of election system design and redesign, the chapter first defines the formal rules encompassing an electoral system and subsequently reviews the literature on election rule design and change, noting the wide range of causal agents connected with this process. Next, it discusses the initial design of post-Soviet election rules and outlines institutional continuity and change over time. The chapter concludes with analytic narratives that assess Russian and Ukrainian decisions to abandon mixed electoral rules in favor of proportional representation.

ELECTORAL SYSTEM DESIGN AND CHANGE

What Are Electoral Systems?

Electoral systems are complex webs of formal rules that directly regulate the behavior of actors in elections (candidates, political parties, voters, contributors, media, and observers) and the electoral process itself, as well as ancillary rules that may apply beyond the active campaign period. Four categories capture the main elements of election legislation.[1]

The first category, *barriers to entry*, includes regulations that affect how citizens exercise their rights to suffrage and how political actors exercise their rights to contestation. To vote, citizens may be required to formally request inclusion on the voter registry by providing documentation proving their right to vote in a particular constituency. The construction of voter lists has been a contentious issue in post-Soviet elections, and many citizens have been denied the opportunity to vote because of exclusion from voter lists.

Election statutes, or ancillary rules, may also control how organizations become officially recognized political parties. Requirements for registration may include submission of party documents (e.g., platforms, rules), membership thresholds (e.g., size, geographic distribution), financial requirements (e.g., disclosure of assets, payment of registration fees), or other provisions that require contestants to reveal personnel, technical, or material resources. In addition to registering as official entities, parties must gain ballot access in specific districts. Candidates and parties are often required to demonstrate some level of popular support (by collecting signatures) or financial backing (by paying a fee or deposit for participation) as a prerequisite for entry to the ballot. As barriers to entry increase, the number and diversity of contestants and voters should decline.

The second category, *campaign regulations*, constrains the conduct of politicians as they attempt to mobilize voters. Legislation or electoral commission regulations generally establish an election calendar, defining when certain activities may begin and when they must end. Regulations also set parameters for appropriate campaign behavior, such as setting limits on solicitation by mail, phone, or in-person; television, radio, or print advertising; or other methods to get out the vote. The rules could obligate the media to allocate free advertising time or space, or provide equal time to candidates in news coverage. Campaign finance regulations may require candidates and parties to disclose personal information and limit the amount and types of funds to be used in elections. Controls over campaign activities could also affect behavior, with more liberal guidelines encouraging wider participation.[2]

The third category, *translation of votes into seats*, encompasses the casting, counting, and compiling of votes. Rules governing the translation of votes into seats are widely regarded as the most important influences on the behavior of political actors. The electoral formula, district magnitude, ballot structure, and thresholds exert well-documented effects on the number of political parties (Taagepera and Shugart 1989; Lijphart 1994; Cox 1997).[3]

The fourth category, *administration and oversight*, addresses the implementation of election rules, including adjudication procedures to resolve disputes. Commissions that implement elections may be organized as partisan, nonpartisan, or mixed bodies, and they may be seated at the national and local levels. Commissions determine who can vote and run for office and often adjudicate procedural complaints along with the courts. If the administration and adjudication process is perceived to be biased or unfair, the number of voters, candidates, and parties willing to participate may decline.

Because they cover a wide range of rights and responsibilities, the rules governing elections may be codified across several documents: the constitution; statutes governing elections, referendums, electoral commissions, courts, media, and public organizations or parties; as well as regulations issued by the executive branch or other administrative agencies.

How Election Rules are Chosen and Changed

A critical gap in the study of elections is a well-developed model of election rule choice supported by solid empirical evidence (Shugart 2005; Benoit 2007). Unlike the literature on the consequences of election rules, which is characterized by a well-defined research program that has evolved over time (Riker 1982b), research on the origins and reform of electoral rules has focused on disparate causal agents, varied countries and time periods, and has used different methods. Kenneth Benoit (2007) notes that scholars have identified parties, nonparty actors, external actors, and nonpolitical experts as agents of change, with history, society, the economy, and even chance as environmental factors in the selection of election rules. Moreover, Benoit indicates that assumptions about the underlying motivation for election system choice and change may focus on office seeking, policy seeking, representation, governance, social engineering, legitimacy, fairness, or other goals (Benoit 2007). Scholarly work on electoral rule design and redesign in postcommunist states has reflected similar variation, with most researchers emphasizing the role of key political actors with normative or strategic commitments to particular election rules, the role of institutional inheritances, or the interaction between these factors.

To explain election rule design and change in the postcommunist region, some scholars have favored normatively defined preferences, focusing on the role of political entrepreneurs. This approach emphasizes the commitment of institutional designers to a particular set of rules because of deeply held beliefs about the rules' positive features and their efforts to seek out or create opportunities to implement preferred rules.[4]

The initial selection of Russia's mixed electoral system may be interpreted through this lens. Viktor Sheynis, a reform-minded politician intensely interested in election systems, was a political entrepreneur with strong a priori beliefs about the system's benefits. Sheynis obtained his preferred outcome via advocacy during the transition period. His early involvement in election system design discussions, and privileged access to elite decision-makers following the suspension of parliament and the Constitutional Court, gave him a direct opportunity to lobby President Boris Yeltsin. Sheynis initially made normative arguments advocating the adoption of a mixed system but noted that Yeltsin was ultimately swayed by the possible political advantage mixed systems could convey to his supporters (McFaul 1999; 2001).

A second approach to understanding institutional design and change emphasizes the pursuit of self-interest rather than normative preferences (Bawn 1993; Smith and Remington 2001; Benoit and Hayden 2004). Politicians may advocate election rule change when different rules could produce a higher yield of parliamentary seats (Benoit 2004; Benoit and Schiemann 2001; Benoit and Hayden 2004), or when new competitors threaten established parties' hold on power (Boix 1999). Politicians situated at critical policy-making choke points may also strive to preserve their advantages by exercising an institutional or partisan veto over efforts to change election rules to a less advantageous alternative (Tsebelis 2002). Recent scholarship on postcommunist election system design has emphasized short-term calculations and strategic errors, noting that election winners often strive to preserve the advantages they accrued in the previous election (Andrews and Jackman 2005). The case studies later in this chapter address self-interest as a decisive factor in election rule change.

The third general approach to explaining election rule change attempts to account for idiosyncratic and exogenous elements.[5] The unexpected collapse of the USSR, civil wars and violent confrontations between political forces, and other events affected the timing, process, and outcome of election rule design. Moreover, because election rules often emerge from elite bargaining, the final form of the rules tends to reflect compromises among competitors at the table. Inherited institutional features and norms, the distribution of power among political elites involved in negotiation, and the contemporary political environment may influence the bargaining process and its outcomes.

For example, some scholars have argued that in countries where bargaining took place over initial election rules, communist parties generally favored majoritarian systems whereas opposition politicians preferred proportional representation. The final outcome of bargaining was determined by the residual power of communist parties: stronger communist parties successfully instituted majoritarian rules, stronger opposition parties instituted proportional representation (PR), and mixed electoral systems emerged when the sides were equal (Elster, Offe, and Preuss 1998; Dawisha 2000). Other scholars have emphasized subnational divisions in parts of the former Soviet Union, with regional actors exerting influence over national and local election rule design (Jones Luong 2002; Moraski 2006). In short, while political actors may seek rules that provide them benefits, they often must respond to the demands of other players or exogenous factors.

The contemporary literature focuses on the identities and roles of the actors engaging in institutional design, the underlying motivations for modifying election rules, and the constraints placed on these actors by the political environment. If the Soviet institutional legacy strongly influences the choice of election rules, one should see evidence of the persistence of Soviet-era practices. Alternatively, the process of election system design may be driven primarily by elite political actors selecting rules designed to benefit themselves and their allies. To the degree that institutional forms differing from Soviet rules are perceived to benefit political actors with the power and authority to institute changes, new institutional forms should emerge.[6] The next section outlines the institutional inheritance from the Soviet period, noting where rules persisted and were abandoned.

ELECTION RULES IN POST-SOVIET STATES

Founding Election Rules

Immediately following the USSR's dissolution, the newly independent states faced pressure to advance along four dimensions of democratic transition: political reform, economic reform, establishing a functioning state apparatus, and developing a national identity associated with the new realities of the post-Soviet era (Kuzio 2001). These formidable challenges, and the absence of a clear roadmap for success, prompted political leaders to sequence their transition efforts differently. The Baltic states addressed all dimensions of transition simultaneously, restructuring political institutions, moving toward a market economy, establishing strong states, and emphasizing a national identity associated with the interwar independence period. Elites in other post-Soviet states did not vigorously pursue all four aspects of transformation equally. Russian leaders, for example, prioritized economic reform over political change, evidenced by the initiation of "shock therapy," while Soviet-era institutions like the constitution and parliament continued to function.

The Russian experience was more indicative of transition in the region. Rather than experiencing rapid, multidimensional change, most corners of the former USSR experienced slow, stalled, or intentionally neglected reform efforts. Several countries became embroiled in conflict: Armenia and Azerbaijan continued their struggles over the Karabakh region, separatists in Transnistria engaged in violence in Moldova, separatists and irredentists challenged Georgian government authority in Abkhazia and South Ossetia, and Tajikistan's regional and ideological divides prompted the bloodiest civil war yet in post-Soviet space. Despite great variation in efforts to reform their systems, and differing political contexts, all of the newly independent countries moved toward holding elections for national offices.

The electoral rules used in initial post-Soviet parliamentary contests reflected both continuity with and change from Soviet-era practices. Table

Table 3.1   Initial and Current Post-Soviet Election Rules (Lower House of Parliament)

Country	Electoral System (Initial)	Electoral System (Most Recent Election)
Armenia	Mixed System (PR and SMD-MR)	Mixed System (PR and SMD-Pl) (2007)
Azerbaijan	Mixed System (PR and SMD-MR)	SMD-Pl (2005)
Belarus	SMD-MR	SMD-MR (2008)
Estonia	PR	PR (2007)
Georgia	Mixed (PR and SMD-Pl)	Mixed (PR and SMD-Pl) (2008)
Kazakhstan	SMD-MR	PR (2007)
Kyrgyzstan	SMD-MR	PR (2007)
Latvia	PR	PR (2006)
Lithuania	Mixed (PR and SMD-MR)	Mixed (PR and SMD-Pl) (2008)
Moldova	PR	PR (2005)
Russia	Mixed (PR and SMD-Pl)	PR (2007)
Tajikistan	SMD-MR	Mixed (PR and SMD-MR) (2005)
Turkmenistan	SMD-MR	SMD-MR (2004)
Ukraine	SMD-MR	PR (2007)
Uzbekistan	SMD-MR	SMD-MR (2004)

Sources: Shvetsova (1999), OSCE reports, and various statutes.

3.1 identifies initial parliamentary election systems and the rules used in the most recent contests. Several countries continued to use single member–district systems with a majority-runoff formula just as in Soviet times (Belarus, Kazakhstan, Kyrgyzstan, Tajikistan, Turkmenistan, Ukraine, and Uzbekistan). Eight countries abandoned this practice, explicitly invoking pre-Soviet election rules or experimenting with new institutional forms. Estonia, Latvia, and Moldova selected proportional representation systems,[7] although Estonia briefly flirted with the single transferable vote (STV)[8] in its 1990 Supreme Soviet elections.

The remaining five countries adopted a relatively new election system: the noncompensatory mixed electoral system. Mixed electoral systems combine a majoritarian rule—usually a single-member district system with plurality or majority formula—with a proportional rule in a single election. These systems were first instituted in the twentieth century, and the long-standing German compensatory model has served as the archetype.[9] Instead of adhering closely to the German model, however, mixed systems are characterized by substantial variation. The formal linkage between allocation tiers, the proportion of seats allocated to different formulas, regulations regarding party and candidate nominations, the number and form of ballots, and other features vary cross-nationally.

Post-Soviet elites did not copy a critical feature of the German model: the linkage between majoritarian and proportional tiers. In the German system, the proportional vote is decisive; it determines overall seat allocation. Seats acquired in the majoritarian component influence the number of positions allocated in the proportional tier, yielding an overall outcome that is proportional in terms of the party list vote. Post-Soviet mixed electoral systems did not formally link the tiers, instead allocating seats independently in the majoritarian and proportional tiers.

Elections for chief executives were less experimental. Although post-Soviet states continued Soviet practices of majority-runoff elections used for republican presidential votes, the popular election of presidents was a new phenomenon associated with the transitional period. Popular election did not extend to the national level; Mikhail Gorbachev created a presidency, but the USSR collapsed before the first public vote was held.[10] For most of the communist era, the leading position in the Soviet hierarchy was the General Secretary of the Communist Party. Although constraints on the general secretary's policy-making authority varied over time and by the identity of the person occupying the office (Roeder 1993), the general secretary wielded significant power.

While some post-Soviet countries eschewed the codification of strong presidential authority, others endowed chief executives with sweeping powers. Based on an assessment of presidential authority over vetoes, decrees, legislation, cabinet, and parliament at the end of the 1990s, researchers ranked Latvia's president as weakest, followed by Estonia; Lithuania and Moldova (tied); Georgia; Tajikistan; Ukraine; Armenia; Russia; Kyrgyzstan; Kazakhstan, Turkmenistan, and Uzbekistan (tied); with Belarus's president rated strongest.[11] Countries with stronger presidents have more closely followed an authoritarian model.

In many countries, first secretaries of regional communist parties successfully navigated the transition to emerge as postcommunist presidents: Heydar Aliyev (Azerbaijan), Eduard Shevardnadze (Georgia), Nursultan Nazarbayev (Kazakhstan), Algirdas Brazauskas (Lithuania), Rakhmon Nabiyev (Tajikistan), Saparmurat Niyazov (Turkmenistan), and Islam Karimov (Uzbekistan). By retaining strong chief executives, and sometimes the person who served as local communist party boss, many post-Soviet societies preserved elements of the Soviet institutional heritage.

Post-Soviet presidential election rules are remarkably uniform. All countries, save Latvia, held at least one public vote for president in the post-Soviet period. Majority-runoff elections are the norm, but institutional designers modified elements of the majority-runoff system. For example, in its sole popular presidential election in 1992, Estonia allowed voters to cast ballots only in the first round of competition. Because the first round did not yield a majority winner, parliament selected the president in the second-round runoff (Raitviir 1996). Selection mechanisms varied slightly in some other countries, but generally adhered to the common practices associated with majority-runoff systems.[12]

Post-Soviet institutional designers continued the Soviet-era principle of voting against candidates, rather than for candidates, in several ways. In some cases the negative ballot, on which voters cross off the names of candidates or parties they do not support, was initially used in Armenia, Azerbaijan, Belarus, Kazakhstan, Kyrgyzstan, Tajikistan, Turkmenistan, Ukraine, and Uzbekistan.[13] In other cases, this method of voting was preserved in part. Latvia and Georgia permitted voters to register both their support for and opposition to candidates. In Russia, the option to vote "against all" was added to the ballot (Lyubarev 2003). Only Estonia, Lithuania, and Moldova solely presented voters with ballots requiring "positive" assessments of the competitors. The presence of multiple candidates and parties on ballots across most of the former USSR eliminated the utility of negative ballots as a method to control voter choices, and most states later abandoned negative ballots as a method of registering voter preferences.

Other elements of Soviet-era election rules were preserved in most states, notably the three-tiered framework for electoral administration, ballot access for nonparty or voter groups, and the use of a mobile ballot box for voters unable to come to the polls. While most initial election rules contained elements that followed the form of Soviet-era institutions, the subsequent decade and a half witnessed substantial election rule reform.

Election Rule Reform

While presidential election rules have been relatively stable, legislative election rules have been quite malleable since the collapse of communism.[14] Table 3.1 illustrates some of the changes by noting the initial election rules and comparing them with the election rules used during the most recent campaign. This table omits several reforms to barriers to entry, the translation of votes into seats, and oversight and adjudication rules. Additional changes are summarized on Table 3.2.[15]

Nine countries retained their primary mode of electing members of parliament: Belarus, Turkmenistan, and Uzbekistan use single member–district systems with a majority-runoff formula; Estonia, Latvia, and Moldova use proportional representation; and Armenia, Georgia, and Lithuania use a mixed system. Despite this continuity, politicians have significantly altered the rules of contestation in all but one of these countries since 1991. Armenia changed the assembly size from 190 to 131, the proportion of seats allocated to PR and single-member districts (SMD) three times, the majoritarian tier's formula from majority-runoff to plurality, the PR threshold by adding a 7 percent barrier for blocs, the number and composition of electoral commissions, ballot access requirements, and deputies' terms of office. Belarus changed the assembly size from 260 to 110, added an upper house, and

Table 3.2   Election Rule Changes, 1992–2008

Country	Assembly Size	Formula	Ballot Access	Threshold	EC Composition	Seat Allocation	Term
Armenia	X	X	X	X	X	X	X
Azerbaijan		X	X	X	X	X	
Belarus	X				X		
Estonia			X				
Georgia	X	X	X	X	X	X	X
Kazakhstan	X	X	X	X	X	X	
Kyrgyzstan	X	X	X	X	X	X	
Latvia				X			X
Lithuania		X		X			
Moldova			X	X			
Russia		X	X	X		X	X
Tajikistan	X	X		X	X	X	
Turkmenistan							
Ukraine		X	X	X		X	
Uzbekistan	X		X				

Note: An X indicates that statutory provisions in the category have changed during the time period under analysis.

Sources: Various constitutions and election statutes.

altered electoral commission composition. Estonia increased party membership requirements for ballot access. Georgia modified its electoral formula,[16] thrice altered the threshold (from 0 percent to 5 percent, to 7 percent, and back to 5 percent), and changed ballot access requirements, the composition of electoral commissions, and deputies' terms of office. Latvia increased its threshold from 4 to 5 percent. Lithuania similarly increased its threshold and briefly altered the majoritarian tier's formula from majority-runoff to plurality. Moldova changed party membership requirements for ballot access, increased thresholds for parties, and decreased the threshold for independent candidates. Uzbekistan altered assembly size and nomination rules. Only Turkmenistan has had no notable changes to parliamentary election legislation since 1991.

The remaining six countries significantly altered the primary method of translating votes into seats, in addition to affecting other changes. Kazakhstan and Ukraine abandoned single member–district majority-runoff rules for a mixed system and later adopted proportional representation. Kyrgyzstan followed a more circuitous path, dropping and reinstating majority-runoff rules bridged by a mixed system and finally adopting pure proportional representation.[17] Russia eliminated its mixed system for the 2007 election, opting instead for proportional representation. Tajikistan adopted a mixed system, replacing its original single member–district majority-runoff system. In addition to instituting major electoral system changes, these countries altered several other aspects of the rules, including thresholds, seat allocation, ballot access, and electoral commission composition. As Table 3.2 demonstrates, rather than exemplifying stability, post-Soviet electoral rules have been prone to change.

This long list of election rule changes includes only those efforts that were successfully implemented. Many attempts to change election statutes have been rebuffed. For instance, Georgia adopted the single transferable vote in place of its mixed electoral system in 1991. After the return of Eduard Shevardnadze and political stabilization, it reinstated a mixed system prior to the 1992 election. Although the election rules were formally changed, no elections were held under the single transferable vote system (Slider 1992; Herron and Mirzashvili 2005), so this redesign effort is generally forgotten.

To fully understand the dynamics of election system change, both successful and unsuccessful efforts must be investigated. The following section addresses the adoption of proportional representation in Russia and Ukraine. While both efforts were eventually successful, election rule reformers endured several unsuccessful attempts to modify both systems along the way.

ABANDONING MIXED ELECTORAL SYSTEMS

Thus far, the chapter has outlined various explanations of election rule choice and change, detailed the institutional rules adopted for founding elections, and outlined election rule reforms implemented in the postcommunist period. The narratives in this section synthesize explanations of election rule change with the dynamics of parallel debates in Russia and Ukraine about the adoption of proportional representation. They also address a puzzle: why did the leaderships of Russia and Ukraine that had opposed proportional representation ultimately support its adoption?

While both countries codified similar forms of proportional representation, the purpose and implementation differed. Russia's reforms support the increasingly centralized character of politics, and Ukraine's reforms support its contentious, nascent democracy. Russia and Ukraine are particularly valuable cases to address because they incorporate both failures and successes in election reform efforts and show how similar institutional forms may be substantially affected by ancillary rules and election administration.

The analysis of Russian and Ukrainian reforms addresses the agents (parties, nonparty actors, external actors, and nonpolitical experts) and environmental factors (history, society, political conditions, and chance) driving election rule change. In both cases, the selection of proportional representation was driven by calculations of self-interest, conditioned by exogenous events that propelled political actors toward the selection of a system that they had opposed.

Russia's Adoption of Proportional Representation

In December 2007, Russia held its first election under the new national closed-list PR system. While PR is generally praised as promoting consensus politics and wide representation (Lijphart 1999), many viewed the election as an extension of President Putin's efforts to centralize power. Yet, Putin and his predecessor, Boris Yeltsin, had long opposed PR, generally expressing preferences for more majoritarian systems. The ultimate adoption of PR under Putin was due to a confluence of events similar to those supporting the initial codification of a mixed electoral system. In both cases, dominant political actors changed the rules to consolidate their decision-making authority, acting when political opposition was weak and extraordinary events justified extreme action.

Russia's initial post-Soviet election system was born out of the resolution to the chaotic struggle between parliament and President Boris Yeltsin in the first two years after Soviet dissolution. Yeltsin's decision to delay political reforms and instead concentrate energies on economic reforms created a political rift that inherited Soviet institutions did not anticipate. Multicandidate elections for the Congress of People's Deputies had produced some political diversity in Moscow, but the Russian legislature was dominated by holdovers from the communist era. These politicians—selected under the rules in force at the time—stymied Yeltsin's reform agenda using existing institutional rules. Yeltsin countered through the use of decrees and by calling a referendum to demonstrate public support for his policies. The conflict escalated, culminating in a series of critical events in autumn 1993: the dissolution of parliament and the Constitutional Court, armed combat between parliamentary protesters and Russian security forces, and the final assault on parliament with heavy weaponry.

By vacating the institutional checks on presidential power, Yeltsin and his team created an environment in which they could quickly restructure the formal mechanisms of Russia's state apparatus. This restructuring included the development of a new constitution, codifying strong presidential powers and weakening parliament, and new elections under an experimental electoral system.

The final discussions leading to the selection of a mixed system were primarily conducted behind closed doors. While scholars and politicians had publicly debated election rules in anticipation of new parliamentary elections, Yeltsin announced the decision to equally split parliament into majoritarian and proportional tiers through a decree. Prior to this declaration, Yeltsin's advisors were divided on the best electoral system to select. Proponents of majoritarian rules pointed to strong performance by the proreform movement in the April 1993 referendum, asserting that this support could be translated into votes for proreform parties via a district-based plurality system. Moreover, no party had the same name recognition as the communists; this advantage could cause proreform parties to underperform in PR.

Proponents of PR pointed to the organizational capacity of communists at the local level and the potential for communist holdovers to use administrative resources to their benefit in majoritarian races. In addition, proreform forces were not adequately organized outside of cities to field strong candidates; PR would allow the candidate list to remain centralized and play to the strengths of Yeltsin's allies (Remington and Smith 1996; Moser and Thames 2001; Marsh 2001). The primary choices on the table at the time did not include a pure PR system, however. The main contenders were a majoritarian or mixed system.[18]

The choice of a mixed system allowed Yeltsin and the proreform wing to hedge bets against potentially disastrous outcomes if they did not adequately anticipate the behavior of voters. As noted above, Viktor Sheynis, a leading proponent of mixed systems in Russia, indicated that Boris Yeltsin was not swayed by normative arguments about the advantages of the mixed system; rather he seemed more swayed by the assertion that allied parties would benefit electorally from a mixed system.[19]

The political context supporting the initial selection of a mixed electoral system included several critical elements: a decision-making environment that did not require consensus or compromise because the opposition had been silenced by the dissolution of parliament; party-based actors advocating rules that they perceived would provide a strategic seat-maximizing benefit at the polls; a normatively driven political entrepreneur who could also muster arguments based on strategic considerations; and a president with the power to rule by decree. The choice of a mixed system diverged from the institutional inheritance by design: from the perspective of Yeltsin and his allies, it was the institutional legacy of the Soviet system, through the formal distribution of powers among the legislative and executive bodies, as well as the legislature elected in the Soviet era, that was stifling needed reforms and sparking the crisis in governance. Creating a strong elected president and parliament selected via party lists and individual constituencies would facilitate Yeltsin's efforts to remake post-Soviet Russian society.

The mixed system did not produce electoral victories for Yeltsin's team, however. The great surprise of 1993's election—the strong performance of Vladimir Zhirinovskiy's Liberal Democratic Party of Russia in the party list component—was portrayed as a protest vote against political and economic developments over the first two years of postcommunism (Sakwa 1995). The results of 1993 elevated dissatisfaction with the mixed electoral system among some politicians, prompting efforts to restructure it.

After the 1993 election, the Duma debated the formal codification of the election law. In the deliberations over election law reform, President Yeltsin proposed a modified mixed system that was markedly majoritarian. This proposal was rejected, with Yeltsin failing to win support from his allies in the Duma. The strongest support was from deputies occupying district seats, the group of deputies most likely to be advantaged by an expansion of majoritarian positions and reduction in party list seats (Remington and Smith 1996;

Smith and Remington 2001). The mixed system used in 1993 was ultimately retained, with minor modifications.

President Yeltsin and his successor, President Vladimir Putin, reportedly continued efforts to alter the electoral system by eliminating PR rather than enhancing it. In 1998, President Yeltsin's envoy to the Duma indicated that the president favored a change to a pure majoritarian system because it would be more democratic.[20] The following year, the new pro-Putin party Unity also advocated for a pure plurality system (Colton and McFaul 2003), and President Putin's advisors indicated his preference for this change.[21] Political analysts suggested that the institution of majoritarian rules would enhance progovernment parties and undermine the opposition. This opinion was apparently shared by officials in Putin's party of power: "[Unity's] founders calculated that a party of power would do better in a district-based system, especially if it could polarize the district races and then prevail in the runoff" (Colton and McFaul 2003, 17).

Rather than eliminating PR, however, President Putin proposed the introduction of a pure PR system in 2004. Putin's praise of PR during his national address at the beginning of 2007 revealed some of the underlying motivation for its ascendance: "It needs to be said directly that the previous elections using single-member districts did not exclude assistance by influential regional structures using administrative resources for their own candidates. I think that we have still not overcome this problem, but the new system significantly reduces the possibilities for using similar methods."[22] President Putin's conception of PR emphasized the benefits of reducing the influence of regional elites and by extension, increasing central authority.

The Beslan massacre—in which Chechen terrorists' occupation of a school, and the poorly coordinated response, resulted in over 300 deaths in September 2004—is an unlikely starting point for electoral reform. Yet, invoking that tragedy, President Putin announced several institutional changes as part of the Russian government's efforts to combat terrorism. Among Putin's proposals were the elimination of elections for regional governors and a change to the electoral system for the Duma, instituting PR in place of the mixed electoral system.

The Beslan event was a catastrophic reminder that Russians are not safe from terrorism; in many ways it prompted the same kind of posttragedy soul-searching that the September 11, 2001 attacks inspired in the United States. The Russian government's response to Beslan focused on strengthening the state's ability to control society and provide security. The tragedy revealed weaknesses in Russia's preparations to defend itself against terrorism emanating from various sources; the institutional changes would further strengthen the state and buttress against future attacks.

In a conversation with a representative of the Central Electoral Commission,[23] I was told that the Beslan incident reinforced the need for Russian citizens to take personal responsibility for politics, and that the reforms would accomplish this goal. Other observers have characterized the reform efforts as a reasonable response, given President Putin's interpretation of Russia's domestic and international position (Lynch 2005). President Putin's majority support in the legislature, and the imperative he ascribed to election system change after Beslan, ensured that his preferences would be accepted by parliament, which easily passed the bill in spring 2005.

The institutional reforms announced in the wake of the Beslan event were not isolated, however (Gurova and Mekhanik 2004; Moraski 2007). President Putin had been conducting ongoing federal reforms to restrict the power of local officials, including the creation of federal districts and the consolidation of some regional units. Further, Russia's Law on Political Parties, enacted in 2001, included provisions requiring political parties to have a national profile and draw membership from across Russia (Herron 2004; Moraski 2006). This ancillary election law was designed to reduce the number of parties and impede the creation of regional parties of power. Beginning with the early stages of his presidency, President Putin was concerned with reconstructing Russia's "power vertical" and reelevating federal-level institutions to the top of the chain of command.

While political observers suggested that majoritarian election rules would undermine the opposition's ability to challenge the party of power (McFaul 2000), national closed-list PR can provide an institutional environment conducive to central control. PR is preferred by institutional designers as a method to maximize diverse representation when it is accompanied by a low electoral threshold that filters out small, poorly supported parties but facilitates representation of a wide range of views. The Russian version of PR, however, coupled with a high threshold, and buttressed by other impediments to open competition, promoted centralization by precluding contestation by independent candidates and regionally focused parties.

Several factors in the 2007 parliamentary election undermined the political environment under PR that generally produces robust multiparty competition. Institutional rules, such as Russia's 7 percent threshold significantly challenged parties that did not have the blessing of officials in central government. Unfair implementation of election rules, manifested by unbalanced media coverage and administrative decisions denying registration to some antigovernment parties, further undermined multiparty competition. Institutional impediments were magnified by Russia's self-destructive opposition that refused to coalesce into a single party.[24] Finally, by placing himself at the top of United Russia's party list, and characterizing the election as a referendum on his presidency, President Putin altered the conditions of the race and enhanced the performance of his party and its allies. While four parties passed the threshold, United Russia, Liberal Democratic Party of Russia, Just Russia, and the Communist Party of the Russian Federation, only the communists could be considered a true opposition party.

Russia's selection of a mixed system, and its subsequent change to PR, did not reflect a Soviet institutional inheritance. Rather, changes in electoral rules accompanied efforts to enhance the decision-making authority of the president and his team. Mixed electoral rules were believed to provide the best option for enhancing the electoral fortunes of proreform elements while mitigating potential losses in the unpredictable environment of founding elections. In the selection of initial election rules, the dissolution of parliament and Constitutional Court, along with bans on many opposition groups, allowed President Yeltsin and his team to select the rules they thought would best serve their interests.

The subsequent change to a PR system is best viewed in the context of President Putin's efforts to centralize Russian decision making. The selection of national closed-list PR with a 7 percent threshold, and ancillary rules controlling party entry into competition, provides strong cover for reducing the effectiveness of opposition candidates. President Putin's majority support in parliament facilitated passage of a new law, but the imperative of national security in the aftermath of Beslan could move politicians who had been reluctant to change the status quo in the past. Efforts to alter the system failed in the 1990s when many parliamentary deputies did not see personal advantages to supporting reform proposals. The PR alternative moved forward only when similar circumstances emerged: a crisis situation that endowed the president with increased authority, a parliament with limited opposition, and a policy-making plan based on enhancing the president's power.

Ukraine's Adoption of Proportional Representation

Like that of Russia, Ukraine's path to proportional representation was circuitous. The institutional reform process incorporated short-term calculations of costs and benefits as the opposition's grassroots and elite support was growing and the semiauthoritarian regime was attempting to engineer a presidential succession. The reversal in PR's fortunes was prompted by a brewing political scandal that galvanized opponents of the president and contributed to the opposition's strong performance in the 2002 parliamentary election. After 2002, the president and his allies came to support the introduction of PR as part of a broader constitutional reform that would reduce presidential powers and enhance those of parliament and the cabinet. Election rule change was once again influenced by strategic calculations, a changing political environment, and exogenous events.

The period following Ukraine's parliamentary and presidential elections in the late 1990s and early 2000s was particularly contentious. Frustrated with the politically divided parliament, President Leonid Kuchma proposed a referendum that would address citizen confidence in the Rada and introduce significant changes to parliament's composition. Some political observers characterized the referendum as an effort to undermine democracy by enhancing the power of the president (Zviglianich 2000), and it was challenged by the parliamentary opposition. The four questions on the April 16, 2000 referendum passed, but were not implemented due, in large part, to a newly unfolding crisis.[25]

The Kuchma regime was often accused of engaging in sinister deeds to silence critics and enhance its power. In November 2000, Socialist Party of Ukraine leader Oleksandr Moroz unveiled secretly recorded audio tapes allegedly implicating President Kuchma and his inner circle in the death of the journalist Heorhiy Gongadze, strong-arm tactics to improperly influence the 1999 presidential election, and other illegal activities. These revelations spawned anti-Kuchma protests as part of the "Ukraine without Kuchma" movement that was active until spring 2001.

Rhetorical support for PR grew as the 2002 parliamentary election approached. Opposition politicians asserted that the majoritarian tier of Ukraine's mixed system facilitated fraud, benefiting corrupt politicians and oligarchs (Kravchenko 2001). The president and his allies generally opposed the introduction of PR, preferring instead to retain the mixed electoral system.[26] Opposition deputies capitalized on the political scandal by taking up the question of election rule change. The first draft law, calling for deputies to be selected via national closed list PR with a 4 percent threshold, came to a vote in January 2001. Table 3.3 shows votes by parliamentary factions on three separate occasions for the proposed PR system. In the first vote, parties of the opposition, as well as some groups traditionally associated with progovernment positions, supported the proposal.

Individual deputies faced additional incentives, depending upon the type of parliamentary seat they occupied. Deputies in majoritarian seats would be more negatively influenced by the reform and more likely to oppose change. This phenomenon is evidenced in the data: among deputies elected to SMD seats, only 86 voted for the proposal, compared to 158 PR deputies.[27]

While the proposal received enough votes to pass, it was vetoed by President Kuchma. PR supporters could not muster enough votes to overturn the veto and instead drafted another version of the law, accepting twenty-three and rejecting sixteen presidential recommendations. Rather than advocating modifications to the proposal, President Kuchma challenged the appropriateness of the PR system itself. Kuchma argued that PR violated the Constitution of Ukraine, providing too much power to parties and not guaranteeing equal treatment of citizens (RFE/RL 2001).[28]

The new draft law passed the parliamentary vote with some changes in faction support (see Table 3.3) in March 2001.[29] Consistent with the expected preferences, majoritarian members of parliament opposed change more vigorously than their PR colleagues, though opposition dissipated from the previous vote. One hundred majoritarian deputies supported a change to PR compared to 169 PR deputies. This proposal was also vetoed by President Kuchma.

The results of the 2002 parliamentary election showed that many of the probable calculations by relevant political actors were realized. Opposition forces—especially Our Ukraine—performed well in the PR tier. The propresidential For United Ukraine bloc performed poorly in PR, but this failure was mitigated by successes in constituency races and later affiliation from deputies elected as independents. Opposition party success influenced the next stage of the election rule reform debate.

In August 2002, President Kuchma announced his support for a new attempt at major institutional reforms. The proposed constitutional changes

Table 3.3 Comparison of Affirmative Votes on PR Proposals

Lean Pro-Government	January 2001	March 2001	March 2004
Democratic Initiative	—	—	10
Democratic Union	—	1	—
Fatherland	28	25	—
Green Party	14	12	—
Labor Ukraine	0	0	33
People's Choice	—	—	11
People's Democratic Party	9	6	9
People's Power	—	—	12
Regions	—	—	50
Regional Revival	0	1	—
Social Democratic Party (United)	0	23	36
Solidarity	0	3	—
Yabluko	14	12	—
Opposition			
Agrarian Party	—	—	15
Communist Party	108	109	56
Our Ukraine	—		0
People's Rukh	16	13	—
Reforms Center	13	14	—
Socialist Party[1]	16	17	20
Tymoshenko Bloc	—	—	0
Ukrainian People's Rukh	21	22	—
Non Faction	13	23	3
Total (226 votes needed to pass)	252	281	255

Sources: Laboratory F-4 and Verkhovna Rada (http://portal.rada.gov.ua/).

would reduce the powers of the president and move Ukraine toward a parliamentary form of government. Kuchma's renewed interest in constitutional reforms was motivated by at least two factors: the increasing popularity of antipresidential politicians and the upcoming 2004 presidential election that would determine Kuchma's successor (Kuzio 2002). But, constitutional reform stalled.

In an effort to energize the reform process, Kuchma and his allies linked election rule change to constitutional reform. This strategy was aimed particularly at co-opting the Socialist and Communist parties that supported PR as well as more modest presidential powers. In early 2004, Kuchma directly courted the Communist Party and Socialist Party by agreeing to support PR, reversing his position from three years before.

While propresidential forces characterized the votes on election rules and constitutional reform as a package, they were conducted separately. The vote on adopting PR was held first in March 2004 (see Table 3.3). Change in positions over time is clear if one broadly groups factions into propresidential and opposition categories.[30] Many opposition factions tended to favor PR in 2001 and oppose it in 2004.[31] The main exception to this observation is among the leftist opposition parties. The Communist Party and Socialist Party factions consistently supported PR in both 2001 and 2004, with few defections of individual deputies from the parties' position. Most propresidential factions opposed PR in 2001 but supported it in 2004.

Faction support for PR parallels positions on constitutional reform. Anticipating the potential for an opposition candidate to win the presidency, Our Ukraine and the Bloc of Yuliya Tymoshenko boycotted the vote, opposing measures designed to reduce presidential powers. Propresidential and left opposition factions supported the constitutional proposals, but were unable to secure the needed supermajority of 300 votes. Ukraine's election rule reform saga thus ended with a victory for PR rules and failure for the president's constitutional changes.[32]

The first section of the chapter outlined several general explanations for election system reform. One explanation privileged the role of political entrepreneurs in the implementation of new election rules. Several Ukrainian politicians, most notably Yuriy Klyuchkovskiy, supported PR and fulfilled some of the criteria of the political entrepreneur model. But when the window of opportunity opened for PR to be enacted, these actors did not provide their votes in parliament. Rather, opposition to constitutional reform, packaged with election rule reform, led many politicians who otherwise promoted PR to retract their support.

Another explanation of election rule reform focused on rational calculations of self-interest. In 2001, the opposition believed that its performance would be enhanced by the use of pure PR; government believed it was advantaged by the retention of the mixed system. Cutting across partisan divisions were differences based on seat mandate. Deputies in majoritarian seats were threatened by the elimination of their path to parliament and were more likely to oppose reform than deputies in PR seats. The 2002 parliamentary election results suggest that opposition and government expectations were reasonable: opposition parties performed well in the PR tier, and progovernment parties performed poorly. Moreover, evidence suggests that administrative resources and fraud contributed to government successes in SMD (Herron and Johnson 2008). Rational calculations of PR's costs and benefits guided decision making, and those calculations also seem to have been reasonably accurate.

Rational calculations about PR's effects do not fully explain decision making on election reform, however. The PR debate became part of a "nested game" (Tsebelis 1990) involving broader constitutional change. In the second round of debates over PR, government actors reflected upon the lessons of the 2002 campaign and noted the looming threat of opposition success, especially in the upcoming presidential election. Progovernment forces were willing to change positions on PR to gain votes from the Communist and Socialist parties on the constitutional reform package. Deputies occupying majoritarian seats were strongly represented among those opposing the change; they also constituted a substantial component of progovernment defectors on constitutional reform. Politicians acted in accordance with their preferences but in the broader context of constitutional change rather than in the narrow context of election rule reform.

Election rule reform in Ukraine succeeded because many political elites perceived that the new rules could enhance their access to power. However, most propresidential politicians viewed the advantages of changing election rules in the context of winning support for constitutional reform. Election rule change was only possible when political actors occupying veto points—notably President Kuchma—assented to new election rules.

CONCLUSION

This chapter assessed the dynamics of election rule design and reform. The first section defined election systems and addressed several explanations for election rule design. The second section revealed that many institutional forms from the Soviet period survived the initial transition, but most of these rules were subsequently replaced. The third section presented narratives of institutional redesign in Russia and Ukraine, exploring how political actors, institutional rules, and the political and social environment influenced recent election system reform. Both cases featured political entrepreneurs favoring particular rules, exogenous events serving as catalysts to propel reform at a particular point in time, political actors assessing the benefits and costs of new election rules, election reform processes encompassed by a broader debate over institutional design, and buy-in by politicians at choke points along the policy-making chain. While these case studies do not characterize all election reform efforts, they nevertheless point to key features in the initiation and successful implementation of high-profile election rule reform in post-Soviet states.

This chapter has also highlighted the importance that political actors ascribe to election rules in both authoritarian and democratic societies. Election rule reform was not limited to democracies in post-Soviet space. Rather, some of the most vigorous advocates of election rule redesign were authoritarian political leaders. Why are politicians so interested in election rules? The next chapter begins to answer this question by assessing some of the outcomes associated with election rules and addressing variation in outcomes across authoritarian and democratic post-Soviet societies.

CHAPTER 4

CONSEQUENCES OF ELECTORAL SYSTEM CHOICE

The previous chapter demonstrated that political actors take electoral system design seriously, even in nondemocratic countries, updating and modifying the rules to benefit themselves and their allies. This chapter investigates a primary output of the electoral rules: political party systems.[1]

Political scientists have intensively investigated the connection between election rules and the party systems that emerge out of the electoral process. This connection is important because the number of parties in a political system is one indicator of how power is distributed. As Giovanni Sartori (1976, 120) observed, "It does matter how many are the parties. For one thing, the number of parties immediately indicates, albeit roughly, an important feature of the political system: the extent to which political power is fragmented or non-fragmented, dispersed or concentrated." The concentration of power in too few hands threatens viable democracy, but significant dispersion of power may undermine effective governance.

This chapter addresses how political institutions, social cleavages, and the postcommunist legacy affect party system development. As noted in Chapter 1, an intense scholarly debate has raised questions about the equivalence of postcommunist cases with their counterparts in other world regions. Rather than assuming, a priori, that postcommunist states differ from other transition countries, this chapter's investigation explicitly controls for the postcommunist experience. The analysis reveals that expectations about party system development may obtain in postcommunist societies, but that these outcomes may be attenuated by regional idiosyncrasies.

The first section of this chapter outlines the debate over the relative importance of institutional and contextual features in determining the contours of party systems. The second section presents interregional and intraregional empirical analyses that assess how institutional, social, and contextual factors influence the number of effective parties.[2] The third section presents deeper discussions of post-Soviet party systems to show how election results have conformed with, and diverged from, expectations about election rules and their consequences.

INSTITUTIONS, SOCIAL CLEAVAGES, AND THE NUMBER OF PARTIES

Much of the political science literature has dichotomized the debate about party system evolution, suggesting that scholars who emphasize the role of institutions trace their lineage to Maurice Duverger's work (1954), while those who emphasize the role of social cleavages are aligned with Seymour Martin Lipset and Stein Rokkan's (1967) approach. Recent research has called this simple dichotomy into question, noting that Duverger himself viewed social factors as a driving force determining the number of political parties and election rules as a constraining force (Clark and Golder 2006). Yet, the two approaches adhere to different logical connections between their primary explanatory factors and political party systems.

Researchers who lean toward Duverger's explanation focus on individual decision making, emphasizing how formal rules create incentives to which political actors respond. Duverger labeled the complementary processes driving behavior the *mechanical* and *psychological* effects. The mechanical effect describes how election rules translate votes into seats. The psychological effect describes how political actors respond to the expected consequences of the mechanical effect.

Single member–district systems (SMD) with plurality rules create a relatively high barrier for victory, although this barrier depends on the number of contestants and their relative strength.[3] To obtain a seat in an SMD plurality system, the winning candidate must receive at least one more vote than the closest rival. If, for example, five candidates compete, and they enjoy equal support among voters in the district, the winner must garner at least twenty percent of the vote, plus one, to exceed the vote total of the second-place candidate. In a two-candidate race, one contestant must exceed 50 percent of the vote to win. Regardless of the number of participants in the campaign, any candidate who exceeds 50 percent plus one vote will win the seat. The mechanical effect in SMD plurality thus benefits large parties and punishes small parties, propelling the psychological effect.

Political actors are faced with two major decisions that significantly impact the structure of the party system: voters must decide whether they will vote sincerely or sophisticatedly (strategic voting), and parties and candidates must determine if they will contest seats (strategic entry) (Cox 1997). After determining which candidate (or party) he or she prefers, a voter must make the final decision of whom to support at the polls.[4] A sincere choice may guide the voter all the way to the ballot box, regardless of the candidate's likely fate. However, many voters are seduced by the logic of strategic voting. If the voter prefers a candidate who appears unlikely to win, perhaps because the party with which the candidate is affiliated has performed poorly in the past, the preferred candidate's competitors have strong financial support, or competitors have out-polled the preferred candidate in preelection surveys, the voter may select a different candidate when filling out the ballot. A strategic voter whose sincere preference is weak would opt instead for one of the two strongest candidates whose positions most closely approximate the voter's preferred candidate. By casting a ballot for a potential winner, the voter does not "waste" his or her vote.

If many people vote strategically, small political parties will lose votes as supporters abandon them for parties more likely to win. Candidates and financiers associated with poorly performing parties will leave them, instead affiliating with parties that exhibit greater potential. As this process occurs over time, the number of effective parties should be winnowed down to two at the district level.[5] This logic led Duverger to conclude that "the simple-majority single-ballot system . . . favors the two-party system" (Duverger 1954, 217).[6] Other researchers have generalized this expectation as the "M+1" rule, which states that the number of effective competitors tends to be one more than the district magnitude (Reed 1991; Cox 1994). The basic principles of strategic entry and strategic voting, and the reductive qualities of SMD plurality rules, have found support in a significant body of scholarship.[7] But, questions remain about exceptional cases and party system aggregation.[8]

Rules that have a less punishing mechanical effect should produce competition among greater than two parties. The logic that encourages the abandonment of small parties in plurality systems promotes more sincere voting behavior and more incentives for entry in majority-runoff and proportional representation systems, benefiting small parties.

As in a plurality system, majority-runoff rules are used in single-member districts; only one candidate emerges victorious. To win an election under these rules, a candidate must gain a majority in the first round or emerge victorious in a second-round contest between the top finishers from the first round. Because a sincere vote cast in the first round is less likely to result in a wasted vote, citizens face reduced incentives to vote strategically. Further, candidates from minor parties may benefit from standing for office as they could use a strong first-round performance to play "kingmaker" in a decisive second round. The incentives associated with majority-runoff systems are likely to produce more effective candidates in the first round of balloting than in a plurality system (Jones 1999).

Depending on the institutional rules in place, especially the minimum threshold for gaining parliamentary seats, voters in proportional representation (PR) systems have an even stronger incentive to support small political parties than voters in plurality or majority-runoff systems. When PR features large districts and low thresholds, the conditions are particularly conducive for small parties to thrive. Rules that are more forgiving to small parties substantially change strategic voting and entry calculations, encouraging voters to support their sincere choices, candidates to remain affiliated with minor parties, and contributors to continue financing small political forces. By retaining voter, candidate, and contributor affiliations, small parties can "stay in business."[9] The different incentives presented by nonplurality systems prompted Duverger to conclude that "the simple-majority system with second ballot and proportional representation favors multipartyism" (Duverger 1954, 239).

The application of Duverger's propositions has not been limited to the three systems addressed directly by Duverger, and research exploring his logic has arguably produced the most developed literature in political science (Riker 1982b). Scholars have applied Duvergerian principles to work on the single nontransferable vote (Reed 1991; Cox 1994), mixed electoral systems (Moser 1999; Shugart and Wattenberg 2001; Ferrara, Herron, and Nishikawa 2005), and other rules. Many scholars, however, have challenged the primacy of election rules in determining party system diversity and have reversed the causal arrow in their work, arguing that the preexisting partisan environment and social cleavages create pressure that leads to the adoption of rules supporting the status quo (Boix 1999; Colomer 2005). That is, societies with many cleavages and political parties are more likely to adopt PR, and those with few cleavages are more likely to adopt a plurality system.

Challenges to institutional accounts are connected with the second major school of thought about what determines the size and shape of party systems. This approach privileges the role of contextual features, specifically political and social cleavages, as the most important influences on the number of competitive parties. As noted above, the quintessential exposition of this view is found in Lipset and Rokkan's (1967) influential chapter, which outlines a puzzle in their observation of party systems in advanced industrial democracies. Lipset and Rokkan found that the cleavages dominating politics in the 1920s had persisted until the 1960s and that the parties dominating political competition changed little.[10] Salient political divisions at the time of mass suffrage heavily influenced party system evolution, and subsequent competition was "frozen" around these cleavages. As parties organized themselves along the main dimensions of political conflict, and voters used positions on these cleavages to distinguish political groups from one another, the party system was conditioned for these divisions to become long-standing.

This explanation suggests that individuals develop attachments in the party system's formative period, and parties that become dominant can reduce the likelihood of successful entry by competitors, weather institutional changes, and survive as viable entities. While scholars have found support for this account in postcommunist states, the cleavage-based approach leaves open several important questions: What makes cleavages adequately salient for political groups to form, and what propels groups associated with salient cleavages to form political parties?

A substantial body of research in the 1990s addressed these questions by emphasizing the interaction of institutional features and social conditions in determining the shape of partisan conflict. Integrating the expectations about institutional and social effects, several scholars showed contingent effects of election rules and social cleavages on party system outcomes (Ordeshook and Shvetsova 1994; Amorim Neto and Cox 1997; Cox 1997; Clark and Golder 2006). While many scholars concede that institutional and social conditions affect party system outcomes, the precise nature of this interaction has not yet been determined.

DETERMINANTS OF THE EFFECTIVE NUMBER OF PARLIAMENTARY PARTIES

This section extends the discussion of electoral rules and party systems to the post-Soviet cases by addressing the following questions: Does the recent history of one-party rule and limited competition affect the evolution of the postcommunist party systems? How well do institutional rules, in democratic and in nondemocratic societies, structure the party system? The first approach in this section uses data from most democratic countries in the post-WWII period to assess how institutional, social, and regime effects influence party systems. The second approach investigates the same factors but uses data solely from post-Soviet states.[11]

Two hypotheses account for institutional effects. The first hypothesis is that election rules affect the number of parties, with PR associated with the most parties, followed by mixed systems (compensatory, then noncompensatory), and majoritarian systems (SMD majority-runoff and SMD plurality).[12] The second hypothesis is that the number of parties is likely to be greater as the assembly size is larger (Taagepera and Shugart 1989). Because the effect of seat size is unlikely to be monotonic, but rather to flatten as assembly size increases, this variable is coded as the natural log of assembly size.

The analysis also accounts for the impact of social cleavages on party systems. Following most of the literature, social cleavages are assessed via ethnic divisions. While ethnic divisions are not the only social cleavages that encourage the proliferation of parties, these divisions are often connected with multidimensional political conflict. In the former Soviet Union, ethnicity has played a crucial role in political disputes—and sometimes violent conflict—in almost all countries. Estonia, Kazakhstan, Latvia, and Ukraine have witnessed nonviolent conflict between the ethnic Russian population and the titular majorities. Ethnicity has been associated with some violent acts in Kyrgyzstan and Uzbekistan and open conflict in Armenia, Azerbaijan, Georgia, Moldova, and Tajikistan. The third hypothesis is that a larger number of effective ethnic groups should be associated with a higher number of effective parties.[13]

An additional, potentially relevant, social condition is the legacy of one-party communist rule. The history of communist rule generates potentially contradictory expectations about its effect on the number of parties, however. On one hand, citizens, desiring order and predictability in the chaotic transition period, may concentrate their support on the "parties of power,"[14] reducing the effective number of parties. Alternatively, freed from one-party domination and empowered to vote sincerely, citizens may support a diverse range of political organizations. While individual voters could respond to both stimuli—the desire for order and freedom to choose in a transitional political environment—the latter explanation will more likely prevail during the period under analysis. The fourth hypothesis is that party systems in post-communist states are likely to feature more parties than party systems else-where in the world. Related to this hypothesis is the expectation that founding elections will produce more parties than subsequent elections, as uncertainty about viability encourages many politicians to contest the first election. The interregional analysis includes a variable to assess first elections.

Finally, regime type should affect the number of competitive parties. While the interregional analysis includes only democratic systems, the intraregional assessment includes all regime types from democracy to autocracy. Election rules and social cleavages should have a predictable and direct effect in demo-cratic states, but restrictions on political competition in authoritarian states may distort institutional effects. While some authoritarian states stage elec-tions with multiple progovernment parties to showcase their "democratic" qualities, authoritarian systems should generally produce fewer parties than democracies. The fifth hypothesis is that higher levels of democracy should be associated with higher numbers of effective parties.

Interregional Assessment

The interregional assessment, featuring data covering elections in all dem-ocratic countries from 1945 to 2004 (Golder 2005), evaluates hypotheses 1 through 3. Selecting only democratic states makes the sample equivalent along an important dimension—regime type—and renders expectations of effects from institutions and social cleavages unaffected by this variation. By omitting nondemocracies, the analysis also parallels the extant literature.

Because the number of post-Soviet states in the dataset is limited, the analysis incorporates all postcommunist states into the variable measuring the Soviet legacy.[15] The expected direction of the effect does not change, but its magnitude may be reduced by Central and Eastern Europe's more limited time under communist rule and the less ideologically dedicated elites in that region. This analysis thus assesses the primary explanatory variables in the literature—institutions and social features—and adds the communist experi-ence as a control variable that may affect party systems.

The dependent variable is the effective number of parliamentary parties. As this index approaches one, it reflects a concentration of seats in a single party. Larger values of the index indicate that the party system is more diverse. The explanatory variables include dichotomous measures for election system types (with PR excluded as the comparison category),[16] the natural log of the parliament's size, and dichotomous variables for concurrent presidential elec-tions, postcommunist states, and founding elections. The analysis in Table 4.1 uses a modified dataset[17] and cross-national and time series methods to assess the hypotheses.[18]

Models 1a and 1b report ordinary least squares results of cross-sectional data, including only the most recent election. Model 1a controls for institutional

Table 4.1 Interregional Analysis of the Effective Number of Parliamentary Parties

Variable	Model 1a Most Recent Election	Model 1b Most Recent Election	Model 2a All Elections (1946–2004)	Model 2b All Elections (1946–2004)
Constant	1.426 (1.214)	1.427 (1.290)	2.367* (0.246)	2.210* (0.358)
Majoritarian	–1.185* (0.480)	–1.156* (0.424)	–1.180* (0.092)	–1.324* (0.116)
MMP	–0.702 (1.194)	–0.433 (0.891)	–0.306 (0.183)	0.270 (0.264)
MMM	0.160 (0.743)	0.357 (0.595)	0.364 (0.731)	–0.119 (0.638)
(ln) Seats	0.521* (0.243)	0.486 (0.247)	0.274* (0.048)	0.263* (0.062)
Presidential Election		–0.616 (0.378)		–0.456* (0.189)
# of Ethnic Groups		0.063 (0.092)		0.157* (0.068)
Founding Election				0.240 (0.258)
Post-Communist		0.306 (0.491)		0.727* (0.271)
Adj. R^2/R^2	0.087	0.112	0.131	0.178
MSE	2.252	1.636		
N	113	90	788	659
Wald Chi Square			328.39*	107.51*

features: parliamentary election rules and the natural log of assembly size. Model 1b adds variables representing the interaction of other institutional rules as well as contextual features: social cleavages and the postcommunist legacy.

Election rules show a direct effect on the number of parties, with majoritarian elections exerting a reductive influence on the number of parties relative to PR.[19] The effect of mixed electoral rules could not be distinguished statistically from those of PR. The impact of assembly size was felt inconsistently across the models; it was statistically significant and positive in sign for model 1a but not significant in model 1b. Concurrent presidential elections, ethnic diversity, and postcommunism had no statistically significant effect.

Results better conform with expectations when the data are expanded to cover elections in the post–World War II period and the method of analysis is adjusted to accommodate time-series data. In Model 2a, majoritarian rules and assembly size exert the expected effect and are statistically significant, similar to the analysis of Model 1a. In Model 2b, institutional features perform consistently, with concurrent presidential elections also producing statistically significant results in the expected direction. Furthermore, contextual features affect the results: the effective number of ethnic groups has an expansive effect on the number of parties, as does the postcommunist experience.

The analysis of both cross-sectional and time-series data shows that institutional rules affect the size of party systems. As anticipated, majoritarian rules generally produce fewer parties than PR systems. Larger assemblies tend to yield a greater number of parties; this variable was statistically significant in three of four models. The effects of other institutions and social conditions were less consistent. Coefficients for concurrent presidential elections, ethnicity, and postcommunism were significant and in the expected direction in the time-series model but not in the cross-sectional model. The results suggest that institutional features and social conditions indeed influence the development of party systems but that institutional factors are more robust. The next question to address is what explains variation across post-Soviet states, for whom the communist legacy is a constant.

Post-Soviet Assessment

While the findings in the interregional analysis mirror those in the general electoral studies literature, the addition of the postcommunist control variable generates some questions about the influence of the communist period on party system development. The analysis in this section incorporates available election data from the whole post-Soviet space and specifically controls for the effect of regime type. As noted above, the general expectation is that authoritarian societies restrict political competition. Yet, some authoritarian elites attempt to manufacture ersatz pluralism by generating results that appear to reflect multiparty competition, with all or most of the parties that gain seats in the legislature serving as shills for the executive.

The next step of the analysis focuses on measuring variation among post-Soviet countries. Restricting the sample creates analytical challenges, however. First, the sample size drops significantly, inflating error terms. Second, instead of assessing countries that are equivalent in terms of regime type, the analysis includes authoritarian systems in which institutional incentives are unlikely to perform according to the same dynamics found in democratic states. Authoritarian systems are likely to have more restrictive competition regardless of the electoral system officially in use. To account for this additional complication, the analysis controls for democratic quality.[20] The models thus include controls for electoral system, cleavage, and regime type effects.

Once again, the dependent variable is the effective number of parties. The institutional controls are the same as in the interregional analysis: election rules and the natural log of assembly size.[21] The models also retain the effective number of ethnic groups and add a measure of democratic quality.

Freedom House scores serve as a proxy for democracy. Combining political rights and civil liberties scores produces a potential score ranging from two (most free) to fourteen (least free). The sample includes fifty-two parliamentary elections, and has at least one election for each post-Soviet state save Turkmenistan (for which no appropriate data are available). Table 4.2 displays the results of the analysis.

Model 3 includes only institutional effects for the fifty-two elections in the sample. The coefficient for majoritarian elections is significant and negative in sign, demonstrating the expected reductive effect. Model 4 includes only the level of democracy and shows that higher-quality democracy is associated with more parties.[22] Model 5 assesses the role of ethnic diversity in determining the number of parties; the coefficient is not statistically significant. Model 6 combines all of the factors together; only level of democracy retains statistical and substantive significance. While institutions exert an effect, it is attenuated by regime type.[23]

In the interregional analysis, institutions generally produced expected effects. In the intraregional analysis incorporating all regime types, only the effect of regime was robust. The impact of regime type in post-Soviet states raises an important question for further assessment: do electoral institutions produce the expected effects in these states, or are the significant results artifacts of another process? To assess this question, the next section evaluates each family of election rules in post-Soviet space and discusses specific elections and results.

DISCUSSION OF ELECTION RULES AND EFFECTS

Following the existing literature, the statistical analysis in the previous section produced results suggesting that election rules matter, but that their effects

Table 4.2 Intraregional Analysis of Institutional and Contextual Effects on the Effective Number of Parliamentary Parties

Variable	Model 3	Model 4	Model 5	Model 6
Constant	2.196	6.103*	3.957*	3.564
	(1.558)	(0.540)	(0.438)	(1.880)
Majoritarian	−1.804*			0.166
	(0.709)			(0.786)
Mixed	−0.628			0.637
	(0.635)			(0.671)
(ln) Seats	0.468			0.343
	(0.305)			(0.293)
Level of Democracy		−0.288*		−0.311*
		(0.058)		(0.069)
# of Ethnic Groups			−0.043	0.350
			(0.252)	(0.390)
R2	0.133	0.242	0.000	0.274
Wald chi square	11.23*	24.30*	0.03	44.27*
N	52	52	52	52

may be attenuated by other factors. Most notably in post-Soviet space, the effect of election rules on party systems was mitigated by the influence of regime type. This outcome could be due to several factors: the party systems are new and inchoate, the rule of law is not well developed, and election rules are fluid, preventing political actors from properly adapting to their incentives. To better understand how election rules are linked to outcomes in post-Soviet states, this section provides a deeper assessment of elections under different rules: plurality, majority, PR, and mixed systems.

Effects of Single Member–District Systems

Scholars attribute three primary benefits to SMD plurality systems: they are simple, they are stable, and they facilitate accountability via direct representation. However, one of the primary disadvantages of SMD plurality is its disproportionality. Because SMD races are winner-takes-all, and candidates need only to gain one more vote than their closest rival to win a seat under plurality rules, national-level seat allocations are more likely to diverge from the overall proportion of votes that the party receives. Disproportional seat allocation helps drive the incentives encouraging two-candidate competition at the district level. Based on Duverger's logic, the reductive effects of the institutional rules should ultimately produce competition between two strong parties.

Assessing these expectations in post-Soviet space is complicated by the paucity of examples. Only one election on the former USSR's territory has followed a traditional plurality formula in single-member districts: Azerbaijan's 2005 contest. This election was not deemed to be free and fair by international observers, who noted significant violations of proper administrative procedures. Depending on how one calculates the effective number of parties, the election produced "too many" or "too few" parties from the perspective of Duverger's Law. If one calculates the effective number of parties, treating independent candidates as a single party and independent candidates supported by the New Azerbaijan Party as a single party, the election produced 2.84 effective parties.[24] This result is rather high for plurality systems.[25] Combining independent candidates formally supported by the New Azerbaijan Party into its total lowers the effective number of parties to 2.32, a result that is consistent with other countries using plurality rules. However, if one combines all independents with the New Azerbaijan Party—as independent candidates were likely to side with the party of power once in parliament—the effective number of parties drops to 1.19. This result is indicative of a single-party dominant authoritarian state. The formal results of Azerbaijan's 2005 contest suggest pluralism, but only due to the presence of nominally independent candidates who inflate the Laakso-Taagepera index.

The traditional consequences of plurality rules manifest themselves just beyond the borders of the former Soviet Union, however. Mongolia, the first Soviet satellite state, adopted a communist regime in 1924. As the "sixteenth republic" of the USSR, Mongolia shares much of the institutional and social history of the countries in this study. Following the collapse of communism, Mongolia has held elections using plurality rules,[26] and it is generally considered to be democratic.[27] While the identities of some parties have changed, political competition revolves around the communist successor party, the Mongolian People's Revolutionary Party, and its rivals in the democratic opposition.

Mongolia's 2000 parliamentary election illustrates an extreme case of disproportionality. In 2000, the People's Revolutionary Party received 50.4 percent of the overall vote, but 95 percent of the seats. Its candidates received between 32 percent and 79 percent of the district-level votes, and the party won twenty-nine seats with less than 50 percent of the district vote. The fragmented opposition split its supporters, allowing the People's Revolutionary Party to gain almost total control over parliament with just over half the votes. The effective number of parliamentary parties reflects the dominance of the People's Revolutionary Party, yielding a result of 1.11. But, the effective number of electoral parties suggests more robust competition. At the district level, the mean effective number of electoral parties was 2.86; competition in the districts ranged from 1.51 effective parties to 4.33. Mongolia's next election in 2004 yielded strong two-party competition; the effective number of parliamentary parties was 2.27, although the election was marred by alleged irregularities.

SMD plurality elections in postcommunist space have not produced solely two-party competition, but this is rare even in developed democracies that employ plurality systems. Instead, the few pure plurality elections that have been held in the region have yielded limited competition and disproportional seat allocation. These results are consistent with the expectations flowing from plurality rules, but because of the limited number of cases, we cannot definitively disentangle country-specific effects from those of the electoral system.

The more common SMD rule in post-Soviet space incorporates a majority allocation rule. The majority-runoff formula has been used in several parliamentary races and in all presidential campaigns, with slight cross-national and temporal variation in the rules. Duverger's propositions indicate that majority-runoff rules should be associated with plural competition in the first round. Moreover, as in plurality-based SMD systems, majority-runoff systems often do not require candidates to be formally affiliated with a political party. Consequently, they should be associated with participation by nonaffiliated candidates, especially in post-Soviet states with inchoate party systems.

Table 4.3 shows the effective number of parliamentary parties for majority-runoff elections in post-Soviet states. The national-level values for the effective number of parliamentary parties range considerably, from 1.25 to 4.67, with a mean of 2.67. The mean value is consistent with expectations, but a deeper assessment of the data producing this outcome raises some questions about how accurately it describes party systems.

The national-level effective number of parties in Ukraine's 1994 parliamentary election was driven primarily by the large number of independent

Table 4.3   Effective Number of Parties in Majority-Runoff Systems

Country	Election 1	Election 2	Election 3
Belarus	3.26 (1995)	1.42 (2000)	1.25 (2004)
Kazakhstan	4.67 (1994)	3.96 (1995)	
Kyrgyzstan	1.34 (1995)		
Tajikistan	2.30 (1995)		
Ukraine	1.98 (1994)		
Uzbekistan	3.88 (2004)		

Source: Author's calculations.

candidates gaining seats; 233 of the 338 deputies initially chosen in the election were not formally affiliated with a political party.[28] Treating independents as a single party, or discarding independents from the calculation, understates Ukraine's political diversity and the competitiveness of the district races. At the same time, these results support one expectation about the effect of single-member district races: they can facilitate participation by unaffiliated candidates.

Other national-level election results are deceptive for the opposite reason; the index suggests robust political competition where little political pluralism exists. The 1994 election in Kazakhstan allowed multiple parties to gain seats in parliament, but international observers noted several problems with election administration. The Ministry of Justice and electoral commissions removed parties and candidates without an adequate appeal process. Ethnic parties were banned, although the construction of districts favored the Kazakh majority. The short election period and concentration of resources on government-sponsored candidates undermined competition (CSCE 1994). Further, President Nursultan Nazarbayev presented a State List allowing him to appoint one-fifth of the legislature.[29] Twelve political parties ultimately gained representation, although most received few seats.

After the results of the 1994 election were vacated by the Constitutional Court and referendums were held to extend President Nazarbayev's term and reconfigure political institutions, Kazakhstan's citizens again came to the polls to select a new parliament in late 1995.[30] The 1995 contest featured many of the same flaws as the 1994 election, but the results in 1995 produced a parliament more in line with presidential preferences. Among the thirty contestants, the leading party was Nazarbayev's People's Unity Party. Legislators loyal to the president, but affiliated with other parties or contesting as independents, filled most of the other seats. While the effective number of parties suggests that a robust competitive environment characterized Kazakhstan's early elections, the 1995 election was closely controlled by the president and his allies.

The national-level effective number of parties measure understated political pluralism in Ukraine and overstated it in Kazakhstan, but it accurately reflects political conditions elsewhere. The election of Alyaksandr Lukash-enka as president of Belarus in 1994 led to swift and significant restrictions of political rights and civil liberties. The rapid decline in Belarus' effective number of parties reflects deteriorating democratic conditions.

In addition to their use in parliamentary elections, majority-runoff rules are the only method used to popularly elect presidents in the post-Soviet region. The bargaining potential that encourages multiple candidates to contest seats in the first round of a majority-runoff system should be particularly evident in presidential elections because the presidential race's stakes are high and presidents have the ability to distribute valuable positions (Jones 1999). The best-known example of interround bargaining occurred in Russia's 1996 election.[31] Boris Yeltsin's vote total slightly exceeded his Communist Party rival in the first round of balloting. Aleksandr Lebed, the former general and maverick candidate, finished in third place. In exchange for a position directing the Security Council, Lebed threw his support behind Yeltsin, who was ultimately victorious.

Table 4.4 shows the effective number of presidential candidates for every election where appropriate data are available. Rather than reflecting robust competition among many contestants, the results suggest more limited competition. While the effective number of candidates rises above two in eighteen elections, it falls below two in twenty-one cases. The latter are most closely associated with consistently authoritarian or semiauthoritarian systems—Azerbaijan, Belarus, Kazakhstan, Kyrgyzstan, Russia, Tajikistan, and Turkmenistan—but also with some countries that have exhibited democratic characteristics, such as Georgia and Lithuania. Constituency-based electoral systems using a plurality and majority formula have followed some expectations

Table 4.4   Effective Number of Presidential Candidates

	Election 1	Election 2	Election 3	Election 4	Election 5
Armenia	2.30 (1996)	3.64 (1998)	2.79 (2003)	2.80 (2008)	
Azerbaijan	2.16 (1992)	1.02 (1993)	1.59 (1998)	1.68 (2003)	N/A (2008)
Belarus	3.84 (1994)	1.68 (2001)	1.29 (2006)		
Estonia	3.14 (1992)				
Georgia	1.58 (1995)	1.42 (2000)	1.06 (2004)	2.76 (2008)	
Kazakhstan	1.44 (1999)	1.20 (2005)			
Kyrgyzstan	1.58 (1995)	1.73 (2000)	1.22 (2005)		
Lithuania	1.97 (1993)	3.28 (1997)	4.73 (2002)	4.53 (2004)	
Moldova	3.92 (1996)				
Russia	3.78 (1996)	2.64 (2000)	1.73 (2004)	1.82 (2008)	
Tajikistan	2.14 (1994)	1.06 (1999)	1.57 (2006)		
Turkmenistan	1.25 (2007)				
Ukraine	3.66 (1994)	4.65 (1999)	2.82 (2004)		
Uzbekistan	1.18 (2000)	1.28 (2007)			

Source: Author's calculations.

from the theoretical literature. But, regime type has constrained their effects, with authoritarian systems both restricting competition and manufacturing false pluralism.

EFFECTS OF PROPORTIONAL REPRESENTATION

The recent trend in post-Soviet electoral system reform has been the adoption of PR. As discussed earlier, some theoretical literature anticipates that PR systems are likely to be adopted in countries with pluralistic party systems to support preexisting multiparty politics,[32] while the institutionalist approach suggests that PR induces multiparty competition. In either case, the expectation is that PR is associated with plural competition. Moreover, some political actors in post-Soviet states have advocated its adoption to combat fraud, arguing that SMD constituencies are more conducive to vote theft.[33]

Increasingly, however, PR has been viewed as a political tool to buttress centralized authority and undermine open competition. Combined with high thresholds, a government-dominated media, electoral commissions that do not behave independently, and administrative barriers for opposition parties to gain ballot access, PR can facilitate central control. PR has been used extensively in Estonia, Latvia, and Moldova and was recently adopted in Kazakhstan, Kyrgyzstan, Ukraine, and Russia (see Table 4.5).

Empirically, we can see the dual nature of PR election outcomes. The average number of effective parties for all PR systems is 4.15. But, if regime type is taken into account, the differences are notable. Omitting results from Kazakhstan, Kyrgyzstan, and Russia, the effective number of parties increases to 4.65. In Kazakhstan, only one party gained seats in the 2007 election. Three parties in Kyrgyzstan and four in Russia passed the threshold in 2007, but in both cases the party of power took most of the seats (79 percent in Kyrgyzstan and 70 percent in Russia), and the remaining parties were loyal to the ruling presidents (except for Russia's Communist Party).[34]

In Estonia and Latvia, PR has promoted robust competition among many political parties. Early elections in both countries were notable for their volatility and inchoate party systems. While ten parties have gained seats in Estonia's parliament in the postcommunist period, the identities of the primary contestants have stabilized over time. The conservative Pro Patria Party and the Res Publica Party merged prior to the 2007 election, forming a major political group. The Center Party and Reform Party have consistently campaigned and performed well in elections since 1995. Together, these parties won 78 percent of the seats in Estonia's 2007 election.

While Latvia also has robust multiparty democracy, its party system is less stable than Estonia's. Fourteen political groups have contested and won seats over the course of five elections. Some of these groups have been independent parties; others have been formed by temporary or permanent mergers of existing political forces. A few parties have demonstrated staying power—such as Latvia's Way, Farmer's Union, For Fatherland and Freedom—but many have been ephemeral (Pettai and Kreuzer 1999).

Table 4.5   Effective Number of Parties in PR Systems

Country	Election 1	Election 2	Election 3	Election 4	Election 5
Estonia	5.90 (1992)	7.95 (1995)	5.50 (1999)	4.67 (2003)	4.37 (2007)
Kazakhstan	1.00 (2007)				
Kyrgyzstan	1.55 (2007)				
Latvia	5.05 (1993)	7.59 (1995)	5.49 (1998)	5.02 (2002)	6.00 (2006)
Moldova	2.62 (1994)	3.43 (1998)	1.85 (2001)	2.31 (2005)	
Russia	1.92 (2007)				
Ukraine	3.41 (2006)	3.30 (2007)			

Source: Author's calculations.

Moldovan political parties have also emerged, disappeared, and joined with other forces. Six different parties or party groups have gained seats in Moldova's parliament since 1994's founding election. In the early 2000s, the Party of Moldovan Communists became the dominant force, especially after the introduction of a 6 percent threshold in 2001. While reflecting multi-party outcomes, the number of parties successfully gaining seats in Moldova's parliament falls below the level of the Baltic states.

The adoption of PR in Ukraine has not enhanced multipartyism but rather has streamlined the array of competitive parties participating in elections. Since the adoption of PR, the effective number of parties in Ukraine has dropped by two. Unlike the mixed system, PR does not accommodate independent candidates, and some parties gained seats only in constituency races when Ukraine used a mixed system. By eliminating this path to parliament, PR reduced party system fragmentation.

Following the Orange Revolution in 2004, Ukraine's national identity cleavage was enhanced, with parties arrayed along the "Orange" (favoring a Western orientation and Ukrainian identity) or "Blue" (favoring a more Russian-focused orientation and preserving the Russophone identity) dimension. The five parties that passed the 3 percent threshold in both 2006 and 2007 could be identified as pro-Orange or pro-Blue, with the exception of the Bloc of Volodymyr Lytvyn in 2007, which attempted to carve out a neutral position. The elimination of the constituency tier, coupled with the dramatic events of 2004, has contributed to short-term party system stabilization in Ukraine.

Just as plurality and majority rules conformed with and diverged from general expectations when applied in the post-Soviet region, so too have PR systems. While they are generally associated with multiparty competition, PR systems in Russia, Kazakhstan, and Kyrgyzstan have been vehicles to enhance central control and reduce the number of competitive parties while maintaining a democratic façade. In democratic states, PR has contributed to multipartyism in two ways. In early adopters, PR allowed many parties to participate in elections and gain seats. In Ukraine, a late adopter, PR has helped to streamline the party system.

EFFECTS OF MIXED ELECTORAL SYSTEMS

Mixed electoral systems were the most popular choice for institutional designers in the early post-Soviet period. Nine of the fifteen post-Soviet states used a mixed system at some point, although mixed systems were subsequently abandoned in all but four countries. Mixed electoral rules promised to combine the advantages of majoritarian and proportional elections, providing local-level and national representation, greater voter choice, and a combination of the reductive qualities of plurality systems with the party-building capacity of PR (Shugart and Wattenberg 2001; Moser 2001; Moser and Scheiner 2004). Some research has challenged these expectations, noting that hybrid systems do not generate the same incentives as their "pure" counterparts (Ferrara, Herron, and Nishikawa 2005).

Mixed systems are expected to fall "somewhere in the middle" between fully majoritarian and fully proportional systems in the number of competitive parties they produce (Nishikawa and Herron 2004). However, the strategic decisions of parties and voters rely on several institutional features of the mixed system, including how the two tiers balance seat allocation (Ferrara and Herron 2005). In post-Soviet mixed systems, this feature varies cross-nationally and temporally. Some countries have consistently balanced the tiers equally, such as Lithuania, Russia, and Ukraine.".[35] Other countries have been markedly majoritarian, such as Azerbaijan,[36] Kazakhstan,[37] Kyrgyzstan,[38] and Tajikistan.[39] Armenia and Georgia altered their allocations over time. Armenia changed from a system with 75 majoritarian and 56 PR seats in 1999 to the reverse in 2003, and finally to 41 majoritarian and 90 PR seats in 2007. Georgia initially balanced its PR and majoritarian seats equally, but changed its assembly size and reduced the number and proportion of PR seats to yield 75 majoritarian and 150 PR seats. Seat allocation was once again modified for the 2008 election, yielding a 150-member parliament with seats balanced equally between PR and SMD.

Data from post-Soviet states provides some support for the contention that party systems produced by mixed electoral rules are positioned in between PR and majoritarian systems. The mean effective number of parties is 3.86, falling below PR systems and above majoritarian ones. However, the coefficients for mixed systems were not significant in the multivariate analysis presented above, and the results cannot be distinguished statistically from those produced by PR.

Mixed systems have also defied some expectations about the relative effects of majoritarian and proportional tiers. Aggregated nationally, majoritarian outcomes have sometimes reflected a proportional distribution of seats (Moser 1999; 2001). Notably, in Russia's 1995 parliamentary election, only four political parties of the forty-three contesting seats passed the 5 percent PR threshold. The deviation from proportionality[40] in the PR race was higher

Table 4.6   Effective Number of Parties in Mixed Systems

Country	Election 1	Election 2	Election 3	Election 4	Election 5
Armenia	2.16 (1995)	3.72 (1999)	5.27 (2003)	3.22 (2007)	
Azerbaijan	2.57 (1995)	2.46 (2000)			
Georgia	9.54 (1992)	3.33 (1995)	2.37 (1999)	1.22 (2003)	1.55 (2008)
Kazakhstan	4.37 (1999)	2.66 (2004)			
Kyrgyzstan	2.15 (2000)				
Lithuania	3.05 (1992)	3.32 (1996)	6.14 (2000)	6.13 (2004)	
Russia	6.19 (1993)	5.21 (1995)	5.50 (1999)	3.34 (2003)	
Tajikistan	2.77 (2000)	1.47 (2005)			
Ukraine	5.26 (1998)	5.87 (2002)			

Source: Author's calculations.

than in SMD, with values of 0.47 and 0.22, respectively.[41] In other words, SMD more proportionally allocated seats than did PR. Other elections in Russia also have produced higher deviations from proportionality in PR than in SMD.[42]

In contrast to expectations from Duverger's propositions, the majoritarian component of mixed systems has witnessed the proliferation of candidates. While participation by independent candidates has inflated the number of competitors, independents are not the only reason for multicandidate competition at the district level. Some researchers have shown that the simultaneous selection of constituency-based and party-list deputies encourages parties to contest seats in otherwise hopeless districts. Nominating candidates associated with a party label can attract voters to the PR ballot, improving the party's overall performance. This "contamination" effect undermines the reductive qualities of plurality rules when they are used in combination with PR in mixed systems (Herron and Nishikawa 2001; Cox and Schoppa 2002; Ferrara and Herron 2005; Ferrara, Herron, and Nishikawa 2005). The contamination phenomenon is not unique to post-Soviet states; it has affected behavior in several elections under mixed systems (Ferrara, Herron, and Nishikawa 2005).

Because scholars have not reached consensus about the effect of mixed electoral rules on party systems, no firm conclusions can be drawn about how the post-Soviet experience complies with or diverges from expectations. But, mixed systems in post-Soviet space have produced a mean effective number of parties that lies between pure PR and majoritarian systems, have generally been favorable to participation by independent candidates, and in some cases have produced more robust multicandidate and multiparty competition in the SMD tier than in PR.

CONCLUSION

This chapter assessed how institutional and social forces affect party systems, explicitly investigating the potential effect of a postcommunist legacy. The results of the interregional empirical analysis conformed with other scholars' findings: institutions and social cleavages affect the number of political parties. Postcommunism also evidenced a significant impact in some models, inflating the number of competitive parties. Whether this outcome is due to the communist legacy, or the newness of elections and inchoate party systems, is a matter for future analysis as more elections are held and the communist era fades into history.

In the evaluation of post-Soviet cases, regime type was the most robust explanatory variable. With controls for institutions and social conditions in place, more democratic systems were associated with a larger number of competitive parties. Deeper assessments of each election rule's impact on post-Soviet party systems followed the cross-national analyses. In some cases, the effective number of parties appropriately reflected local political diversity. At other times, it understated or overstated the level of political pluralism as regimes artificially restricted competition, or created ersatz pluralism.

The use of the Laakso-Taagepera index assumes that the units comprising the system—the parties themselves—are meaningful. Chapter 6 revisits this question, addressing the qualities of post-Soviet parties and the characteristics of their supporters. The intervening chapter explores the potential impact of institutions, social effects, and the postcommunist legacy on decision making in elections. Instead of focusing on strategic entry decisions by parties, however, Chapter 5 explores why citizens cast ballots.

CHAPTER 5

CITIZENS AND THE
INCENTIVES TO VOTE

On a cold, dark election day morning in January 2004, I watched as a dozen citizens in Kutaisi, Georgia lined up to cast ballots, well before the polling station's doors were scheduled to open. Over the course of the day, almost two million fellow citizens (88 percent of registered voters) followed their lead, visiting polling stations and dropping sealed ballots into clear plastic urns. The eventual winner, garnering 97 percent of the vote, was the leader of the 2003 Rose Revolution, Mikheil Saakashvili. While many Georgians were energized by the promise of improved conditions under "Misha's" leadership, why did they bother to participate when Saakashvili's victory was all but guaranteed?[1]

While voting is a fundamental form of political participation, it requires citizens to invest a substantial amount of time and energy. In addition to visiting the polls to cast a ballot, voters must register to participate and identify their preferred candidate, party, or position. The previous chapter brought voters into the analysis, discussing how election rules provide incentives for individuals to cast strategic votes and assessing the consequences of voter choices on party system evolution. This chapter's analysis combines individual- and aggregate-level data to investigate how voters in post-Soviet states make decisions about participating in elections, evaluating how rational calculations, social factors, and Soviet-era conditioning influence turnout.[2]

WHY VOTE?

As the Soviet Union entered its waning years, modes of acceptable political participation changed. Through his reform policies, Mikhail Gorbachev encouraged citizens to become more engaged in decision making. Like

Nikita Khrushchev decades before, Gorbachev recognized that resuscitating the moribund Soviet economy required more efficient practices informed by market principles and nonparty experts. Through greater openness in public discourse, Gorbachev encouraged honest evaluations of the Soviet system, especially critiques that might reduce bureaucracy and improve performance. He also proposed more democratic decision making by initiating competitive elections, introducing choice to the Soviet ballot where before there had been none.

Increasingly, Soviet citizens recognized that a new choice lay before them: to vote or not to vote. As noted in Chapter 2, elections were an important socialization tool for the Soviet state that served many purposes. By the time of the Congress of People's Deputies election in 1989, the goals of socialization had changed. Elections were no longer mandated to demonstrate loyalty to the Soviet state but rather allowed citizens to voluntarily make more meaningful choices.[3] While deputies still lacked formal decision-making authority, they were imbued as never before with rhetorical power to engage in open dialogue about the failures of the Soviet state.

Most citizens participated in late-Soviet-era elections. In the 1989 election, national turnout was 90 percent (Birch 1995), with the lowest regional participation rate recorded in Armenia (72 percent) (Rutland 1994). Despite high turnout by international standards,[4] the Congress of People's Deputies election failed to command participation rates typical for most of the Soviet period. The increase in abstentions signaled a change in Soviet citizens' behavior—or a change in the information that Soviet authorities were willing to reveal.[5] In either case, it became clear that voting was increasingly viewed as voluntary. After the USSR's collapse, voting in most of the newly independent states evolved into an even more voluntary enterprise, reflected by the further decrease in participation rates. What explains this phenomenon?

Political scientists have attacked the puzzle of voter turnout from two angles. One approach focuses on the socioeconomic characteristics associated with participation and abstention. The second approach focuses on the "calculus of voting," emphasizing the costs and benefits of the voting act. Layered on top of these theoretical approaches are analyses using both individual- and aggregate-level indicators of turnout. Empirical analyses have revealed a wide array of potential effects on turnout, with scholars generating complementary and contradictory conclusions about why people vote.

At the individual level, most research focuses on the United States and assesses the impact of socioeconomic and institutional features on an individual's self-reported intention to vote and past voting practices. Scholars have reported contradictory findings, concluding that economic difficulties positively (Lipset 1960) and negatively (Rosenstone 1982) affect the likelihood of voting. The argument for the former effect is that grievances stimulate participation. The argument for the latter effect is that economic challenges elevate concerns over basic needs; politics is rather unimportant for citizens who lack reliable employment, food, water, or shelter. Studies of socioeconomic explanations also feature race, gender, social class, and education as potential influences on turnout (Leighley and Nagler 1992), with some work suggesting that minority,[6] female,[7] lower class,[8] and lower educated voters[9] are less likely to participate.

Research focusing on early socialization is related to the approach emphasizing socioeconomic influences. Socialization may affect voting behavior in several ways: voting may become habitual behavior beginning in early adulthood (Plutzer 2002), or past voting practices may guide future behavior (Gerber, Green, and Shachar 2003). A norm of participation or abstention could emanate from the political environment, the effect of participation on feelings of efficacy, or attitudes about civic duty.

The rational choice explanation for turnout differs from the socioeconomic approach. While initially sketched out by Anthony Downs (1957), the "formula" for voting was later introduced by William Riker and Peter Ordeshook (1968) and informed many subsequent studies. The basic notion is that, like other forms of political participation, voting has costs and benefits. The benefits can be direct but elusive, such as casting the decisive vote, or indirect, such as the psychological satisfaction of participating in the democratic process.[10] Research on the calculus of voting tends to favor formal modeling because the explanatory factors can be challenging to directly measure.[11] However, a recent cross-national analysis of turnout derives its analytical models from the rational choice tradition (Franklin 2004).

Not only did Downs' work and early research on turnout spawn a vast literature investigating individual-level decisions to participate in elections, but it also informed the research using data aggregated at the national level. Like the research on party systems discussed in the previous chapter, national-level research on turnout has emphasized how institutional incentives and social conditions induce participation.[12] The argument for institutional effects on turnout is straightforward: rules create conditions in which citizens perceive a vote as more or less likely to "count," or the rules affect participation costs. As rules generate incentives to participate, individuals should be more likely to cast ballots, and aggregate measures of turnout should increase. While the general argument for institutional effects is straightforward, the rules sometimes generate contradictory incentives,[13] and institutional influences may be intertwined with political effects.

In addition to assessing the effects of institutions, early cross-national research on national-level turnout emphasized political variables. G. Bingham Powell (1986) noted how competitive districts and connections between political parties and social groups affected turnout. Robert Jackman (1987) found that electoral competitiveness, proportionality, party system fragmentation, compulsory voting,[14] and the existence of a single legislative body directly influenced turnout in parliamentary elections.[15] Subsequently, other scholars have investigated similar institutional and political factors all over the world.[16]

Aggregate-level turnout studies have also measured the effect of socioeconomic variables. Some research has connected country size to the likelihood of casting a decisive vote, noting that as population decreases, the likelihood of an individual's vote determining the winner increases (Blais 2006; Geys 2006). Other scholarship has focused on social pressures to vote, suggesting that urbanization, population stability, and ethnic homogeneity[17] may increase participation (Geys 2006).

The legacy of the communist period may also affect voter participation. Pacek, Pop-Eleches, and Tucker (2009) identify two potential perceptual mechanisms that may drive citizen choices: "disenchantment" and "discernment." "Disenchantment" describes how voter dissatisfaction with economic and political change might dissuade citizens from participating. "Discernment" suggests that the relative importance of the election might influence decisions to participate, with voters recognizing when decisions at the polls really matter and adjusting their behavior accordingly. The individual- and aggregate-level analyses in the following sections are informed by the extensive literature on voting behavior and speak to "disenchantment" and "discernment" as motivators.

INDIVIDUAL-LEVEL ANALYSIS OF TURNOUT

The individual-level analysis uses data from the Central and Eastern Eurobarometer (CEEURO) and Comparative Study of Electoral Systems (CSES) to assess the determinants of turnout.[18] These datasets provide valuable insight into citizen attitudes about voting across post-Soviet space during the initial decade of postcommunism.

The dependent variable is an individual's response about the intention to vote (CEEURO) or report on participation in the most recent election (CSES) during election years in countries with available data.[19] Independent variables include respondents' views of the economy and democracy, and demographic features. Following previous assessments of socioeconomic influences on turnout, attitudes about economic conditions could encourage participation to register grievances or encourage abstention because economic deprivation renders politics a remote concern. Variables focusing on the respondents' financial conditions measure these attitudes.[20] With CEEURO data, the economic questions assess the respondents' financial situation in the previous or next twelve months. The CSES questions only permitted retrospective evaluations, asking respondents to assess economic change in the last twelve months. The Appendix describes the data and variables in greater detail.

Respondent attitudes toward democracy speak to their assessments of efficacy; if democratic quality is poor, then participation in elections is likely to be viewed as less meaningful. The analysis also includes demographic characteristics: age, gender, and education. Older voters are expected to participate more consistently than the young, whether due to habituation or a heightened sense of civic duty accumulated over the years. Gender could play a role, but its direction of effect is difficult to predict. Given traditional gender roles, women may be less likely to participate. But, the official Soviet-era emphasis on gender equality could render traditional roles insignificant. Finally, based on existing literature, more educated respondents are likely to cast ballots.

Table 5.1 shows the statistically significant variables in multivariate assessments of the likelihood to abstain from voting in analyses of twenty-three election years in ten countries. The cell entries show the year in which the coefficient is significant, and its direction.

Voters' assessments of past and future economic conditions affect the likelihood of their abstaining in several cases. A positive coefficient indicates that increasingly negative assessments of economic conditions are associated with a higher probability of abstaining from the vote. In one case, respondents were more likely to abstain as their assessments of the economy were more positive. In eight other cases (one prospective and seven retrospective), voters with more negative evaluations of economic conditions showed a greater propensity to abstain from voting. This outcome supports the idea that difficult economic circumstances—or the expectation of difficult economic circumstances—may depress voter turnout.

Respondents with more negative views of democracy displayed a greater likelihood to abstain in twelve cases. This outcome supports the contention that feelings of efficacy influence individual decisions to vote. A belief that democracy is developing well implies that citizens may affect political outcomes, encouraging participation.

Age was significant and negative in sign in eighteen cases, reflecting the greater likelihood of younger respondents to abstain from voting. Older respondents may be more likely to participate in voting because of habituation, especially under Soviet political conditions, or because attitudes about civic duty evolve over time. Gender was significant in two instances, with men more likely to abstain than women. Education was significant in twelve cases, with lower levels of achievement associated with abstention, except in one instance.

The individual-level analysis shows that assessments of economic conditions, attitudes about democracy, age, and education level influence the propensity to abstain.[21] Age was the most consistently significant variable, followed by education, attitudes about democracy, and retrospective assessments of economic conditions. Gender and prospective economic assessments were significant in only two cases each. These results suggest that "disenchantment"—reflected in prospective and retrospective economic evaluations—affects the likelihood of participation. "Discernment"—measured by attitudes about democracy—also plays a role, with voters expressing a greater likelihood of abstaining if they believe that democratic conditions are not present in their country.

AGGREGATE-LEVEL ANALYSIS OF TURNOUT

Reported turnout data for presidential, parliamentary, and referendum votes in the post-Soviet period serve as the raw material for the dependent variable in the aggregate-level analysis.[22] The use of regional turnout data requires several caveats. The most obvious challenge is the high likelihood of manipulation in many elections. Some results—such as Turkmenistan's fantastic

Table 5.1 Probit Analysis of Intention to Abstain in Election Years

	Armenia	Belarus	Estonia	Georgia	Kazakhstan	Kyrgyzstan	Latvia	Lithuania	Russia	Ukraine
Prospective Economic								1992 (−)		1994 (+)
Retrospective Economic			1995 (+)	1995 (+)				1992 (+) 1996 (+) 1997 (+)	1999 (+) 2000 (+)	
Satisfaction with Democracy		2001 (+)	1992 (+) 1995 (+)	1992 (+) 1995 (+)		2005 (+)	1995 (+)	1996 (+)	1999 (+) 2004 (+)	1994 (+) 1998 (+)
Age		1995 (−) 2001 (−)	1995 (−)	1992 (−) 1995 (−)	1995 (−)	2005 (−)	1995 (−)	1992 (−) 1996 (−) 1997 (−)	1995 (−) 1996 (−) 1999 (−) 2000 (−) 2004 (−)	1994 (−) 1998 (−)
Gender								1996 (−)	2004 (−)	
Education	1995 (+)	1995 (−)	1995 (−)			2005 (−)		1992 (−) 1996 (−) 1997 (−)	1996 (−) 1999 (−) 2000 (−) 2004 (−)	1994 (−)

Sources: CEEURO and CSES datasets.

Note: Cell entries indicate the model (country/survey year) in which the coefficient was statistically significant at the .05 level and the direction of the coefficient.

reports of nearly complete participation—are artifacts of the authoritarian governments producing them. To address this problem, most studies of turnout include only elections that are deemed free and fair or mostly free and fair. This selection mechanism assumes away the potential problem of inaccurate data reporting, especially in semireformed societies. While using democracy scores to select cases can improve the quality of data in the analysis, poorquality data are not solely found in authoritarian societies.

Rather than a priori excluding authoritarian states from the analysis, the multivariate models test for the effects of regime type in two ways. The initial model includes a measure of democracy—Freedom House scores—in an analysis of all post-Soviet elections for which data are available. Subsequent models systematically exclude states based on the quality of democracy and assess the effects of institutional and socioeconomic explanatory variables to determine the impact of regime type on turnout.

Another challenge for turnout data is provenance. The data set includes figures from International IDEA, central electoral commissions, nongovernmental organizations, and the media. These sources do not always agree on the final result, however, due to differing methods of calculation or inaccurate reporting. The Appendix includes a detailed discussion of discrepancies and coding decisions.

A few patterns emerge in the turnout data. As anticipated, authoritarian states report high turnout, though exceptions exist (for example, Belarus reported 56 percent and 61 percent turnout in the 1995 and 2000 parliamentary elections, respectively). Contrary to expectations, turnout does not necessarily fall off following initial elections. Reported turnout from founding elections is lower than at least one subsequent election for president in Armenia, Azerbaijan, Belarus, Georgia, and Ukraine; for parliament in Armenia, Belarus, Estonia, Kyrgyzstan, Russia, and Tajikistan; and for referendums in Belarus, Kyrgyzstan, and Lithuania. Also, presidential elections and referendums seem to yield similar turnout, whereas parliamentary elections and EU parliamentary elections inspire fewer voters to cast ballots.

Average turnout for various types of elections is consistent with the notion of discernment; voters understand which votes are more important. The mean turnout for presidential elections is 76.8, followed by referendums at 72.8, parliament at 70.3, and EU parliamentary elections at 38.7. The high turnout for presidential elections and low turnout for EU parliamentary elections is not surprising. Presidents are generally the most powerful political figures in post-Soviet states,[23] and their elections garner the highest reported participation levels. Low turnout for EU parliamentary election is consistent with patterns in other EU countries.

The relative placement of turnout for referendums and parliamentary votes may reflect how referendums are used in the region. Authoritarian rulers have been particularly fond of referendums to directly modify constitutions and extend presidential terms, although they have been used in more democratic states to make decisions about policy and membership in international organizations.

Because scholars have inconsistently defined the dependent variable and applied explanatory variables in cross-national turnout research (Geys 2006), no single replicable model exists. This analysis follows the lead of research that has focused on the postcommunist region (Kostadinova 2003; Pacek, Pop-Eleches, and Tucker 2009; Kostadinova and Power 2007) and includes institutional, political, and socioeconomic explanatory variables.

Most of the turnout literature has focused on measuring voter participation in parliamentary elections. The advantage of selecting only legislative elections is that this uniformity allows scholars to assess the effects of variation in election rules. The inclusion of parliamentary, presidential, referendum, and EU parliamentary ballots in this chapter's analysis restricts the available range of institutional variables. The models include two institutional variables: election type and simultaneous elections. Election type is represented by four dichotomous variables for parliamentary, presidential, referendum, and EU parliament votes (with presidential elections excluded as the comparison category). The first hypothesis states that turnout for presidential elections is likely to be the highest, followed by referendums, parliamentary elections, and EU parliamentary elections.

Further, because of the increased attention directed to the electoral process that is likely to accompany multiple elections, turnout should be higher in these races than in single-election contests.[24] The second hypothesis states that turnout is likely to be higher when elections are combined.

The analysis incorporates three political variables: founding elections, political fragmentation, and level of democracy.[25] Many studies note that first elections after democratic transition are more likely to engage voters, with a subsequent decline in participation after the initial euphoria has dissipated. The third hypothesis is that founding elections are likely to yield higher turnout than later elections.

Regime type is addressed in two ways. First, the initial model includes the summary score from Freedom House. Second, subsequent models systematically remove authoritarian states from the analysis to evaluate how authoritarian election data influence the results. The fourth hypothesis is that elections held by authoritarian governments are likely to be associated with higher turnout.

Political fragmentation could affect turnout, and scholars often use the effective number of parties to measure this factor. Several models include the effective number of parliamentary parties for the most proximate previous parliamentary election. However, because this variable by definition excludes the first election after political transition, it cannot be present in models that include controls for founding elections.

The analysis also includes three socioeconomic variables: urbanization, economic development, and population homogeneity. Following Kostadinova and Power's (2007) analysis of turnout, the models include urbanization and gross domestic product measures (in logged purchasing power parity terms) from the World Bank. The analysis also includes an index of the effective number of ethnic groups to account for differences in the population that could influence social pressures to participate.

Table 5.2 displays the results of the analysis. Models 1a and 1b include all elections, with a variable assessing democratic quality. Models 2a and 2b exclude the least free cases, those with Freedom House composite scores of 13 and 14. Models 3a and 3b relax the threshold of exclusion, omitting cases with scores higher than 10. Models 4a and 4b include only democratic elections, omitting those with scores higher than 5.

In all of the models, the type of election exerts a strong effect on turnout. Parliamentary and Euro-parliamentary elections produce a negative effect relative to presidential elections. However, as more authoritarian governments are excluded from the analysis (Models 4a and 4b), parliamentary elections no longer exhibit turnout rates statistically different from presidential races. The increased importance of the parliamentary vote relative to the presidential vote encourages turnout.[26]

Referendums yield results that are not statistically different from presidential turnout when more authoritarian regimes are included in the analysis (Models 1a-2b, 3b) but show statistically significant and negative results when only unambiguously democratic states are included (Models 4a-b). Referendums in post-Soviet authoritarian states are often used as proxies for presidential elections, enhancing the importance of turnout. In democratic states, they are more typically used to make lower stakes policy decisions.

Parameters for founding elections, simultaneous elections, gross domestic product, and ethnic concentration are significant in only one model. In Model 3a, first elections are associated with higher turnout, and simultaneous elections are associated with lower turnout. Gross domestic product exhibits a small negative effect and ethnic concentration is significant and positive, showing that less homogeneous populations are associated with higher levels of participation. The coefficients for the effective number of parties are not significant.

Regime type's influence is evidenced in two ways. First, Freedom House scores exhibit a significant, positive effect in Models 1a and 1b. Consistent with expectations, more authoritarian regimes are associated with higher reported turnout. In Models 2a–4b, the effect of regime type is controlled via case selection. As more authoritarian states are removed from the analysis, the effects of explanatory variables change. Coefficients for parliamentary elections become statistically indistinguishable from the excluded category, presidential elections.

The aggregate-level analysis provides additional support for the "discernment" explanation. Turnout is higher in elections where the outcomes are more likely to have direct policy implications or the elected office is more powerful. Authoritarian systems witness higher turnout, whether through enhanced participation by citizens who comply with regime expectations or through data manipulation. The former explanation again supports the notion of "discernment," but in a profoundly different manner than in democratic

Table 5.2 Multivariate Analysis of the Determinants of National-Level Turnout

	Model 1a (All Elections)	Model 1b (All Elections)	Model 2a (FH<13)	Model 2b (FH<13)	Model 3a (FH<10)	Model 3b (FH<10)	Model 4a (FH<5)	Model 4b (FH<5)
Constant	0.785*	0.745*	1.244*	1.214*	0.834*	0.767*	0.014	-0.262
	(0.183)	(0.216)	(0.206)	(0.231)	(0.132)	(0.205)	(1.965)	(1.770)
Parliament	-0.058*	-0.073*	-0.074*	-0.087*	-0.064*	-0.076*	-0.114	-0.109
	(0.023)	(0.028)	(0.026)	(0.024)	(0.023)	(0.029)	(0.070)	(0.072)
Referendum	0.007	-0.033	-0.005	-0.035	-0.050*	-0.101	-0.202*	-0.205*
	(0.030)	(0.039)	(0.034)	(0.034)	(0.023)	(0.041)	(0.068)	(0.066)
EU Parliament	-0.275*	-0.302*	-0.325*	-0.340*	-0.366*	0.377*	-0.417*	-0.428*
	(0.101)	(0.081)	(0.113)	(0.082)	(0.080)	(0.078)	(0.103)	(0.083)
Simultaneous Elections	-0.030	0.005	-0.044	-0.053	-0.050*	-0.019	-0.079	-0.083
	(0.030)	(0.033)	(0.044)	(0.048)	(0.019)	(0.043)	(0.074)	(0.077)
First Election	0.022	—	0.022	—	0.042*	—	—	—
	(0.026)		(0.023)		(0.010)			
Effective # of Parties (Prev. El.)	—	-0.002	—	0.003	—	-0.004	—	-0.009
		(0.007)		(0.008)		(0.009)		(0.017)
FH Score	0.017*	0.015*	—	—	—	—	—	—
	(0.003)	(0.004)						
Urbanization	-0.256	-0.162	-0.201	-0.214	0.219	0.398	1.085	1.271
	(0.184)	(0.189)	(0.258)	(0.199)	(0.152)	(0.397)	(2.520)	(2.125)
GDP/PPP	-0.010	-0.013	-0.055	-0.053	-0.057*	-0.054	-0.029	-0.008
	(0.036)	(0.037)	(0.045)	(0.039)	(0.014)	(0.046)	(0.119)	(0.105)
Ethnic Concentration	0.026	0.046	0.034	0.043	0.116*	0.093	0.123	0.129
	(0.024)	(0.027)	(0.036)	(0.026)	(0.058)	(0.054)	(0.100)	(0.075)
N	110	77	100	75	67	51	22	22
R²	0.532	0.492	0.474	0.485	0.460	0.424	0.544	0.549
Wald	128.18*	125.39*	52.71*	101.68*	1675.02*	47.51*	26.20*	43.68*

societies. The primary measure of "disenchantment" was significant in only one case; poorer economic performance encouraged participation.

CONCLUSION

In Soviet times, participation in elections was obligatory. After the USSR's collapse, many citizens of the newly independent states faced a decision similar to their counterparts elsewhere in the world: to vote or not to vote. This chapter explored citizen participation in the vote by conducting analyses of turnout using individual- and aggregate-level data.

In this investigation, Soviet-era conditioning potentially reveals its continued influence in at least two ways. First, the most authoritarian post-Soviet societies continued to emphasize participation, though only Turkmenistan consistently reported nearly perfect participation, as in most Soviet-era elections. Second, the analysis of survey data revealed that older voters tended to participate more readily than younger voters. This finding could be due to habituation during the Soviet period. But, older voters were more often saddled with the negative effects of reform efforts, and their participation also could be related to grievances. Furthermore, maturation may lead to an enhanced sense of civic duty, promoting participation in the vote.

In determining the relative importance of "disenchantment" versus "discernment," the data tell a mixed story. At the individual level, negative assessments of economic conditions were more closely associated with abstention from voting. This supports an account based on disenchantment. Negative assessments of democracy's progress were also associated with a greater likelihood of abstention, consistent with an account based on discernment.

The aggregate-level analysis suggested that voters are discerning and are more likely to respond to the invitation to vote when more powerful institutions are involved. This motivation was reflected in the effects of election type and regime type. Democracy scores were directly related to turnout; higher turnout was associated with more authoritarian states. Further, when all countries were included in the analysis, turnout in presidential elections was not different statistically from referendums but was greater than parliamentary or Euro-parliamentary elections. As more authoritarian countries were eliminated from the analysis, turnout for parliamentary elections became statistically indistinguishable from presidential elections, and referendums tended to yield lower turnout. Dictators continue to use elections as mobilization and control tools, heightening the importance of participation by citizens. Citizens understand when their presence at the polls is more important and respond accordingly.

This chapter addressed the first question facing citizens: to vote or not to vote. After deciding if they should participate in the vote, citizens face another critical question: whom should they support? The next chapter continues the analysis of voter decision making, turning to the growth and development of political parties in post-Soviet space.

CHAPTER 6

POLITICAL PARTY EVOLUTION

Functional political parties are essential participants in democratic politics.[1] Ideally, a party is a robust and responsive organization promoting a clearly defined ideology or set of views on pertinent policy matters that regularly contests elections, wins seats, and participates in policy making as a member of a governing coalition or the loyal opposition. While some groups in post-Soviet space purporting to be parties have developed consistent policy platforms and stable organizations, many more are ideologically ambiguous, organizationally hollow, personalistic, and incapable of formal participation in governance.

Previous chapters defined political parties in simple terms—a party was any group that contested an election—and deferred a deeper discussion of the issue to this chapter. While the definition used in earlier chapters simplifies coding and analytical procedures, it avoids addressing important features that qualitatively differentiate groups labeled as political parties from one another.

This chapter investigates the forms and functions of political parties, following other scholars who have characterized party system development in terms of party "supply" and "demand." In one conceptualization of market-driven party competition, Richard Rose (2000) argues that citizen demand for parties and elite supply interact. Citizens demand particular outcomes, and parties compete to provide what voters want. Alternatively, Henry Hale (2005; 2006) proposes that the main market relationship exists between party organizations as suppliers of valuable services and candidates as consumers who demand those services. He notes that many small parties supply few, if any, resources for candidates, in contrast to larger parties, patronage networks, and business organizations that offer valuable electoral goods and services. The chapter refers to concepts of both supply and demand but adheres more closely to Rose's notion of elite supply and citizen demand for political parties.

The chapter assesses the role of political parties in post-Soviet politics in four sections. The first section defines political parties and their functions in the post-Soviet context. The second section shows how regional party systems have begun to stabilize. The third section describes families of parties that have emerged on the ballots in the postcommunist period. The fourth section assesses the determinants of voter support for parties and reflects on the potential for parties to create long-term connections with the voting public.

WHAT ARE POLITICAL PARTIES?

Scholars often use the term "political party" in the post-Soviet context as simple shorthand covering a diverse set of political organizations: parties, blocs, factions, and deputy groups. However, the roles of these varied organizational forms in electoral and legislative politics differ. *Political parties* are the primary groups that form policy platforms, create organizations, and participate in elections. But, many officially registered political parties do not perform these functions, instead existing as shell organizations for various financial and political purposes.

Blocs, combining more than one party into an electoral alliance, may contest in some states. Blocs may be subject to higher thresholds than individual parties, or they may be treated as equivalent to parties in vote counting and seat allocation. *Factions* and *deputy groups* are political organizations in the legislature. These "parties in parliament" may be directly connected with a party or bloc that was on the ballot. They also may be subsidiary groups carved out of existing party-based factions, experiencing a full life cycle in the legislative period, with deputies rejoining parties and blocs during election campaigns.[2]

The diverse collection of party-like organizations operating in post-Soviet space begs the question: what is a political party? Although scholars have developed many explanations of how parties emerge and what functions they serve,[3] they generally concede that in a democratic society a political party's key activity is to contest elections.[4] In addition, parties may offer ideology, mobilize voters, communicate information between citizens and government, contribute to leadership recruitment, help elites coordinate to overcome collection action problems, and govern (LaPalombara and Weiner 1966; Lipset and Rokkan 1967; Janda 1980; Eldersveld 1982; Schlesinger 1991; Aldrich 1995). In authoritarian societies, parties perform many of these tasks as well, but the absence of electoral competition fundamentally alters how political elites and party organizations behave.

Almost all post-Soviet states regulate political parties via ancillary statutes that accompany their primary legislation on elections. The language in these laws typically defines parties as *voluntary citizen organizations designed to articulate citizen interests and to participate in politics.* Generally, parties

are granted rights to contest elections, mobilize citizens, disseminate information, own property, charge dues, and pursue other activities to achieve
their political goals. Laws often contain prohibitions on parties that challenge
the integrity of the state or incite ethnic or religious hatred. Many statutes
also prohibit party membership by government officials such as judges, law
enforcement, and in some cases, presidents.[5]

Post-Soviet governments consistently require parties to formally register
as public organizations, independent of their efforts to gain ballot access,
although the registration requirements vary substantially. The most onerous
statutory registration requirements are in Kazakhstan, where parties must
have fifty thousand members (or one out of every 306 Kazakh citizens based
on recent population data) distributed across many regions of the country.
Armenia, Moldova, Russia, Tajikistan, Ukraine, and Uzbekistan also have
regional distribution requirements for signatures or membership. In some
cases, registration gains a party access to state financing, such as in Armenia,
Azerbaijan, Estonia, Kyrgyzstan, Moldova, Russia, Ukraine, and Uzbekistan,
although the amount of public financing varies. Formal regulatory guidelines
only tell part of the story, however, as oversight bodies may create additional
impediments for parties to register and participate in elections.

PARTY SUPPLY

A party system is a collection of groups, labeled as parties, that contests elections. As the analysis in Chapter 4 showed, knowing the number of parties provides important insights into the distribution of power, the system's
political cohesion or fragmentation, and the relative stability or fluidity of
politics. But, the number of parties only tells part of the story; it does not
indicate what kinds of parties participate and how they enter or depart from
competition (Stokes 1999).

The Communist Party of the Soviet Union was the sole legal party entity
in the USSR. While party-like groups began to emerge in the Congress of
People's Deputies, no formal political parties were legally permitted to compete with the Communist Party. As the USSR moved toward collapse, civil
society organizations emerged across the Soviet Union, and regional elections featured multiple proto-party groups. Some of these organizations
transitioned into political parties, such as Sajudis in Lithuania.

After the USSR's disintegration, hundreds of parties registered across the
region, and many successfully gained seats in parliament during founding
elections. In Georgia, for example, candidates representing twenty-two parties received seats in the 1992 parliamentary election. While all of these organizations could not survive in the long term because of an inadequate supply
of voter, financial, and personnel resources, some party organizations grew
and prospered, others merged with stronger groups, and many more ceased
to exist as competitive entities.

Party genealogies are complicated—political elites move from party to
party, and organizations merge and change. The example of the democratic

opposition in Moldova illustrates the challenges of analyzing party systems in the region.[6] In Moldova's early post-Soviet period, parties proliferated across the ideological spectrum. An initial ban on the Communist Party created new parties on the left, but the reinstatement of the Party of Communists of Moldova, and the party's strong performance in elections beginning in 1998, prompted several shifts in the strategies and fortunes of opposition forces in local and national elections.

As Figure 6.1 illustrates,[7] the Moldovan Democrats Bloc was founded in 2005 to participate in the national parliamentary election, uniting several parties that had previously coalesced under the Our Moldova label for the 2003 local elections with the Democratic Party of Moldova and Social Liberal Party. The Our Moldova bloc featured an even more complicated family tree and consisted of four major parts. The first branch included the Social Democratic Alliance of Moldova, which evolved from the Civic Alliance for Reforms and a merger with the Motherland Party. The second was the Liberal Party, which evolved from a merger of the Party of Rebirth and Reconciliation, the National Peasant Christian Democratic Party, and the Social Liberal Union.[8] The third component was the Independents' Alliance, which united municipal-level leaders. The final piece was the Democratic People's Party. After the 2005 election, the Bloc of Moldovan Democrats broke into four parts, with the Social Liberal Party and Democratic Party reestablishing

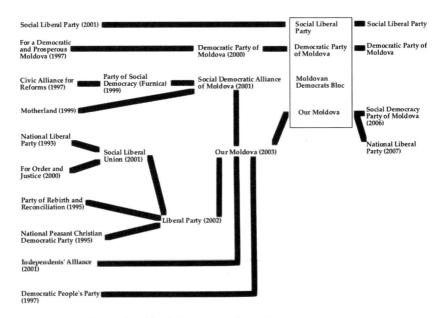

Figure 6.1 Evolution of Moldova's Democratic Opposition

their independent activities and the Social Democracy Party and National Liberal Party emerging from the remains of Our Moldova.

The twists and turns of the Moldovan democratic opposition echo several patterns found in other parts of the former USSR. Parties emerge and disappear frequently, generating high information costs for voters and complicating the assessment of party system growth and development. Parties are often closely associated with individual politicians. Underscoring the personalistic nature of politics in the region, many political organizations are even named for their leaders. For example, Dumitru Braghis' Social Democratic Alliance of Moldova was also known as the Braghis Alliance. In addition to Moldova's Braghis Alliance, eponymous parties and blocs have participated in elections in Latvia,[9] Lithuania,[10] Russia,[11] and Ukraine.[12] Moreover, Braghis' party's participation in short-term alliances or blocs[13]—Our Moldova in 2003 and Moldovan Democrats in 2005—underscores the popularity of party blocs, which have been found in elections in Armenia,[14] Estonia,[15] Georgia,[16] Latvia,[17] Lithuania,[18] Russia,[19] and Ukraine.[20] The inability of the democratic opposition to coalesce permanently also characterizes politics elsewhere in the former Soviet Union and has hindered the ability of these parties to win elections and effectively govern when they have been victorious.[21] Indeed, party systems across the newly independent states have been inchoate, characterized by many shifting participants, parties with weakly developed organizational features, limited voter attachments to parties, and a sometimes tenuous connection between elections and policy making (Mainwaring and Scully 1995).

Two indexes facilitate the assessment of party system stability. The volatility index—measuring the difference in the proportion of votes cast for parties from election to election—gives insight into how voters allocate their support across multiple elections and how participants in elections change (Pedersen 1979). If the same parties achieve similar electoral outcomes over time, volatility scores are low. The replacement index—measuring the proportion of the vote cast for new parties—also shows how voter support changes, but focuses on new entrants to the party system (Birch 2001). Volatility scores do not differentiate new entrants from established parties; replacement scores provide additional information about whether voter support moves among a restricted set of "usual suspects," or if new parties enter competition and achieve success against established parties.

Table 6.1 shows volatility and replacement scores for nine countries where appropriate data are available.[22] Many of the countries evidence declines in volatility and replacement scores over the 1990s and 2000s, suggesting increased stability among the competitors and decreasing fluidity in votes distributed among those parties.

The scores are best interpreted in relative terms. The highest volatility score on Table 6.1 is associated with Moldova's 1994–1998 election cycle. The corresponding replacement score is also relatively high, showing that 36 percent of votes were cast for parties that had not appeared on the ballot in the previous election. The 1998 election yielded a seismic shift in the Moldovan

Table 6.1   Replacement and Volatility Scores

		1st–2nd Election	2nd–3rd Election	3rd–4th Election	4th–5th Election
Armenia	Replacement	23.7 (1999)	11.4 (2003)	28.2 (2007)	
	Volatility	18.3 (95–99)	24.6 (99–03)	32.3 (03–07)	
Estonia	Replacement	36.7 (1995)	4.3 (1999)	25.6 (2003)	7.1 (2007)
	Volatility	38.1 (92–95)	25.8 (95–99)	28.1 (99–03)	21.9 (03–07)
Georgia	Replacement	57.6 (1995)	21.3 (1999)	79.6 (03/04)	14.3 (2008)
	Volatility	N/A (92–95)	36.4 (95–99)	51.9 (99–03/04)	18.7 (03/04–08)
Kazakhstan	Replacement	N/A (1995)	37.4 (1999)	26.9 (2004)	4.5 (2007)
	Volatility	N/A (94–95)	N/A (95–99)	46.3 (99–04)	17.7 (03–07)
Latvia	Replacement	19.0 (1995)	44.3 (1998)	30.2 (2002)	4.83 (2006)
	Volatility	41.5 (93–95)	38.9 (95–98)	23.1 (98–02)	16.0 (02–06)
Lithuania	Replacement	15.9 (1996)	2.1 (2000)	2.0 (2004)	
	Volatility	38.7 (92–96)	55.8 (96–00)	25.2 (00–04)	
Moldova	Replacement	36.0 (1998)	5.8 (2001)	0.0 (2005)	
	Volatility	63.9 (94–98)	31.3 (98–01)	28.4 (01–05)	
Russia	Replacement	42.1 (1995)	43.4 (1999)	16.6 (2003)	2.2 (2007)
	Volatility	42.3 (93–95)	37.8 (95–99)	23.0 (99–03)	21.6 (03–07)
Ukraine	Replacement	32.7 (1998)	45.5 (2002)	11.2 (2006)	1.8 (2007)
	Volatility	31.8 (94–98)	20.0 (98–02)	39.7 (02–06)	9.9 (06–07)

Sources. Author's calculations. See the Appendix for more information about sources.

party system: the reemergence of a strong Party of Communists as well as a reversal in fortune for many parties that had participated in the 1994 election. As the Party of Communists further consolidated its position as the leading party, volatility dropped in half. Replacement dropped even more, to zero in 2005. Voter preferences continued to shift among competing parties, but the identity of those parties stabilized.

The lowest volatility score is associated with Ukraine's 2006–2007 electoral cycle. Four of the five top parties in the 2006 election obtained similar levels of electoral support in 2007, with some shifts in the vote benefiting the Bloc of Yuliya Tymoshenko. The replacement score in 2007 was also low: under 2 percent of the vote was cast for parties that did not appear on the ballot in 2006. Ukraine's scores show a substantial decrease in instability from the early transition period when volatility and replacement scores were in the 30s.

In both the Moldovan and Ukrainian cases, party system stabilization is emerging in the context of democratic competition. Recent research has underscored how postcommunist states have developed more predictable competition, with significant reductions in volatility after the first decade of postcommunism (Tavits 2005). But, increased predictability in party systems is not only associated with democratic mechanisms. Declines in volatility and replacement scores in Kazakhstan and Russia occurred in the context of increasing centralization of executive power. Strong performance by the parties of power, coupled with institutional mechanisms to impede new entrants (such as party registration rules with high membership requirements, and high electoral thresholds to gain seats), also contributed to a decline in volatility and replacement scores.

The identity of election contestants has begun to stabilize across many post-Soviet states. In other words, the "supply" of competitive parties has become increasingly consistent, although the mechanisms introducing this increased stability vary. The next section provides more detail on party supply, identifying what types of political parties typically contest seats.

PARTY FAMILIES

While institutional rules, regime types, demographic features, and salient cleavages vary substantially across post-Soviet space, several "families" of political parties have emerged. Instead of producing an encyclopedic list of all parties and political persuasions, this section identifies several functional categories of parties that are active in the region using labels that should be familiar to even casual observers of postcommunist politics.

Communist Successor Parties

Perhaps no group of political parties in postcommunist space has been subjected to as much analysis as the successors to communist parties.[23] While communist parties occupy a specific ideological space, they also have a functional purpose outside of their political views. These parties provide continuity for voters between past and present and also provide an example to emerging parties of how to create regional networks and disciplined organizations. As inheritors of many of the Communist Party of the Soviet Union's personnel resources and a loyal electorate, communist successors were arguably the only organizationally coherent parties in the early postcommunist period.

The coup attempt in 1991 precipitated a backlash against the Communist Party, leading to bans in several republics.[24] While these bans were later lifted, the lack of formal continuity can render identification of the "true" successor a challenge. For instance, some members of the banned Communist

Party in Moldova formed the Socialist Party in 1992. But, Vladimir Voronin and other party members successfully worked to have the ban reversed and the party reinstated. Which group is the "real" successor to the Communist Party in Moldova? While many consider the Party of Communists headed by Voronin to be the heirs, one could argue that the Socialist Party also deserves that designation (Ishiyama 1997). Similarly, in Kazakhstan, some researchers argue that the Communist Party of Kazakhstan is not a direct descendant of the Soviet-era party (Cutler 2004), while other sources indicate that it is.[25]

Simply donning the label "communist" does not render a party a successor to the Soviet-era organization. In Georgia, parties called the Georgian Communist Party, Stalin Communist Party, and Georgian United Communist Party have contested elections. In Russia, the Communist Party of the Russian Federation has been joined on the ballot by Communists–Working Russia–For the Soviet Union. In Ukraine, the Communist Party of Ukraine, Communist Party of Workers and Peasants, and Communist Party (Renewed) have participated in elections. Moreover, communist successor parties in Estonia (Estonian Democratic Labor Party), Latvia (Socialist Party of Latvia), and Lithuania (Lithuanian Democratic Labor Party), jettisoned the labels and trappings of their predecessors to remain as electorally relevant as possible in societies with strong antipathy toward the Soviet past.

The following parties are considered to be the inheritors of the Communist Party tradition: Armenian Communist Party, Azerbaijan Communist Party, Communist Party of Belarus, Estonian Social Democratic Labor Party, Georgian United Communist Party, Communist Party of Kazakhstan, Party of Communists of Kyrgyzstan, Latvian Socialist Party, Lithuanian Democratic Labor Party, Party of Communists of Moldova, Communist Party of the Russian Federation, Communist Party of Tajikistan, Communist Party of Ukraine, and People's Democratic Party of Uzbekistan.

The decline in communist parties' electoral prowess has varied across post-Soviet space. These parties have fared well in countries in which they have reimagined themselves as European-style social democratic parties. For example, communist successor parties in Latvia and Lithuania received 14 percent and 21 percent respectively in the most recent elections. Less reformed parties have performed well in recent elections in Moldova (46 percent), Tajikistan (21 percent), and Russia (12 percent), less so in Belarus, Kyrgyzstan, and Ukraine (with 5 percent in each), and have collapsed electorally elsewhere.

Parties of Power

Parties of power occupy a special place in the post-Soviet political context. The term generally describes not just a traditional party but a political machine and its trappings.[26] These parties are closely associated with presidents, although the chief executives of post-Soviet states have generally eschewed formal membership status in their own parties of power. The close connection of these parties to executive power provides them access to material, personnel, and financial resources unavailable to other political groups.

The political opposition often accuses these parties of using "administrative resources" for nefarious purposes. A party of power's access to administrative resources may be manifested in more intense positive media coverage,[27] favorable decisions by administrative bodies like electoral commissions and the courts, and the ability to formally or informally dole out rewards and punishments to citizens during an election campaign.

Because these parties rely upon executive resources, they are most commonly found in systems with strong presidents. Examples of current parties of power include the Republican Party (Armenia), New Azerbaijan Party, Nur-OTAN (Kazakhstan), United Russia, People's Party of Tajikistan, and the Democratic Party of Turkmenistan. Not surprisingly, the electoral performance of parties of power reflects their privileged status. In the most recent elections, all but one of the parties of power received the majority of seats in parliament: the New Azerbaijan Party received 65 of 123 seats,[28] United Russia 315 of 450, and the Peoples Party of Tajikistan 49 of 60. Nur-OTAN and the Democratic Party of Turkmenistan received all of the seats in their respective parliaments. The lone failure to secure an outright majority was the Republican Party of Armenia, which received 65 of 131 seats.

Several post-Soviet states are absent from the above list because they lack formal parties of power. In some cases, such as Belarus and Uzbekistan, strong leaders have not vested powers in a single party, relying instead on loyal "independents" or several parties for support. In Kyrgyzstan, former President Askar Akayev had party support, Alga Kyrgyzstan and Adilet, but neither rose to the level of an exclusive party of power. Rather, Akayev relied on his regional and familial connections for his power network. Current president Kurmanbek Bakiyev may be working toward creating a party of power (Ak Zhol), but the necessary machinery is not yet in place. The Baltic states and Moldova are also absent from this list. The Baltic countries do not have parties-of-power largely due to the weakness of presidents and more democratic political competition. In Moldova, the party that most closely fills this role is also a communist successor party and is addressed in that section.

Because of their connection to chief executives, these parties may disappear when their patrons leave the political scene or form a new party of power. Examples of parties of power that have lost their position include the Citizen's Union of Georgia, Our Home is Russia, and People's Democratic Party (Ukraine). Despite the failure of some parties of power to persevere, they have proven to be an enduring feature of the post-Soviet party landscape.

Opposition Parties

Political groups attempting to serve as a counterweight to parties of power are generally labeled the "opposition." Like opposition parties anywhere in the world, post-Soviet opposition parties challenge dominant parties in elections and in policy making. Unlike opposition parties in European democracies that expect eventually to win elections and become governing parties, many post-Soviet opposition parties are mired in perpetual opposition status.

In the early postcommunist period, opposition parties arose from independence movements and some, like Sajudis (Homeland Union) in Lithuania, successfully became governing parties. Unlike the categories of communist successor parties or parties of power whose members are relatively easy to identify, opposition parties have been more diverse, ephemeral, and greater in number. This classification constitutes a peculiar mix of parties, some oriented toward a market economy and democracy, others to more populist economic policies and dubious attitudes toward democratic governance, and still others that are primarily personal vehicles for ambitious politicians. What opposition parties share is a disadvantaged position in the party system, challenging dominant parties often without access to the full range of resources at the disposal of progovernment parties.

A partial list of recent opposition parties includes the Rule of Law Party (Armenia);[29] Democratic Party, Musavat, Popular Front, and Umid (Azerbaijan); United Democratic Forces[30] (Belarus); Ak Zhol and Social Democratic Party (Kazakhstan); Ar-Namys and Ata-Meken (Kyrgyzstan); Union of Right Forces and Yabloko (Russia);[31] Islamic Renaissance Party and Social Democratic Party (Tajikistan); and Erk (Uzbekistan). Opposition party performance varies substantially, although they often perform poorly when they gain ballot access. In the most recent elections, parties listed above received 9 of 131 seats (Armenia), 8 of 125 (Azerbaijan), 2 of 60 (Tajikistan), and no seats in the remaining states. Their failure to garner electoral support and legislative seats is due, in part, to the institutional impediments placed in front of them by ruling parties, and also to their unwillingness to coalesce into a single opposition force.

The "Colored Revolutions" demonstrated that opposition parties can oust incumbent governments when they overcome the reticence to ally with one another. The National Movement in Georgia, the "Orange" forces in Ukraine, and a motley assortment of opposition protesters in Kyrgyzstan parlayed pent-up citizen dissatisfaction with corrupt politics into victories on the streets and in the ballot boxes. In Georgia and Kyrgyzstan, former opposition politicians began to exhibit some of the corrupt behaviors as their ousted predecessors. In Ukraine, postrevolutionary politics have been contentious but increasingly democratic.

Technical Parties

A large contingent of groups that are labeled political parties meet only minimal criteria. While they contest elections with an identifiable label, these "parties" lack important ancillary features and serve diverse purposes. Some technical parties are created as "twins" or "clones," to divert votes from other parties by mimicking the names of existing groups, historic parties, or famous politicians. They may be designed to promote candidacies in district races rather than national-level politics or to help improve a politician's competitiveness in a future contest. Technical parties are also created to funnel money and shelter business interests,[32] serve as backup organizations in case ballot access for a major party is challenged,[33] or allow major parties to stack electoral commissions in their favor.[34]

Examples of technical parties abound. For example, in Ukraine's 2007 parliamentary election, several competed. The All Ukrainian Hromada Bloc and KUCHMA Bloc invoked the names of political forces of the recent past but were unrelated to their namesakes.[35] Similarly, the Communist Party of Ukraine (Renewed) was unrelated to the Communist Party of Ukraine, but many supporters of the latter feared that it would draw votes from that party. None of these parties received many votes, but technical parties can undermine electoral success for major competitors.

Institutionalized Competitive Parties

The final, and smallest, family of parties emerging slowly across post-Soviet space includes political organizations that have relatively clear platforms, extensive organizations and networks, participate in and win elections, and generally function like developed West European parties. These parties have also demonstrated staying power and are beginning to develop stable roots in society. Major parties in the Baltic states have arguably developed into modern competitive parties. Parties in Ukraine have recently moved in this direction, although they remain highly personalistic.

PARTY DEMAND

The previous section addressed the "supply" side of the party system equation, describing the complex family trees associated with many post-Soviet parties and categorizing several types of parties offered by elites to voters during elections. This section of the chapter assesses individual voters' decision-making processes, asking how voters determine whom they will support.

Scholars of voting behavior have investigated the role of group membership,[36] psychological attachments to parties,[37] and assessments of economic conditions[38] as the main determinants of party support. Over the half-century following publication of the seminal *The American Voter*, the voting behavior literature has evolved theoretically and methodologically. Although some work suggests that concepts such as party identification do not travel well (Thomassen 1976; Mughan 1981), researchers have employed this and other concepts from the American voting behavior literature outside the United States, extending the analysis to many post-Soviet countries.

Russia has been the primary focus of most voting studies in the region, accounting for more than half of the articles and books published in the first decade of postcommunism. Aside from Ukraine and the Baltic states, most of the remaining former Soviet territories are virtually ignored in scholarship on voting (Tucker 2002). Like their colleagues in the American voting behavior literature, postcommunist scholars have investigated how attitudes about politics and the economy, as well as objective demographic features, affect voter tendencies (White, Rose, and McAllister 1997; Birch 2000; Colton

2000). While some literature on regional political parties, especially in Russia, suggests that they are weak and undifferentiated (White et al. 1997),[39] other work argues that consistent attitudes toward parties are developing at the individual level, setting the stage for voters to develop long-term psychological attachments (Brader and Tucker 2001; Miller and Klobucar 2000; Miller et al. 2000). This section addresses voting behavior, investigating how respondent attitudes and demographic features affect citizen support for major post-Soviet political parties.

Voting Behavior in Post-Soviet States

To assess voting behavior across several post-Soviet states, this chapter uses data from the Central and Eastern Eurobarometer (CEEURO) and the Comparative Study of Electoral Systems (CSES).[40] The dependent variable is an unordered, discrete measure of respondent support for the main political parties and a residual other category. Results from the multinomial logit models use the communist successor party and party of power as referent groups. Consistent with the voting behavior literature (White and McAllister 2003; Brader and Tucker 2001), the analysis measures public attitudes about politics and the economy, assessments of economic status, and various demographic features.

In studies of mass partisanship in post-Soviet states, supporters of communist successor parties distinguish themselves from other voters based on attitudes about the market economy (Miller et al. 2000; Brader and Tucker 2001). Moreover, in elite and mass surveys, communist successor parties anchor the left side of the economic policy dimension, with parties of power and opposition parties less clearly distinguished from one another by economic policy orientation (Miller et al. 2000; Miller and Klobucar 2000). These observations from research conducted in a few post-Soviet states should apply to a wider range of countries included in this chapter's analysis.

Researchers who have attempted to isolate the effects of inherited cultural attitudes on voting have relied on region (Roper and Fesnic 2003) or views about strong leadership (Mishler and Willerton 2003) as proxies. While the former variable is available in the data, the applicability of region is undermined by population mobility and the limited geographic scope of areas with unequal Soviet experience. Questions assessing leadership qualities more directly address one of the region's ostensible cultural inheritances: a preference for strong rulers. Unfortunately, the datasets do not offer appropriate questions about leadership qualities.

Attitudes about the market economy and future relations with Russia serve as proxies for respondent connections to the Soviet past. While these measures are imperfect substitutes for cultural inheritance, as antipathy toward the market and positive feelings about Russia do not necessarily equate with Soviet nostalgia, they are the best variables available to assess this concept. The models also include controls for objective economic conditions (income and employment) and demographic variables, including place of residence and age. Rural residents and older respondents should be more likely to evidence Soviet nostalgia and consequently support the communist successor parties over their rivals.

Table 6.2 shows partial results of the analysis, comparing support for parties of power relative to communist successor parties from surveys held in the mid-1990s. The cell entries are "relative risk ratios," terms that show the likelihood of changes in the variable rendering the outcome in the comparison or the referent group category. A value above one means that the result in the comparison group is more likely; a value under one indicates that a result in the referent group is more likely. For example, with a value over four in the Armenia model, support for the market is significantly more likely to be associated with respondents who favor the party of power (comparison group) rather than the communist successor party (referent group).

The four countries with clearly identifiable parties of power did not yield a consistent set of variables differentiating party support. But, some explanatory variables are more often associated with vote choice. Most notably, economic variables and satisfaction with democracy distinguish support for parties of power in three of four countries. In two countries, older voters are more likely to support communist successor parties relative to parties of power. Support for Armenia's party of power is associated with market support, a belief that Armenia's future is not tied to Russia, confidence that economic conditions are likely to improve, urban residence, and greater satisfaction with the level of democracy. In Georgia, support for the market, negative views of past economic performance, higher income, younger voters, and more satisfaction with democracy are connected with support for the party of power relative to the communist party. In Kazakhstan and Russia, few variables differentiate support for the party of power from the communist successor party. In the former, younger voters are more likely to support the party of power. In the latter, more positive views of past economic performance and more positive views of democracy are connected with support for the party of power.

Similarly, economic variables drive voter decisions about supporting opposition parties versus the communist successor party. Table 6.3 shows results for nine countries, also in terms of relative risk ratios. While some of the parties match the definition of opposition parties offered above, some cases require additional commentary. Most notably, in the Baltic states, the parties included in this analysis are leading parties, not opposition parties. Because parties of power are absent in the Baltic states, the most successful electoral parties serve as substitutes.

Overall, few strong patterns emerge. In five of nine cases, support for the free market strongly differentiates respondents favoring the opposition party from those who prefer communist successor parties. Other economic coefficients are also significant in several cases. Many coefficients, such as those for the country's future being tied with Russia, age, and satisfaction with democracy, are significant in only three of nine cases. While economic variables predominate, support for opposition parties is idiosyncratic.

Table 6.2 MNL Analysis (Relative Risk Ratios), Party of Power[1] vs. Communist Successor

Party of Power > Communist Successor	Market	Future with Russia	Retrospective Economic Views	Prospective Economic Views	Income	Unemployed	Urban	Education	Gender	Age	Satisfaction with Democracy
Armenia (1995)	4.318*	0.445*	1.056	0.635*	1.017	0.726	1.821*	1.106	0.713	0.991	0.445*
Georgia (1995)	2.708*	1.206	2.131*	0.734	1.175*	—	0.786	1.054	0.969	0.975*	0.446*
Kazakhstan (1995)	1.471	1.108	0.958	0.919	0.973	0.588	0.959	2.084	1.619	0.938*	1.071
Russia (1995)	2.253	—	0.624*	0.843	1.030	2.730	1.580	1.211	1.566	0.992	0.356*

Table 6.3 MNL Analysis (Relative Risk Ratios), Main Opposition[1] vs. Communist Successor

Major Opposition > Communist Successor	Market	Future with Russia	Retrospective Economic Views	Prospective Economic Views	Income	Unemployed	Urban	Education	Gender	Age	Satisfaction with Democracy
Armenia (1995)	2.684*	0.281*	0.923	0.803	1.021	0.260	2.209	0.633	1.118	0.981	0.954
Belarus (1995)	5.864*	0.373*	0.887	1.681*	1.055	3.865	1.633	1.215	1.071	0.933*	1.287
Estonia (1995)	1.184	0.147	1.227	1.212	1.197	—	0.164	0.448*	14.203*	0.988	0.737
Georgia (1995)	1.806	0.729	2.750*	0.664	1.199*	—	1.275	1.226	0.764	0.949*	0.489*
Kazakhstan (1995)	0.802	1.949	1.505	0.818	1.075	1.388	0.589	2.551	1.510	0.942*	0.468*
Latvia (1995)	0.251*	0.577	0.535*	0.841	1.173	1.954	0.521	1.436	0.759	1.032	0.580
Lithuania (1996)	4.252*	1.083	1.976*	1.794*	1.104	—	1.251	1.791	1.267	1.021	1.964*
Russia (1995)	4.043*	—	0.674*	0.690*	0.956	0.705	2.192*	1.862*	1.375	0.994	0.700
Ukraine (1994)	3.404*	0.125*	0.931	1.101	0.970	1.782	—	0.809	0.218*	0.984	0.502*

Table 6.4 MNL Analysis (Relative Risk Ratios), Main Opposition[1] vs. Party of Power

Major Opposition> Party of Power	Market	Future with Russia	Retrospective Economic Views	Prospective Economic Views	Income	Unemployed	Urban	Education	Gender	Age	Satisfaction with Democracy
Armenia (1995)	0.622	0.631	0.874	1.265	1.003	0.358	1.213	0.572	1.568	0.990	2.146*
Georgia (1995)	0.667	0.604	1.290	0.904	1.020	—	1.623	1.163	0.789	0.973*	1.096
Kazakhstan (1995)	0.545	1.760	1.572	0.890	1.106	2.361	0.615	1.224	0.933	1.004	0.437*
Russia (1995)	1.794	—	1.080	0.818	0.928	0.258	1.387	1.537	0.878	1.002	1.964*

When the referent category is changed to the party of power (see Table 6.4), the explanatory power of the models is reduced substantially. In the four cases with clearly defined parties of power, only attitudes about democracy (in three cases) and age (in one case) distinguish voters for opposition parties from those supporting the party of power. In Armenia and Russia, greater dissatisfaction with democracy yields greater support for the opposition relative to the party of power. In Kazakhstan, the relationship is reversed.

Findings from later in the 1990s match several aspects of those from the mid-1990s. In surveys associated with Russia and Ukraine's elections in 1998 and 1999 (see Table 6.5), satisfaction with democracy is consistently associated with support for parties of power and opposition parties, relative to communist successor parties. In two cases, more positive assessments of economic change are connected with supporters of the party of power (Russia) and opposition party (Ukraine). In Russia, older voters are more likely to be associated with support for the communist party, and support for opposition parties is associated with more educated voters in both Russia and Ukraine.

Changing the party of power to the referent category yields less consistent results. Higher levels of education are associated with opposition-party support relative to the party of power in both countries, and urban dwellers are more likely to support the opposition in Russia. Whereas economic variables tended to distinguish support of the parties of power and opposition relative to the communist successor parties, attitudes about democracy and education distinguished party of power supporters from opposition voters, but this relationship was weak.

Table 6.5 MNL Analysis (Relative Risk Ratios), CSES Data[1]

Party of Power> Communist Successor	Economic Change	Income	Unemployed	Urban	Education	Gender	Age	Satisfaction with Democracy
Russia (1999)	0.740*	1.034	1.002	1.082	1.115	1.364	0.964*	0.600*
Ukraine (1998)	0.684	1.174	0.473	1.707	0.990	1.021	0.940	0.481*
Major Opposition>Communist Successor								
Russia (1999)	0.733	1.234	1.523	3.087*	1.396*	2.155*	0.970*	0.622*
Ukraine (1998)	0.529*	0.945	1.447	0.777	1.325*	0.896	1.005	0.579*
Major Opposition>Party of Power								
Russia (1999)	0.991	1.193	1.519	2.855*	1.252*	1.580	1.006	1.037
Ukraine (1998)	0.774	0.805	3.059	0.455	1.410*	0.877	1.015	1.202

The data available to assess citizen attitudes toward political parties provide mixed results. First, economic variables often differentiate support among political parties when communist successor parties are the referent category. Because the policy preferences of communist successor parties generally promote greater state ownership of the economy than the policies of other parties, differentiation of voter attitudes along this dimension is not surprising. Moreover, the ability of voters to distinguish among these parties on economic matters suggests that parties are providing reasonably meaningful choices in this policy area. Second, attitudes about democratic quality differentiate voters in some cases. Supporters of communist successor parties are more likely to express dissatisfaction with the status of democracy than are supporters of the parties of power or the opposition. The pessimistic assessment of democratic quality among these voters may be related to the disadvantaged position of communist successor parties compared with their recent past. Third, consistent with demographic accounts of party support, older voters are more likely to support the communist successor parties when age is statistically significant. Also, higher levels of education tend to be associated with opposition-party support. While inconsistent, the features connected to voter support of political parties generally conform to findings in other voting behavior research.

CONCLUSION

This chapter defined political parties and analyzed how voters differentiate among them. Although few post-Soviet political parties organizationally measure up to their counterparts in established democracies, some are developing technical capacities, consistent platforms, and stable electoral support. Volatility and replacement scores from across the region support this interpretation; while voters have distributed support among a wide range of party organizations, the diversity of many party systems has declined over time. Despite this progress, old party forms persist across the region, with parties of power dominating the political landscape in many post-Soviet states.

Based on survey data from the mid- and late-1990s, a few patterns of party support emerge. Attitudes about the economy and democracy tend to differentiate party supporters, while other variables inconsistently delineate partisans from one another. These findings suggest that post-Soviet voters exhibited some clarity about their own preferences and could distinguish among major participants along key dimensions of politics, even in the early transition period. Post-Soviet parties are generally weak, but they are beginning to evolve into more stable political forces.

The next chapter continues the discussion of electoral choice in post-Soviet states but alters the questions facing voters. Instead of focusing on elections where citizens choose among candidates and parties, Chapter 7 covers referendums where voters weigh in directly on policy preferences.

CHAPTER 7

REFERENDUMS AS
DIRECT DEMOCRACY

As Russian citizens prepared to vote in late 2007, political rhetoric relabeled the upcoming parliamentary election a "referendum"[1] on President Vladimir Putin's rule. Nearly two months before election day, parliamentary speaker Boris Gryzlov announced that "we are in fact not conducting parliamentary elections, but a referendum on confidence in the president" (Rosbalt Information Agency 2007). United Russia's political advertisements reminded Russian citizens that a vote for the party was a vote in support of its leader, President Putin. Politicians and the media repeated this mantra, with Putin himself characterizing the election as a type of referendum (Ivanov 2007). Just as his predecessor, Boris Yeltsin, succeeded in his public confidence vote fourteen years earlier, so too did Putin.

The effort to portray Russia's 2007 parliamentary election as a referendum illustrates the perceived power of this form of voting. By allowing citizens to directly vote on their preferred policy outcome, rather than having policy mediated through elected representatives, referendums are often considered to be the most direct form of democracy.[2] Some scholars question this assessment, suggesting that referendums do not offer real choices because political elites often determine question wording and tend to initiate referendums only when they are convinced that their preferred policy will be victorious.[3] Moreover, many question the capacity of voters to fully understand complex policy matters and cast a meaningful vote consistent with their true preferences.[4]

Despite these concerns, the use of referendums has increased in recent decades (Mendelsohn and Parkin 2001), with over half of the world permitting national-level votes on policy matters.[5] In the post-Soviet region, referendums have been a popular policy-making device since Mikhail

Gorbachev's March 1991 vote on preserving the union. Prior to Gorbachev's tenure, Soviet political elites did not offer citizens the opportunity to directly influence policy; policy making was the exclusive domain of high-ranking party and government officials (Roeder 1993). By calling the referendum, Gorbachev attempted to use public support to ward off challenges from conservative members of the ruling elite and defuse nationalist sentiments in many corners of the USSR. However, Gorbachev miscalculated both public attitudes about retaining the Soviet system and the tactical responses of his emerging rivals in the republics. The referendum inspired boycotts and counterreferendums in the regions, allowing local leaders to enhance their authority vis-à-vis Moscow. Only four of the fifteen republics held the referendum as Gorbachev planned, with a single question about preserving the union, and six republics boycotted the vote. While Gorbachev declared victory, the win was hollow. Instead of helping to preserve the USSR, the vote provided a mechanism for republics to enhance their independence claims and move toward dissolving the union a few months later (Walker 2003).

Since 1991, referendums have been important political tools in both democratic and authoritarian post-Soviet societies. Every successor state has held at least one referendum on questions ranging from institutional design to accession to international organizations. This chapter assesses the role of referendums in politics, focusing on how political elites use referendums.[6] Specifically, it investigates whether referendums have granted the public an opportunity to make important policy decisions, or if they have been controlled by political elites to create an illusion of legitimacy.

The chapter addresses this issue in two parts. The first section assesses referendums using various classification tools: based on how referendums are initiated, their outputs,[7] the relative competitiveness of the process,[8] and the substance of the issues addressed. The second section provides detailed information on each referendum that has been held in post-Soviet space, categorizing them by the substantive questions facing voters. The chapter concludes by reviewing when political elites have used referendums strategically to enhance their authority and claim popular support for their initiatives and when referendums have offered voters a meaningful choice.

TYPES OF REFERENDUMS

The use of referendums as policymaking tools is constrained by the institutional rules dictating who may place issues on the ballot and what issues may be decided via direct public voting. Constitutional rules and statutes typically spell out the range of actors who may call a referendum and the process by which the vote may be initiated. Although the specific circumstances and limitations on the ability to call a referendum vary, referendums may be initiated by post-Soviet presidents in twelve countries, parliament in twelve countries, citizens in ten countries, and government in two countries.

The content of referendums is subject to restrictions in each country. While specific provisions vary widely, commonly prohibited issues include budget and tax matters (eight countries), granting amnesty or pardons (seven coun-tries), the dismissal of public officials (six countries), emergency measures (five countries), and international treaties (four countries). Referendums can produce outcomes that are binding on political actors, enacting a law or mandating a particular action. Alternatively, the result of the referendum may suggest a certain course of action or recommend an outcome.

Most post-Soviet referendums have been binding, such as approving initial constitutional texts or subsequent changes. But several votes have been consultative, recommending a policy outcome. Consultative referen-dums have included questions on voter support for the principle of con-stitutional changes (Belarus 1995), removing Russian troops and receiving reparations (Lithuania 1992), supporting continued independence (Moldova 1994), expressing confidence in the president and his policies (Russia 1993), and authorizing the president to move forward on constitutional changes (Ukraine 2000).[9] Consultative referendums are not impotent, as they can affect policy decisions and provide political actors with bargaining leverage.

Scholars have also assessed referendums by analyzing the type and com-petitiveness of questions, distinguishing referendums that benefit the regime (prohegemonic) from those that do not (antihegemonic), as well as refer-endums initiated by government actors (controlled) and those that are not (uncontrolled) (Smith 1976; Qvortrup 2000). Although government-initi-ated referendums may be more likely to succeed, especially in post-Soviet states, one must exercise caution in classifying referendums based on the results.[10] Yet, because of state interference in election processes, controlled, prohegemonic referendums gain advantages in many countries. Even Gor-don Smith, the creator of this classification scheme, noted that "control" is "partly based on the right of initiation and partly according to the actual events which lead to a particular vote."[11]

Instead of classifying referendums based on outcomes, but remaining mindful of how control overlaps with election quality, this chapter's coding of controlled or uncontrolled votes is based on the initiator as well as election quality. Controlled referendums are those in which governments allegedly use their access to the media and administrative resources to generate a favor-able outcome. Uncontrolled referendums are those in which the playing field is reasonably free and fair. For example, Armenia's 2003 presidentially initi-ated referendum on constitutional change was prohegemonic and controlled, albeit unsuccessful.[12] A similar referendum in 2005 passed and is also classi-fied as prohegemonic and controlled. In both cases, observers and the media reported allegations of manipulation and fraud, although the allegations were arguably more serious in 2005.

Table 7.1 categorizes all of the referendums in the post-Soviet states along two dimensions: pro- or antihegemonic and controlled or uncontrolled (Smith 1976; Qvortrup 2000). Referendums that include multiple ques-tions falling into more than one category are classified in 0.5 increments.[13] For example, the 1996 Belarusan referendum that included both president-initiated prohegemonic constitutional changes and parliament-initiated

Table 7.1   Types of Referendums

	Controlled/ Prohegemonic	Controlled/ Antihegemonic	Uncontrolled/ Prohegemonic	Uncontrolled/ Antihegemonic
Armenia	3	0	0	0
Azerbaijan	2	1	0	0
Belarus	2.5	0.5	0	0
Estonia	0	0	1.5	0.5
Georgia	2	0	0	0
Kazakhstan	2	0	0	0
Kyrgyzstan	6	0	0	0
Latvia	0	0	3	1
Lithuania	0	0	6	1
Moldova	0	0	1	0
Russia	1	0	1	0
Tajikistan	3	0	0	0
Turkmenistan	1	0	0	0
Ukraine	1	0	0	0
Uzbekistan	2	0	0	0
Total	25.5	1.5	12.5	2.5
Success Rate	24.5/25.5	1/1.5	7.5/12.5	0/2.5

Source: Author's calculations based on data from central electoral commissions and media sources.

antihegemonic constitutional changes (along with other questions) is coded as 0.5 prohegemonic and 0.5 antihegemonic.[14]

Consistent with scholarship suggesting that elites tend to initiate beneficial referendums when they are confident in victory, most post-Soviet referendums have been prohegemonic and controlled (25.5 of 42). Prohegemonic and uncontrolled referendums constitute the second-largest category (12.5 of 42), with few antihegemonic referendums making it to the ballot (1.5 controlled and 2.5 uncontrolled).

The success rate for referendums varies by content and process. Controlled prohegemonic referendums almost never fail. Uncontrolled prohegemonic referendums have a success rate of 60 percent, with 7.5 of 12.5 cases yielding victories. Antihegemonic referendums typically fail. The only possible exception is the 1992 vote in Azerbaijan that ousted the president. However, this vote could be considered prohegemonic, as the opposition to President Abulfez Elchibey controlled the process. The results of post-Soviet referendums provide additional support to the idea that public officials tend to call referendums when they are confident of success; not only do prohegemonic referendums predominate, but they tend to succeed, whereas antihegemonic referendums tend to fail.

Referendums may also be classified by the content of the questions. Thirty-four referendums have asked voters to weigh in on institutional design and power: approving or changing constitutions, modifying election rules, or extending the presidential term of office. Four referendums have addressed membership in international organizations such as the EU or NATO. Ten referendums have asked policy questions related to citizenship, public benefits, foreign policy, and other matters.[15]

The Baltic states have conducted the most competitive referendums, while referendums in Belarus, the South Caucasus, and Central Asia have almost exclusively favored the dominant regimes in content, process, and outcome. Moldova, Russia, and Ukraine have held few referendums, but they have tended to favor the incumbent regimes. To better inform the assessment of referendums in post-Soviet states, the next section outlines the details of each referendum.

Referendum Questions in Post-Soviet States
Constitutional and Election Rule Changes

The most common questions addressed via referendums are related to the approval or change of the constitution. In the post-Soviet period, initial constitutional texts were approved by voters in Armenia, Azerbaijan, Estonia, Kazakhstan, Lithuania, Russia, and Tajikistan. Constitutions often include public-approval provisions for change, and eleven[16] post-Soviet constitutions include clauses requiring a referendum to alter part or all of the constitution. All but four countries have put constitutional questions before voters, and government-initiated changes typically pass.

A rare example of failure met President Robert Kocharian's efforts to amend Armenia's constitution in 2003. The referendum proposed several changes, including limits on the president's authority to dissolve parliament due to its inactivity (or in prescribed postelection periods), reducing parliament's size, establishing dual citizenship, eliminating the death penalty, creating a human rights ombudsman's office, and allowing foreign individuals to buy land (BBC 2003e; CSCE 2004). The opposition challenged the legality of the referendum, claiming that Kocharian had violated several laws and regulations (BBC 2003b). European officials reacted cautiously, questioning the appropriateness of a public vote on these issues (BBC 2003c). The referendum failed; while over 50 percent of those casting ballots supported the measures, the total number of voters constituted less than the constitutional minimum of one-third of registered voters.

In November 2005, a referendum was once again placed in front of the public to alter presidential powers, lift limitations on dual citizenship, and expand individual constitutional rights. The proposed amendments altered the standing constitution, transferring authority to form government, appoint the prosecutor general, and call emergency legislative sessions from the president to parliament. The amendments also removed the president as the chief of the Council of Justice and added several civil rights to the constitution: consumer defense, a clean environment, bans on forced and child labor, and enhancements to other rights such as movement and assembly. The amendments also, in principle, established enforcement mechanisms to ensure that citizen rights would be upheld, including the creation of a human rights ombudsman's office and expanded appeal rights to international organizations and the constitutional court (RFE/RL 2005a).

The Armenian opposition did not object to the content of the amendments as much as it objected to the right of the president to hold a referendum, arguing that he was illegitimate and obtained office through fraudulent means. But, in addition to receiving presidential support, the revisions were backed by the European Union (BBC 2005d), the Venice Commission, and the United States (Peuch 2005). Unlike the 2003 referendum, the 2005 version passed, with 64 percent of voters taking part in the election and 61 percent of voters approving the changes. However, the opposition claimed that these results were due to massive fraud and that turnout was much lower (BBC 2005a; 2005b).

In Azerbaijan, opposition forces also challenged a constitutional referendum. The 2002 vote addressed dozens of changes to more than twenty constitutional articles. The most significant proposal was to alter parliamentary election rules, abandoning the mixed electoral system and adopting a single-member district system with plurality formula (van der Schriek 2002). The preparatory phase was contentious, with the opposition announcing a boycott, and cautious statements by international actors, including a recommendation to postpone the referendum (BBC 2002c). Despite claims of widespread fraud (BBC 2002a; 2002b), the referendum was deemed successful by Azerbaijan's Central Electoral Commission.[17]

In May 1995, Belarusan voters faced four policy questions put forth by President Alyaksandr Lukashenka. One question was consultative but spoke to the increasingly authoritarian nature of Belarusan politics after Lukashenka's 1994 election victory. This question asked voters if they would support constitutional changes that would allow the president to dissolve parliament in the wake of its "systematic or gross" violations of the constitution. Citizens were also given the opportunity to vote on elevating the Russian language to equal status with Belarusan, approving a new flag and state seal that were much closer in form to their Soviet-era counterparts, and pursuing economic integration with Russia. The Belarusan Popular Front claimed that the results of the referendum and the simultaneous parliamentary election were falsified (BBC 1995). All of the proposals passed.

After success in the consultative referendum in 1995, Belarusan authorities moved forward on formal constitutional changes in 1996. President Lukashenka continued to consolidate power and stifle dissent, and the opposition was increasingly placed under direct pressure to halt its activities. In response to Lukashenka's actions, Belarus' parliament initiated impeachment proceedings. Belarusan voters faced seven questions on the November 24 referendum, four proposed by President Lukashenka and three by parliamentary deputies. The most critical question was on constitutional amendments that would allow President Lukashenka to extend his term of office, reconstitute parliament, and increase presidential powers by appointing members of parliament and the Constitutional Court. In addition, the president asked voters about changing Belarus' Independence Day, land privatization, and elimination of the death penalty. Members of parliament also posed three questions on constitutional changes to abolish the presidential office and create a strong prime minister, elections of local officials, and transparent financing of government institutions.

The referendum was contentious. Parliament, supported by the Constitutional Court, asserted that only two questions could be binding according to Belarusan law: changing Independence Day and the election of local government officials (BBC 1996c). A Russian-brokered compromise that would have rendered the referendum nonbinding was rejected by parliament; Lukashenka vowed to hold a binding vote and declared the Constitutional Court decision null and void (BBC 1996b; Gordon 1996). The proposals on constitutional changes and Independence Day passed, but land sales and elimination of the death penalty, along with the deputies' proposals, were rejected. Lukashenka ignored domestic claims of fraud as well as international condemnation of the vote (BBC 1996a; Zaks 1996) and quickly moved to form a new parliament that was under his control, enhancing his powers. The new parliament immediately ended the impeachment efforts (Deutsche Presse-Agentur 1996d). Russia, which had attempted to mediate the conflict, accepted the referendum results. This referendum was a tipping point in Belarusan politics, consolidating authoritarian rule under Lukashenka.

The stakes in Georgia's constitutional reform referendum in November 2003 were also high. The opposition to President Eduard Shevardnadze was emboldened and expected a victory in the simultaneous parliamentary election. Allegations of fraud led to massive street demonstrations, culminating in the ouster of Shevardnadze in the Rose Revolution, followed by new presidential and parliamentary elections in 2004. While the referendum on changing the size of parliament passed, it did not come into force in 2004 because the elections were invalidated.

Amid accusations of increasing authoritarianism under the Rose Revolution's hero, Mikheil Saakashvili, opposition groups took to the streets in protest in late 2007. In November, riot police aggressively dispersed protesters, using water cannons, tear gas, and physical force. Human rights organizations criticized the crackdown, and international opinion began to swing away from support of Saakashvili (BBC 2007b). In a compromise, President Saakashvili agreed to hold early presidential elections as well as referendums on NATO membership and early parliamentary elections. The January 5, 2008, vote on early parliamentary elections passed.

Rather than responding to opposition concerns, referendums in Kazakhstan have been used to undermine opposition successes and consolidate power under President Nursultan Nazarbayev. Although President Nazarbayev and his allies created conditions for the 1994 election to produce an obedient legislature, parliament did not comply with Nazarbayev's plans. While the propresidential People's Unity Party won the most seats, the president did not fully command loyalty among a solid majority of deputies. Parliament began to act independently, opposing government policies and passing a no-confidence vote (Olcott 1997). The Constitutional Court nullified the 1994 election in response to a court challenge filed by a candidate.[18] After the dissolution of parliament, President Nazarbayev ruled without a legislature until 1995.

In the interim, the president called two referendums. The April 29, 1995, referendum asked voters if they agreed to extend President Nazarbayev's term until December 2000. The referendum passed with 95 percent of the votes cast in favor (Rossiya 1995). On August 30, 1995, another referendum was held on a new constitution establishing a bicameral parliament and increasing presidential powers. This referendum also passed, with 89 percent support (ITAR-TASS 1995).

Kazakhstan's neighbor, Kyrgyzstan, is one of the most active post-Soviet states in the use of referendums, holding four separate votes on major constitutional changes. In 1994, President Askar Akayev called a vote to establish a bicameral parliament and change the number of seats (Deutsche Presse-Agentur 1998b). The existing parliament, elected in 1990, had resisted Akayev's efforts to reform Kyrgyzstan's economy, and the referendum facilitated new parliamentary elections. The second question on the referendum enhanced the use of referendum voting. In the wake of his victory, Akayev called for a constitutional assembly to prepare additional constitutional changes (BBC 1994).

The next round of constitutional reform was held less than two years later. The successful February 1996 referendum expanded presidential powers, extending Akayev's ability to hire and fire ministers, dissolve parliament if it were to reject his nominee for prime minister three times, and form policy (Deutsche Presse-Agentur 1996b). The president announced another referendum in 1998 to address the legalization of land privatization, change immunity for parliamentary deputies, increase media freedom, and alter seat allocation in parliament. According to the referendum, the number of deputies in the Legislative Assembly (the upper house) would grow from thirty-five to sixty-seven, while the number of deputies in the People's Assembly (the lower house) would drop from seventy to thirty-eight. This move was seen as an effort to create an even more compliant parliament that would agree to Akayev's reform efforts (Deutsche Presse-Agentur 1998b). The successful referendum enhanced Akayev's powers and made Kyrgyzstan the first Central Asian country to allow private ownership of land.[19]

President Akayev placed another significant package of institutional reforms before Kyrgyz citizens in 2003. Akayev enacted a decree for the February 2 referendum on January 14. Even presidential supporters on Akayev's constitutional committee questioned the short timeframe between the announcement and the vote (BBC 2003g), and opposition politicians planned a boycott (BBC 2003f). International organizations expressed concern about the constitutional reforms and the limited amount of time for voters to study the significant policy changes (BBC 2003h). The referendum went ahead as planned, but many international organizations, such as the OSCE, did not send observation missions. The referendum's two questions asked voters to extend Akayev's term of office until the end of 2005 and approve constitutional changes. The constitutional amendments were designed to expand the president's power to dissolve parliament and remove deputies from office, eliminate the bicameral parliament, and abandon the mixed electoral system.[20] Both questions passed.

After the ouster of President Akayev in 2005, President Kurmanbek Bakiyev indicated that he would modify the constitution, reducing presidential powers that Akayev had amassed. Bakiyev's failure to fulfill this promise led to protests in 2006 and a power struggle with parliament that initially reduced, then restored, strong presidential authority (Eurasia Insight 2006). In September 2007, the Constitutional Court issued a ruling that declared unconstitutional both documents approved during the fall 2006 power struggle. Bakiyev called a new constitutional referendum in the wake of the court decision. The referendum also asked Kyrgyz voters to accept a new parliamentary electoral system and increase the number of parliamentary deputies to 90. Opposition politicians objected to the content of the new constitution as well as the timing of the referendum (BBC 2007a). Amid allegations of fraud, both questions on the referendum passed, leading to the dismissal of parliament and new elections (Stern 2007).

Like Kyrgyzstan, Lithuania has also actively used referendums for constitutional changes and policymaking. Prior to approving its constitution in October 1992, Lithuania held a referendum on institutional design. Facing a parliament elected in the Soviet period that featured significant representation of leftist forces, Vyatautis Landesbergis and the Sajudis movement advocated new institutional rules to reduce the influence of communist-era holdovers (BBC 1992e). Specifically, Landesbergis aspired to increase the powers of the chief executive and establish a presidency. The referendum failed to garner the necessary votes to pass. While a majority of those casting ballots supported the measure, it required a majority of registered voters to be successful. Mutual recriminations characterized the postreferendum fallout, with representatives who opposed the vote (BBC 1992a) and its supporters (BBC 1992c) claiming that the other side was attempting to reestablish authoritarian rule.

In 1996, accompanying both rounds of the parliamentary election, several questions were placed in front of voters. The Lithuanian Democratic Labor Party proposed amendments to the constitution, reducing the number of parliamentary seats to 111 from 141, adding guarantees of social support in the budget, and rescheduling elections. The conservative opposition proposed to restore savings that citizens lost in the transition (Deutsche Presse-Agentur 1996c). During the second round of the parliamentary election, the Democratic Labor Party proposed another provision that would have allowed the sale of agricultural land (Deutsche Presse-Agentur 1996a). Once again, support for the measures exceeded opposition, but none of the questions cleared the majority requirement among registered voters.

Russia's dual referendums in 1993 significantly affected the style and institutions of Russian politics for the last decade and a half. After the collapse of the Soviet Union in late 1991, President Boris Yeltsin concentrated on economic reform, leaving in place Soviet-era political institutions. Like the early transition period in Lithuania, the composition of parliament was weighted heavily toward the political left, as deputies had been elected during the waning days of the Soviet Union when the Communist Party still monopolized the selection process. Parliament not only opposed Yeltsin's reform efforts but increasingly began to challenge him on constitutional grounds. The Soviet-era constitution vested significant authority in parliament, though parliament had not been able to exercise its power until the USSR's collapse. After proposing competing referendums, the two sides agreed to hold a vote on constitutional matters. Parliament rejected the questions that Yeltsin proposed, revoked the emergency powers he gained after the coup attempt in 1991, and canceled the planned referendum. After acrimonious debates and counterproposals, Yeltsin agreed to hold a referendum in April 1993 that would serve as a vote of confidence in the president and his policies. The four questions addressed trust in the president, support for his socioeconomic policies, and early elections for the president and parliament. Yeltsin won the critical vote of confidence, but the referendum did not resolve Russia's constitutional crisis (Brady and Kaplan 1994).

Disagreements between the president and parliament became more antagonistic, leading Yeltsin to dissolve parliament, suspend the Constitutional Court, and physically evict members of parliament in a dramatic and bloody confrontation at the Russian White House. After eliminating his rivals, Yeltsin and his allies crafted a new constitution that strengthened presidential power and developed new rules for parliamentary elections. The constitutional referendum and elections to the lower and upper houses of Russia's new parliament were held in December 1993. While some observers alleged that fraud was used to enhance turnout, victory was declared in the constitutional referendum.

After experiencing the bloodiest civil war on post-Soviet soil, Tajikistan worked toward reconciliation among the former combatants. A critical part of the process was a 1999 referendum on amendments to twenty-seven articles of the constitution, including an extension of the presidential term to seven years, the establishment of a bicameral parliament, and provisions permitting religious parties to compete (BBC 1999c). The referendum was proposed by the National Reconciliation Council and the president and was portrayed as a major step toward peaceful conflict resolution (BBC 1999d). The referendum process received little criticism, particularly in comparison with the subsequent presidential election. While some parties opposed elements of the referendum, especially the bicameral parliament (BBC 1999b), it passed.

In Ukraine, a constitutional referendum passed in 2000 but was never implemented. The parliament elected in 1998 was particularly contentious, and President Leonid Kuchma saw it as impeding policymaking. After his reelection in late 1999, Kuchma announced a referendum designed to push parliamentary deputies to cooperate with him on his policy initiatives. The referendum was criticized not only by domestic politicians but also by international bodies (BBC 2000d). Primarily leftist parties organized rallies against the referendum (BBC 2000b; 2000c) and recommended that voters refuse to participate. The four questions that were included on the referendum addressed conditions for the president to dissolve parliament, proposed the elimination of deputy immunity, and authorized the creation of a smaller lower house in a new bicameral parliament. Amid allegations of fraud, all of the proposals passed with over 80 percent of the vote. Not long after his victory, however, President Kuchma was embroiled in a scandal that undercut his authority to implement the referendum.[21]

Changing the President's Term

In all but one case, referendums to change the term of office for the president have extended the president's rule. By failing to provide an alternative candidate and by using the machinery of the state to ensure victory, these referendums create the illusion of citizen input in choosing a chief executive. Referendums to permit presidents to stand for office when their terms expire or extending the presidential term have been held in Belarus (2004), Kyrgyzstan (1994), Kazakhstan (1995), Tajikistan (1999 and 2003), Turkmenistan (1994), and Uzbekistan (1995 and 2002). All of these referendums passed amid accusations of fraud and government manipulation.

The sole exception to the use of a referendum to extend a president's term in office occurred in Azerbaijan. The first president of Azerbaijan, Ayaz Mutalibov, abdicated his post in March 1992 after Azeri forces suffered several battlefield defeats and Azeri civilians were victimized in a mass killing in the disputed Karabakh region. He returned to his position in May 1992 as the presidential election approached. The following month, voters selected Abulfez Elchibey as the first popularly elected president of post-Soviet Azerbaijan. Elchibey's decision to disarm a military garrison for insubordination led to a mutiny, and the soldiers threatened to invade Baku. With an attack looming, Elchibey fled to the Nakhichevan region (*New York Times* 1993). Heydar Aliyev, speaker of parliament and former First Secretary of the Communist Party, increasingly asserted himself, calling for Elchibey's impeachment and a referendum on ending his presidency. The August 29, 1993, vote removed Elchibey, paving the way for Aliyev to become president.

Accession to International Organizations

In addition to asking voters to weigh in on domestic institutions, governments have held referendums on their countries' international position with votes on the maintenance of an independent state (Moldova), membership in the EU (Baltics), and potential membership in NATO (Georgia).

Voters in Moldova's March 1994 referendum were asked about their support for Moldova's continued independence within its current borders.

Added to the Soviet Union as part of the Molotov–Ribbentrop Pact, Moldovan citizens were encouraged to think of their ethnic group as separate and distinct from Romanians; the Cyrillic alphabet was adopted for the language, and a mythology about Moldova was encouraged. While the Transnistrian region boycotted the polls, the remainder of Moldova's citizens overwhelmingly voted to remain independent, with over 90 percent supporting a separate state (*Wall Street Journal* 1994).

In 2003, all three Baltic states held referendums on joining the European Union.[22] Lithuania held its referendum first, followed by Estonia and Latvia. Despite some skepticism about accession, especially in Estonia and Latvia (Szczerbiak and Taggart 2005), the EU bids received strong public support, with 67 percent of voters in Estonia, 67 percent in Latvia, and 90 percent in Lithuania supporting EU membership. While other post-Soviet states have also proposed referendums about their place in the international order, only Georgia has held such a vote. In January 2008, along with the early presidential election and referendum on an early parliamentary election, Georgia held a consultative vote on NATO membership. The proposal passed, with 73 percent of voters in favor.

Miscellaneous Policy Questions

Post-Soviet states have also used referendums to address a wide range of domestic policy matters. While not limited to the Baltic states, this use of referendum voting has been most common in Estonia, Latvia, and Lithuania.

During the constitutional referendum in June 1992, Estonian voters were faced with a second question: whether or not to allow noncitizens who had applied for citizenship to vote in future parliamentary and presidential elections. While the provision would affect approximately five thousand of the six hundred thousand Russian-speakers on Estonian soil who had applied for citizenship, the issue was wrapped in the broader context of contentious ethnic politics in Estonia. Citizenship and participation was a grave concern of the titular nationalities in Estonia and Latvia, both of which hosted large Russian populations and had suffered significant population displacement under Soviet rule. The restoration of Estonia's 1938 citizenship law excluded hundreds of thousands of Russians from the vote (Barrington 1995). Considered by some to be colonists (BBC 1992b), many ethnic Russians had lived for several generations in Estonia and considered it to be their homeland (Barrington, Herron, and Silver 2003). But, relatively few ethnic Russians had learned the Estonian language, reinforcing negative stereotypes of Russophone residents as occupiers. Despite the deep ties of many Russians to Estonia, the referendum results excluded noncitizens from participation in later elections.

Latvia also explored citizenship matters in a referendum. In October 1998, Latvian voters faced two questions about liberalizing the citizenship process. The first question addressed extending citizenship to children born in Latvia after 1991 without subjecting them to a language test. The second question asked voters to eliminate age requirements in the naturalization process, allowing anyone to participate (Deutsche Presse-Agentur 1998c). The proposals were endorsed by a wide array of actors: the EU, the OSCE, Russia, and the Latvian parliament (Deutsche Presse-Agentur 1998a). Latvia's bid to join the EU had been scrutinized because of its citizenship policies, and the vote was viewed as crucial to improving relations with the West and Russia. Both questions on the referendum passed, easing restrictive citizenship policies.

A year after the citizenship referendum, Latvia held another vote to review changes to the pension system that raised the retirement age and reduced benefits for senior citizens who continued to participate in the workforce (Deutsche Presse-Agentur 1999a). While opposition parliamentarians encouraged a yes vote, the prime minister encouraged voters to stay at home. The referendum failed due to low turnout (Deutsche Presse-Agentur 1999b).

Latvia's 2007 referendum on security issues also failed due to inadequate voter participation. The vote reflected a political struggle between outgoing President Vaira Vike-Freiberga and the government. The controversial laws included amendments allowing government ministers and their staff members to access information in criminal investigations. Because the files could include information related to national security, the president argued that the legislation could undermine Latvia's relationships in the European Union and NATO. After her veto was overridden by parliament, President Vike-Freiberga referred the matter to a referendum through a constitutionally vested presidential power. Although the supporters of the amendments withdrew them, the referendum moved forward. Supporters of the referendum noted that government could once again attempt to enact the rules after the end of the president's term of office; the referendum would preclude this action. While voters registered significant support for the president's position, turnout was too low for the referendum to formally succeed (Deutsche Presse-Agentur 2007a; 2007b; Associated Press 2007; Peach 2007).

In addition to constitutional questions detailed above, Lithuania has held several referendums on policy issues.[23] In 1992, acrimonious relations between the left and right, intensified by the referendum to establish a strong chief executive, were further inflamed by another vote. Lithuanian voters approved measures calling for the withdrawal of Russian troops that were still on Lithuanian territory following the collapse of the USSR and reparations from Russia. The Russian government unsurprisingly expressed opposition to the referendum, calling for diplomatic activity to resolve the issue (BBC 1992d). Although the referendum could not force Russian troops to leave, strong support enhanced the Lithuanian government's negotiating position.

In August 1994, Lithuanians once again were asked to go to the polls for a referendum on policy. This poll addressed eight issues related to privatization and economic matters, including a review of the legality of the privatization process and a plan to help citizens recover savings lost in revaluations from 1991 to 1994. Landesbergis, in the opposition due to his party's election loss in 1992, spearheaded support for the referendum (Bivens 1994). The

Democratic Labor Party and Lithuania's president, along with international financial institutions like the World Bank and International Monetary Fund, and the governments of Estonia and Latvia, expressed opposition (*New York Times* 1994; Baltic News Service 1994). Despite the prospect of directing government to improve their personal economic conditions, supporters could not muster enough participation at the polls. While the majority of voters supported the measures, turnout fell well below the requirement for the provisions to be enacted.

CONCLUSION

The use of referendums does not have a long history in the post-Soviet region. Although the Soviet constitution permitted national referendums,[24] Soviet-era officials closely controlled access to policy-making, eschewing public votes. Mikhail Gorbachev's introduction of the referendum as a method to gain support, and the tactical responses of his regional rivals, demonstrated the utility of referendums to legitimize decisions and mobilize citizens. In the postcommunist era, referendums have become a common tool for political elites.

The main question posed in this chapter was *how* do political elites use referendums? Do referendums provide citizens a meaningful opportunity to directly influence policy decisions? Or, do they present a false choice, with political elites offering questions for public vote only when they are confident in a favorable outcome? The evidence from former Soviet states suggests that referendums serve both purposes but tend to be legitimization tools for the political elite.

As illustrated in the first section of the chapter, referendums are most often prohegemonic and controlled, with questions and processes favoring the ruling elite's preferences. In addition, the choices facing voters often serve to enhance the authority of politicians in power through changes to the constitution and the extension of presidential terms of office. In a more limited subset of cases, notably but not exclusively in the Baltic states, referendums offer voters a legitimate chance to influence domestic and international policies. Voters have been given the opportunity to state their views on citizenship, pensions, and economic policies, and accession to international organizations. While some of these votes were consultative, many were binding.

Post-Soviet elites are likely to continue using referendums as a mechanism to enhance their authority and gauge public views on policy. Examples of potential referendums abound. Prior to the 2007 parliamentary election in Ukraine, politicians from different parties proposed referendums on the semi-presidential system, language issues, foreign policy, and local self-government to mobilize core constituencies. Following the election, the Party of Regions proposed a referendum on potential NATO membership in response to the Ukrainian government's efforts to move closer to Western institutions.[25] The main question for the future of referendums is whether they will increasingly offer citizens legitimate choices or if they will continue to be used as a legiti-mization tool for predetermined policy decisions.

The next two chapters more deeply address the question of whether elec-tions offer citizens real choices, or if they are political theater controlled by elites. An issue that has been looming over the analyses of presidential, parlia-mentary, and referendum voting is the process by which elections are imple-mented. While the quality of election administration varies cross-nationally and temporally, it has not yet been systematically addressed. The following chapters ask how the quality of elections and election administration has affected outcomes in the post-Soviet region. This analysis begins in Chapter 8, focusing on the administrative bodies charged with implementing elections and the domestic and international organizations that monitor campaigns.

CHAPTER 8

ADMINISTRATIVE
ARCHITECTURE OF ELECTIONS

Research on elections focuses on most aspects of the voting process: how political actors select and modify election rules, how these rules influence behavior, how citizens decide to vote and develop attachments to parties and politicians, and how parties emerge and function. By contrast, research on the administrative architecture of elections plays a modest role in the electoral studies literature.[1] Yet, the organizations charged with administrative and oversight responsibilities determine who can contest seats, which voters may participate, and if the rules have been violated, as well as managing the casting, counting, and compiling of results. These institutions also create incentives that may influence the behavior of political actors. As the infamous saying suggests, "It doesn't matter who votes, but who counts the votes."[2]

The primary institutions that implement election laws and adjudicate disputes are electoral commissions and the courts. Election administration is typically led by a national-level electoral commission, with subordinate regional- and precinct-level commissions. Each layer of election administration has unique responsibilities, but generally all levels participate in dispute adjudication along with the courts. Depending on the issue at hand, and the statutes governing elections, claims may be directed to local or regional courts, or national courts such as a Supreme Court or Constitutional Court.

By hearing complaints and ruling on disputes about election procedures, commissions and courts play an important role in oversight. In addition, election observation teams, typically sponsored by international organizations and nongovernmental actors, provide essential oversight functions by directly assessing the quality of election processes and recommending improvements.

Political scientists have identified two approaches to oversight[3] that can be applied to election management. "Fire alarm" oversight is a relatively decentralized process in which institutional rules provide mechanisms for citizens and public organizations to observe and assess decisions, challenging these decisions if they violate proper procedures or statutory guidelines. "Police patrol" oversight is a more centralized process in which an identified agent monitors a portion of an organization's actions, identifying procedural violations. In principle, not only does the act of observing activities potentially reveal problems, but it may serve as a deterrent to improper behavior.[4] In the context of elections, courts and electoral commissions generally operate on the "fire alarm" approach. By contrast, domestic and international observer groups operate on the "police patrol" approach, albeit for a limited time frame.[5]

This chapter bridges the earlier analysis of election rules and their consequences with the final two chapters that assess the quality of election data and the consequences of election fraud. The first section describes how election laws are implemented and provides a general evaluation of election administration performance in several post-Soviet states. The second section addresses dispute adjudication by focusing on the role of courts in managing election-related disputes. The third section assesses oversight mechanisms, notably domestic and international observer missions designed to evaluate the integrity of electoral processes. The chapter concludes with a discussion of recent controversies surrounding election observation, especially those prompted by Russian government complaints about the politicization of the observation process.

ADMINISTERING ELECTIONS

Electoral commissions are charged with the multifaceted task of administering elections, including interpreting and issuing opinions on the implementation of election law; hearing disputes and appeals; ensuring that candidates and parties have fulfilled registration requirements; determining the boundaries of election districts; monitoring campaign finances; designing and distributing ballot forms; providing election infrastructure, including the designation of polling places and the distribution of ballot boxes and voting booths; developing and maintaining voter lists; addressing requests for early or special voting; and managing the process of casting, counting, and compiling votes until the final decision is announced and certified.

In the Soviet period, election administration was managed by commissions at the national, republican, regional, and local levels. Commissions were composed by and primarily accountable to administrative units at the corresponding level of hierarchy rather than the higher level electoral commission. For example, the Supreme Soviet determined the composition of the Central Electoral Commission at the federal level; the republic-level Supreme Soviets determined the composition of the republic-level Central Electoral Commissions.[6] The commissions' composition, especially for positions of authority, favored members of the Communist Party (Schapiro 1977). Institutionally, post-Soviet election administration has changed from the communist era. In practice, however, interference in the implementation of elections, control by authorities over election commission activities, and engineered results reflect continuity with past practices.

Post-Soviet election commissions tend to be vertically integrated, with a national-level body (commonly referred to as the Central Electoral Commission [CEC])[7] at the top of the hierarchy, and lower-level commissions subordinated to it. CECs typically bear primary responsibility for implementing and interpreting election laws, registering parties or candidates, supervising lower level commissions, hearing appeals from lower level commissions, confirming and certifying final election results, and registering elected representatives.

The responsibility for determining the composition of post-Soviet election commissions varies substantially, with the executive, legislative, and judicial branches, as well as local government, involved in the selection process. In Armenia, Belarus, Kyrgyzstan, Moldova, and Russia, the president and parliament nominate some positions on the CEC. Parliamentary parties appoint members in Armenia, Azerbaijan, Georgia, and Lithuania. The president nominates CEC members but requires parliamentary confirmation in Kazakhstan, Tajikistan, and Ukraine.[8] Parliament appoints the CEC in Uzbekistan. Local governments play a role in personnel decisions in Georgia, Russia, and Turkmenistan. Estonia primarily relies on the judiciary to compose its commission; several members of commissions in Lithuania and Moldova are also associated with the judicial branch.

While formal rules suggest power sharing in the creation of election commissions, often the formal rules do not reflect actual practices. In states where appointments are formally divided among different institutions, but parliamentary seats disproportionately favor the chief executive's preferred party and the executive branch exerts significant informal leverage over judicial decisions, statutory rules for creating election commissions create an illusion of diversity. Indeed, biased commission membership is cited frequently in observer reports of fraud and manipulation.

Mid-level election commissions manage the aggregation of votes from the polling stations and pass along information to the CEC. If mid-level commission boundaries correspond to geographically defined constituencies, they may register candidates and announce the results of those contests as well. These commissions typically confirm voting results and monitor, guide, and hear appeals from lower-level commissions.

At the lowest level of the election administration hierarchy are precinct, or polling station, commissions. Precinct commissions constitute the "front line" in the election process: they manage voter lists, set up polling stations, hear and adjudicate complaints, and conduct the casting and counting processes. In precinct commissions, typically three commission members serve as officers—a chair, deputy chair, and secretary—and they exert substantial influence over the conduct of the vote and vote count. While the specific process of voting varies cross-nationally and temporally, voting procedures tend to be similar across post-Soviet space. Electoral commissions make voter lists available for public scrutiny prior to election day and hear complaints about errors on the list. After receiving blank ballots, boxes, and materials for booths, precinct commissions set up the polling sites. On election day, the commissions assemble prior to the polls' opening to seal the ballot boxes and secure other documents and materials.

Once the polling station opens, each voter presents approved identity documents to officials, who find the voter's name on the registry. The voter signs the registry and receives ballots that may be countersigned by election officials with a "coupon" removed and collected to undermine ballot-box stuffing. The voter fills out the ballot paper and places it in the ballot box and in some cases has a finger marked with indelible ink to undermine fraud. After the polls close, the precinct commission secures unused and spoiled ballots, verifies that ballot box seals are secure, opens the boxes, counts the total number of ballots cast, sorts the ballots by candidate or party, identifies and makes a determination about the validity of questionable ballots, finalizes the results in a formal document (called the protocol), securely packs the election materials, and transports them to the higher-level commission.

The impartiality and transparency of these procedures significantly affects election quality. In an analysis of twenty-six elections, Sarah Birch scored the electoral process in five categories: compliance of party and voter registration with the law, state interference in the electoral process, access for observers, and an overall assessment of performance.[9] Eleven of the twenty-six elections evidenced poor performance, including contests in Azerbaijan, Belarus, Georgia, Kazakhstan, Kyrgyzstan, Tajikistan, and Uzbekistan. While officials permitted competition and oversight in some cases, primarily through wider ballot access and international observer accessibility, they also interfered significantly in the voting process. Many of these countries performed well in voter registration, consistent with the tendency of authoritarian states to encourage "appropriate" citizen participation. The next tier included nine elections in Armenia, Georgia, Kyrgyzstan, Moldova, Russia, and Ukraine. These elections evidenced higher-quality implementation, with better performance in ballot and observer access, but still suffered from significant state interference. The best elections included six contests in Estonia, Latvia, Lithuania, and Moldova. These elections were characterized by relatively open registration procedures for voters and parties, wide access for observers, and limited government interference in the process.

ADJUDICATING DISPUTES

In most post-Soviet states, electoral commissions hear appeals. However, election legislation also envisions a role for the courts in adjudicating disputes involving voters, candidates, or parties over perceived injustices. The courts may play a secondary role as an alternate venue for dispute resolution along with electoral commissions or a primary role as the initial body ruling on cases.

In the Soviet period, the judiciary was the most impotent branch of government, often resolving disputes through "telephone justice," in which party officials would contact judges and dictate the verdict (Boylan 1998).[10] During the post-Soviet period, judicial independence and the rule of law have evolved slowly and unevenly across East Europe and Eurasia. Judicial power, a key element in this evolution, also varies substantially. In the only cross-national assessment of judicial power in the region, Smithey and Ishiyama (2000) rated Estonia's courts as the weakest, followed by Russia, Belarus, Azerbaijan, Ukraine, Georgia, Latvia, Lithuania, Moldova, and Armenia. In principle, stronger courts are more capable of maintaining independence and issuing decisions that better reflect the merits of the cases rather than succumbing to external pressure. While the formal strength of judicial institutions provides some insight into their abilities to independently adjudicate election disputes, most post-Soviet judicial institutions have been accused of failing to follow proper procedures or making decisions in a biased manner.[11]

Just as assessments of formal judicial power can be undermined by informal practices, other measures of election quality and judicial independence must be interpreted with caution. Because courts can be used as political instruments to challenge an election loss, delay government formation, or otherwise influence the governing process, large numbers of appeals alone do not serve as evidence of flawed elections. Moreover, large numbers of denials (i.e., cases in which the plaintiff loses) also do not signify that the courts are behaving in a biased manner. Yet, courts in many post-Soviet states have issued allegedly biased rulings that inconsistently apply the law to pro- and antigovernment politicians.

This section outlines the major questions that courts adjudicate in the election process and presents some examples of court behavior that has been questioned by international observers. While some matters have been appealed to international courts, the review covers disputes that have been directed to domestic courts at all levels,[12] employing the richest sources of information: reports from election observers and the media. This review is selective, due to the limited research on the intersection of courts and elections. Moreover, the examples are not uniformly distributed across the region; the most democratic and most authoritarian societies produce fewer disputes for the courts to resolve.

Election Rules. Disputes about election rules have been referred to the courts in several post-Soviet states, and court rulings have forced legislators to alter laws. Prior to the 1998 parliamentary election in Ukraine, the Constitutional Court ruled that several provisions in the election law violated the constitution. Most notably, dual candidacy—the right of candidates to simultaneously contest constituency and party list seats in the mixed system—was deemed to be illegal. The decision was binding but did not take effect until the 2002 parliamentary election (Herron 2002b; OSCE 1998d).

In Russia's 1995 parliamentary election, nearly half of the votes in the proportional representation component were wasted on parties that did not pass the 5 percent threshold. This result raised concerns about how effectively parliament could represent citizens when only four of 43 political parties on the ballot gained seats through the party list tier. A Constitutional Court decision prompted a relaxation of the threshold in 1999: if over 50 percent of the votes cast were "wasted" on parties that did not pass the threshold, a lower 3 percent barrier would apply (OSCE 2000g, 5).

Kyrgyzstan's Supreme Court also ruled on a dispute about electoral thresholds. The 2007 parliamentary election law controversially included a regional threshold requiring parties to obtain no less than 0.5 percent of the vote in each region (based on national turnout) in addition to the national 5 percent threshold. When the preliminary results were announced, only one party secured seats in parliament, the propresidential Ak Zhol party. Ak Zhol challenged the fairness of the regional threshold with the Supreme Court and the Court declared that the regional threshold was unconstitutional (Namat-bayeva 2007).[13] As a result, two additional parties gained seats.

While court rulings in Russia, Ukraine, and Kyrgyzstan led to election rule changes, court rulings are not always decisive. In Georgia, ambiguity in the election law created a dispute about how a party's vote total should be calculated. Specifically, the law did not clearly state whether a party's vote percentage should be based on overall turnout or valid votes cast. Using overall turnout would depress party performace, making it more difficult to clear Georgia's high 7 percent threshold. Court decisions on the eve of the 2004 election did not resolve the matter (OSCE 2004c, 10).

Voter List Disputes: Voter lists determine which citizens have the right to cast a ballot. Individuals who are excluded from voter lists may file for reinstatement, and in many post-Soviet states courts actively participate in reviewing and resolving these disputes up to and on election day. Voter list disputes constitute the most prevalent form of court intervention in terms of the number of cases filed. For example, in Armenia's 1999 parliamentary election, 22,157 citizens appealed to courts for resolution to voter list problems (OSCE 1999a, 20). The number was halved by the 2003 presidential election, to 10,400,[14] but was still significant (OSCE 2003b, 7). Armenia's case is not isolated,[15] as poor quality voter lists plague many regional elections.

Registration Denials. Perhaps the most politically charged issue that courts address are appeals by candidates or political parties for reinstatement after registration denials. While registration denials are often based on the submission of faulty signature sheets, the failure of candidates to disclose required information, or other violations of election procedures, these decisions may also be motivated by partisan considerations. Moreover, election commissions do not always make consistent decisions, denying registration to applicants whose errors are analogous to other applicants who successfully gain ballot access. Appeals directed to the courts have been similarly scrutinized, and courts have been accused of partisanship and inconsistency in rendering decisions.

In some cases, bias against candidates opposing incumbent governments seems clear. In the 2000 parliamentary election in Belarus, 218 of 768 nominated candidates were denied registration, with opposition candidates rejected at a higher rate than progovernment candidates. Of the rejected candidates, 146 appealed and 28 were reinstated by the CEC or Supreme Court (OSCE 2001a, 7–8). In 2004, 312 of 692 candidates were denied registration, with 48 reinstated.[16] In addition, the Belarusan Party of Labor was closed by order of the Supreme Court in 2004 (Karmanau 2004).

The prominent Kazakh opposition candidate, Akezhan Kazhegeldin, was barred from participation in the 1999 presidential election due to a court sanction for participating in a meeting of an unlicensed organization promoting free and fair elections. Because only some attendees were detained and formally charged, his registration denial was interpreted by many observers as politically motivated (OSCE 1999c, 9–10). In the 2004 parliamentary election, 32 of 623 candidates in single-member district races were taken off the ballot. Ten candidates were removed from the ballot three days before the election, precluding appeals for reinstatement. Observers affiliated with the Organization for Security and Cooperation in Europe (OSCE) asserted that deregistration in many cases was "questionable" (OSCE 2005c, 10). In addition, in 2005, Democratic Choice of Kazakhstan was closed by court order due to allegations of extremism (Associated Press 2005).

Nine parties were denied ballot access in Kyrgyzstan's 2000 parliamentary election due to improperly composed documents or their failure to be registered as public organizations more than one year prior to the election. After it added members of a deregistered party to its list, the Democratic Movement of Kyrgyzstan was subsequently deregistered itself. Not only was the inclusion of candidates from deregistered parties within the bounds of the law, it was permitted in the case of a progovernment party in the same election (OSCE 2000b, 5–6). Registration problems characterized other elections in Kyrgyzstan as well. Three candidates challenged their exclusion from the ballot in the 2005 presidential race (OSCE 2005b), and several parties and candidates were denied registration in the 2007 parliamentary election, including the leader of an opposition party who was deregistered on the eve of election (OSCE 2008b). These decisions underscore the courts' inconsistency in interpreting and applying the law, a conclusion that OSCE observers reached in several Kyrgyz elections.

Other examples of registration decisions do not directly imply commission or court bias but rather illustrate how many elections hinge on the outcomes of such cases. The most prominent case of deregistration in Russia's 1999 parliamentary election involved Vladimir Zhirinovskiy's Liberal Democratic Party of Russia and the smaller Russian Conservative Party of Entrepreneurs. Both parties were removed from the ballot because of inaccuracies on candidates' registration paperwork. The Russian Conservative Party of Entrepreneurs challenged the decision, and the Supreme Court sided with the party. After regaining ballot access, both parties were removed again when the Supreme Court reviewed the matter a few days later and altered its ruling. Zhirinovskiy ultimately gained access via secondary parties that were partners to his primary party organization (OSCE 2000g, 14–15).[17]

During Tajikistan's 1999 presidential election, the courts faced a peculiar registration controversy. Initially, opposition candidates were refused registration, leaving the incumbent Emomali Rahmon on the ballot as the sole contender. Subsequently, government officials registered the candidate from the Islamic Renaissance Party, but the candidate filed a complaint with the Supreme Court asserting that his own registration was illegal. The opposition argued that it could not accept a registration that initially had been deemed illegal because the process was a "trap" set by government to subsequently deny future nominations (Associated Press 1999).

Latvia's ban on candidates with ties to Soviet-era security services and the publication of lustration information has also been challenged and upheld by the courts. In 2002, candidates were rejected for failing to pass lustration barriers (OSCE 2002a). While no applicant was denied registration due to these provisions in 2006, the rules could discourage potential candidates from seeking office (OSCE 2007c).

Campaign Violations. In some cases, the media has been targeted by both progovernment and opposition forces for court challenges. Prior to Georgia's 2003 parliamentary election, the courts levied a substantial fine against an independent television station, Imedi TV, for improperly broadcasting opposition advertisements (OSCE 2004b). In Belarus' 2004 parliamentary election, a journalist was fined for publishing remarks about the president that were considered to be insulting (OSCE 2004d, 15–16).[18] Following Armenia's 2007 presidential election, the defeated Lev Ter-Petrossian filed a complaint with the Constitutional Court claiming that state-owned television improperly participated in the effort to undermine his candidacy. The Constitutional Court dismissed Ter-Petrossian's suit (BBC 2008).

Mundane campaign activities, such as distributing literature or organizing events, have also prompted legal intervention. In Kazakhstan's 2004 parliamentary election, a candidate was deregistered for hanging posters in improper locations and allegedly inciting ethnic violence (OSCE 2005c, 18). In Belarus' 2006 election, the courts supported law-enforcement actions that undermined opposition campaigning, such as fining oppositionists who were distributing campaign literature for littering, and restricting opportunities for assembly by arresting event organizers (OSCE 2006b, 13–14). Due to his leadership in a postelection protest, one of the losing candidates was sentenced to over five years in prison (Associated Press 2006d), and domestic election observers were convicted for up to two years of imprisonment because their organization was unregistered (Associated Press 2006c).

Electoral Commission Actions. Electoral commission interpretations of the rules have also been questioned in court. For example, in Armenia's 1999 parliamentary election, CEC decisions about precinct boundaries were challenged and altered by the courts (OSCE 1999a, 25). In Georgia, CEC appointments of district commission heads were challenged, but the CEC's decisions were upheld (OSCE 2004b, 14). Several candidates alleged bias in the appointments of electoral commission officers prior to Ukraine's 1999 presidential election. While the local prosecutor did not pursue the case, a candidate representative filed a complaint with a regional court, which found in the plaintiff's favor. Despite the court decision, electoral commission personnel did not change (OSCE 2000i, 8).

Criminal Prosecution for Fraud. In rare cases, individuals have been tried for fraud or other violations of election law. After fraud prompted the invalidation of eleven district results in Azerbaijan's 2000 parliamentary election, some perpetrators were prosecuted (OSCE 2001c, 2). In the wake of hundreds of invalidated precinct results in 2005, Azerbaijani officials fired all members of 108 precinct commissions and six constituency commissions, along with three local administration leaders (OSCE 2006a, 24–25). In Russia, a local court removed a member of parliament for bribing voters (Yablokova 2004). Finally, following Armenia's 2007 parliamentary election, three people were convicted of bribery, and members of a precinct electoral commission were tried for falsification. All of the accused were convicted, but only the PEC chair was sentenced to prison (OSCE 2007a, 27).

Final Election Results. Appeals of final election results are common, but courts overturn results at the precinct or district level more frequently than they vacate national results. For example, in Armenia's 1999 and 2003 elections, the Constitutional Court invalidated elections in two single-member districts (OSCE 1999a, 26; OSCE 2003b, 2). Further, in Azerbaijan's 2000 parliamentary election, results were invalidated by the judiciary and CEC in eleven districts, prompting by-elections. However, only the constituency races were rerun; any fraud perpetrated in the proportional tier was not remedied (OSCE 2001c). In the subsequent parliamentary election in 2005, results were annulled in ten districts and 625 polling stations (over 12 percent of all polling stations) (OSCE 2006a, 23).

National-level election results have been declared invalid by the courts in Georgia (2003), Kazakhstan (1994), Kyrgyzstan (2005), and Ukraine (2004). In three of these cases, court decisions served as a catalyst for widespread public protest and the ouster of the incumbent regime.

EVALUATING ELECTION QUALITY

To ensure the propriety of government processes, independent or external evaluators are often engaged to provide a thorough, objective analysis and make recommendations for improvement. For decades, international and nongovernmental organizations have assessed the quality of elections across the globe. The intervention of external groups in the election process can be extensive, such as the OSCE's supervision of elections in Bosnia-Herzegovina during the 1990s. But, most oversight missions are passive, with observers collecting data and issuing reports that detail problems and suggest remedies.[19]

While election observation took place during the Soviet-era (Padilla and Houppert 1993), the enterprise expanded substantially after the USSR's dissolution. Immediately after the collapse of communism in Eastern Europe, newly liberated countries invited Western organizations to monitor founding elections. In the former Soviet territories, Estonia, Georgia, and Lithuania welcomed the first delegations from the Council of Europe and Commission on Security and Cooperation in Europe (CSCE) to observe elections in 1992 (Beigbeder 1994).

Since that time, a cottage industry of election observation has grown. From 1989 to 2002, international election observer teams were deployed to evaluate 86 percent of national elections in ninety-five countries (Bjornlund 2004, 43). The major international organizations that conduct missions in the postcommunist world include the OSCE's Office for Democratic Institutions and Human Rights (ODIHR), the European Union, the Council of Europe, and the Commonwealth of Independent States. Nongovernmental organizations, such as the European Network of Election Monitoring Organizations, the National Democratic Institute, the International Republican Institute, and the International Foundation for Election Systems, also conduct observation missions and provide technical assistance. In addition, many national parliamentary or diplomatic delegations and smaller nongovernmental organizations (NGOs) organize observer missions.

Organizations sponsoring observer deployments must address three issues: what aspects of the electoral process they intend to observe, whether they will cover pre- and postelection developments or focus on election day activities, and how they will manage data collection and analysis to produce generalizable findings (Beigbeder 1994; Carothers 1997; Elklit and Svensson 1997; Bjornlund 2004). The most extensive missions, such as those sponsored by the OSCE, evaluate a wide range of election activities and employ long-term and short-term observers. Long-term observers are sent into the field several weeks or months before the election to assess the electoral environment across the country, monitor the election campaign, and make logistical preparations for short-term observers. Short-term observers arrive a few days before the contest and focus on the counting, casting, and compiling of votes on election day.[20]

The size of observation missions varies substantially, but they are often based on the size of the country, the number of participating organizations, the intensity of interest in the election, and the willingness of host governments to provide credentials. In the most extensively observed election, Ukraine's repeat second round of the 2004 presidential contest, the CEC registered over twelve thousand international observers (TASS 2004). The size of this observation mission would have permitted a foreign observer to be permanently stationed in one out of every three polling stations for the duration of election day. Typically, deployments are smaller, numbering in the hundreds.

Data collection and assessment present significant challenges in all observation missions. The professional preparation of short-term observers varies widely, potentially affecting data quality. Observers may not know how to identify evidence of improper behavior or may miss subtle signals of illicit activities. Further, because the primary objective is to evaluate overall election quality and observers cannot monitor all activities across the entire country, planners must select a sample of precincts, regions, and events to carefully analyze. Site selection is often affected by the region's geography and transportation capabilities, however, undermining the collection of representative data. If observers are granted flexibility in site selection, the problem of generating a representative sample is exacerbated.[21] In my experience as an observer, teams were informed of potentially problematic precincts in their region of responsibility and made an effort to visit them. This approach risks oversampling troubled precincts and potentially generates bias in the final assessment. Lastly, election observation groups often poorly coordinate their activities and do not share data in a systematic manner.[22]

Although planning and implementing an observation mission is logistically challenging, perhaps the greatest challenge is reaching a judgment on the election's overall quality. Ideally, observer reports are objective analyses of the election process based on predetermined criteria for free and fair election practices. In an essay on the definition of free and fair elections, Elklit and Svensson (1997) argued that "the phrase 'free and fair' cannot denote compliance with a fixed, universal standard of electoral competition: No such standard exists, and the complexity of the electoral process makes the notion of any simple formula unrealistic." While standards in fact exist, they are not universally accepted, nor are they translated into clear, objective criteria for distinguishing a free and fair election from a compromised one. Moreover, the tenor of reports may be affected by the economic and political interests of mission sponsors (Beigbeder 1994; Bjornlund 2004), concerns about future access to the country if negative reports are filed, or fears that negative reports would spark civil unrest (Carothers 1997).

Preliminary assessments of election quality are often released on the day following elections, undermining a careful analysis of the data and precluding the evaluation of postelection dispute adjudication (Bjornlund 2004). While more comprehensive reports are often issued later (for example, ODIHR releases a final report several weeks after elections), the preliminary findings substantially affect how the election is viewed domestically and internationally.

In some cases, preliminary reports have diverged from final reports issued after more thorough analysis, undermining organizations' credibility and claims of impartiality.[23] For example, OSCE officials reportedly disagreed on the content of the preliminary report for Armenia's 1998 election. The conclusions of the more positive initial report were challenged by a more critical final report issued several weeks later (Bjornlund 2004). Initial evaluations of other elections, such as Armenia's 2007 parliamentary election and Georgia's 2008 presidential election, have been similarly criticized.

Despite these problems, internationally sponsored observation missions have made important contributions to the evaluation of election quality. International observers have a less direct stake in the outcome of elections than domestic observers, enhancing the perception of objectivity. International teams often bear the imprimatur of respected organizations, facilitating access to politicians and administrators and lending weight to their assessments.

Moreover, in the early postcommunist period, international teams brought needed expertise to the region and improved electoral processes through technical assistance. However, international missions have been accused of bias, fielding underprepared observers, and failing to have enough staff members who speak local languages.

International observation teams are not alone in evaluating election quality in the region. Domestic observers range from representatives of parties or candidates to NGOs and the media. Local NGOs such as Viasna (Belarus), Partnership (Belarus), International Society for Fair Elections and Democracy (Georgia), Georgian Young Lawyers Association, Republican Network of International Monitors (Kazakhstan), Coalition for Democratic and Civil Society (Kyrgyzstan), League for the Defense of Human Rights (Moldova), Golos (Russia), and the Committee of Voters of Ukraine have observed and assessed elections. Local observers know the landscape well, can effectively communicate, and are often more adept at picking up subtle signals from their conationals. Because domestic teams are often larger than international ones, they have also been key players in producing parallel vote counts, a valuable tool in assessing the quality of the vote aggregation process.[24] But, in many countries, local observation groups are under pressure from government and experience restricted access to information.[25] Because their work often implicitly challenges incumbent regimes, domestic groups have been accused of partisanship and their assessments dismissed as biased (Carothers 1997).

Observation missions, especially internationally sponsored missions, have come under greater scrutiny from countries that have received negative evaluations. The most prominent critic of election evaluation, especially missions led by the OSCE, has been the Russian government. In 2007, Russia's representative to the OSCE accused the organization of double standards in mission deployment and of political bias in its activities and assessments.[26]

Led by Russia, several post-Soviet states proposed modifications to election mission deployment standards in September 2007. The proposal would have capped the size of missions at fifty observers, prevented the publication of reports until after official results were announced, and involved all members of the OSCE Permanent Council in the composition of the final report. The proposal enjoyed the support of Armenia, Belarus, Kazakhstan, Kyrgyzstan, Tajikistan, and Uzbekistan (Chivers 2007) but was not adopted.

Although the OSCE's deployment procedures were not changed, the Russian government limited the size of observation missions for its 2007–2008 election cycle. Russia offered to admit seventy OSCE observers for short-term observation. The OSCE argued that the mission size and duration was inadequate to properly assess the elections, noting that four hundred observers were admitted to observe the 2003 parliamentary election. After visa delays, the OSCE canceled its observation missions for both the 2007 parliamentary and 2008 presidential elections. President Putin responded by alleging that pressure from the United States caused the OSCE to withdraw its observation team (Ponomarev 2007). In response, the United States accused Russia of efforts to undermine the efficacy of election monitoring.

While election observation has been hampered by several problems associated with data collection and analysis, such as inadequately specific definitions of the processes constituting free and fair elections; barriers to the complete and objective collection, assessment, and reporting of observations of the electoral process; and backlash against the enterprise, it remains an essential tool for the assessment of election quality.

Conclusion

While election administration, dispute adjudication, and quality assessment have been under-studied, they are critical elements in the development of free and fair electoral practices. As noted in the introduction to this chapter, these institutions operate on different oversight principles. Election commissions and courts adhere most closely to the "fire alarm" approach, and observers adhere most closely to the "police patrol" approach. The fire alarm approach is generally considered to be more effective, but only when institutions function properly. The assessments in this chapter suggest that in many former Soviet states, administrative, judicial, and observation processes require improvements before oversight can deter inappropriate behavior and encourage best practices.

The institutional shortcomings undermining proper administration, adjudication, and oversight have produced an environment conducive to the perpetration of election fraud. The next chapter addresses fraud directly, using data from observer reports as well as election data produced by electoral commissions.

CHAPTER 9

ASSESSING ELECTION QUALITY

Many post-Soviet elections illustrate the perils of accepting the "electoral fallacy," the notion that implementing elections is equivalent to introducing democracy. The "Colored Revolutions" that swept out the corrupt leaderships of Georgia, Ukraine, and Kyrgyzstan from 2003 to 2005 were sparked by evidence that systematic fraud substantially influenced election results. Post-"revolutionary" politics in these countries has diverged, with Ukraine showing signs of nascent, if contentious, democratic politics; Georgia again slipping toward authoritarianism; and Kyrgyzstan quickly returning to the cronyism and corruption associated with the toppled regime.

While Kyrgyzstan was characterized as authoritarian at the time of the regime's ouster, Georgia and Ukraine were deemed by Freedom House to be "partially free" and had conducted elections moving toward international standards. It is in these "grey area" regimes that the electoral fallacy is most likely to be applied. "Partially free" states evidence some of the pluralism and competition associated with democratic politics but also restrict freedoms that undermine their classification as fully democratic societies. A principal factor in determining if the regime tends to present more features of liberal democracy or more features of autocracy is the quality of the election process.

The assessment of election quality—like the assessment of democratic quality generally—requires several components. First, the basic contours of an appropriate election contest should be articulated, along with any internationally defined standards that guide the definition. Chapter 1 addressed this issue. Second, institutions or organizations that can protect against subversion should be identified and their quality assessed. Chapter 8 covered this component. Third, methods of undermining the quality of the election process should be identified and investigated (Beetham 2005). This chapter focuses on the last element, evaluating the how free and fair electoral practices may be subverted.

Studies of improper influences on the vote address several processes, including biased media coverage, questionable administrative decisions on registration and ballot access, efforts to bribe or intimidate voters, and actions that directly affect the casting, counting, and compiling of ballots on election day. Some of these activities are illegal, such as ballot-box stuffing, while others are legal or semilegal. Unequal media coverage, for example, may afford certain candidates an advantage in the campaign. However, unbalanced attention may not directly violate election statutes and is challenging to definitively prove. Further, administrative decisions to remove candidates may follow the law but also may be applied unevenly across the party system. *Manipulation* includes those legal or semilegal activities that violate the spirit of free and fair competition. *Fraud* includes illegal activities surrounding the casting, counting, or compiling of election returns.

Some research on manipulation and fraud focuses on the election process, while other work emphasizes the results, implying that manipulation and fraud are important primarily when they make a "winner" into a "loser" (Sutter 2003).[1] While accusations of manipulation and fraud are associated with many elections, these elections often meet a reasonable definition of fairness: the elections pass muster with international observers, and opposition candidates take seats that they earn (although the total number may be lower than the opposition "should" have earned) (Kuenzi and Lambright 2001). Even in elections that pass this relaxed standard of fairness, however, seat allocation may be substantially affected by vote theft, potentially undermining citizen confidence in the system's legitimacy. While the intellectual argument for emphasizing outcomes is understandable, the analysis in the chapter focuses instead on the process.

This chapter asks if final vote tallies reported by authorities accurately reflect the voters' wishes when they cast ballots at the polls and addresses the question in two sections. The first section reviews the diverse forms of manipulation and fraud, providing examples from the post-Soviet world. The second section presents results from detailed analyses of election data, focusing on specific forms of fraud and detection techniques. The chapter concludes with a discussion of the implications of manipulation and fraud for post-Soviet elections.

A PRIMER ON MANIPULATION AND FRAUD

Inappropriate influences on elections that undermine fair competition among candidates and free expression of voter preferences are not a new phenomenon, nor are they limited in their geographic scope. Complaints of interference by officials and intimidation of the electorate date back to the first council elections in England (Cox 1868), spreading to early electoral contests in colonial, post–Civil War, and contemporary America (e.g., Argersinger 1985–1986; Bensel 2004; Campbell 2005; Cox and Kousser 1981), and across the globe from the eighteenth to the twenty-first centuries (e.g., Callahan and McCargo 1996; Mikhailov 2000; Lehoucq and Molina 2002; Lehoucq 2003; Myagkov, Ordeshook, and Shakin 2005). Evidence of fraud's pervasiveness across countries and time suggests that the primary question is not *whether* manipulation and fraud occur but *at what level of magnitude*.[2] Despite the universality of manipulation and fraud, they have been peripheral concerns in the study of elections until recently.

Evidence of improper influences on the vote emanates from several sources: domestic and international observers, parallel vote counts, aggressive investigative media reports, and whistle-blowers in government. The diversity of information sources is paralleled in the scholarly literature, with researchers relying on surveys, ethnographic work, memoirs, formal complaints and legal cases, news accounts, reports from civil society, and election data to evaluate election quality (Lehoucq 2003). Studies in American politics (e.g., Cox and Kousser 1981; Wand et al. 2001; Herron and Sekhon 2003) and comparative politics (e.g., Sobyanin and Sukhovolskiy 1995; Mikhailov 1999; Myagkov and Ordeshook 2001; Lehoucq and Molina 2002; Birch 2007) have used various sources of data and techniques to calculate systematic error in elections attributable to manipulation and fraud.

Measuring the scale and scope of improper influences on elections depends upon how widely scholars define the target of their analyses. In the most general sense, manipulation and fraud could include any action on the part of government officials, political parties, candidates, partisan supporters, or other political actors that interferes with the dual rights of contestation and participation. But, what actions constitute "interference?" While threats of violence and ballot-box stuffing are clear violations of open and free competition, what about the hazier areas of electoral "malpractice" (Birch 2007)?

As discussed in Chapter 8, election administrators exert considerable influence over the process of registering voters and candidates, monitoring the propriety of the election campaign, and overseeing voting and counting. A primary responsibility of election administrators is to determine who is eligible to vote and to ensure that each voter casts only one ballot. The integrity of voter lists—and the inclusion and exclusion of voters from those lists—has been challenged in many elections. The most flagrant violations have included the disenfranchisement of large numbers of voters allegedly for partisan reasons or padding voter lists with ineligible or deceased voters to inflate the vote for one or more contestants.

Administrators also exert a strong effect on ballot access for candidates and parties. Questionable interpretations of election laws or unequal application of the laws have negatively affected contestation rights by excluding prominent candidates from the ballot. Yet, even proper application of the rules can prompt accusations of partisan machinations on the part of election commissions.

While government actors are able to use the considerable resources of the state to influence elections through administrative commissions, government may also use its powers to reward and punish other participants.[3] In many countries, the list of government employees is long; in addition to bureaucrats and military personnel, the state may employ teachers and school administrators from primary through higher education, hospital staff, and other professionals as civil servants. These employees may be pressured to "deliver the vote" for the national or local power broker's preferred party, and they consequently may attempt to exert influence over their charges (e.g., soldiers, students, and patients) through promises of rewards or threats of punishment. In some cases, compliance can be closely monitored so that rewards and punishments can be meted out to individuals; at other times monitoring is more diffuse, requiring collective judgment. For example, the votes of incarcerated citizens or bedridden patients may be closely observed, encouraging compliance with the preferences of overseers through implicit or explicit threats of punishment for failure to comply.[4] In many university districts, precincts are located in dormitories; individual compliance cannot be as effectively monitored as in prisons or hospitals, but students—or the faculty—may be punished collectively for failure to deliver the vote. This type of administrative influence over the vote is cited extensively in observer reports of elections in post-Soviet space.[5]

Political parties and candidates have also been accused of improperly influencing the election process. In some cases, parties work through administrative organs to gain undue influence over election administration. For example, supporters of Viktor Yanukovych in Ukraine's 2004 presidential election gained positions on local electoral commissions by "representing" minor candidates who were on the ballot in the first round of the contest. As an election observer during the second-round presidential runoff, I encountered two rural precinct electoral commissions where the chair, deputy chair, and secretary all claimed to represent Yanukovych. When confronted with legal provisions demonstrating that this arrangement contravened the law, the officials searched the records to find their official "sponsors," noting that they in fact represented minor candidates who failed to pass through the first round. Stacking the deck on precinct commissions potentially influences outcomes. In the same election, I observed an unbalanced electoral commission admit questionable ballots that supported Yanukovych and invalidate similarly mismarked ballots on which the voters showed a clear preference for Viktor Yushchenko.[6]

The media plays an important role in influencing the tenor of the campaign and voter awareness of issues and candidates. Incumbents generally enjoy greater access to the media because their actions as elected representatives constitute "news." But, in many states—especially where the major media outlets are owned or controlled by government entities—the media is used to actively support certain parties or candidates. Media monitoring reports, such as those produced by the European Institute on the Media and Organization for Security and Cooperation in Europe (OSCE), often point to preferential treatment for parties of power. For example, reports on the 2004 parliamentary election in Belarus illustrate how government-sponsored television and radio provided extensive positive coverage of

President Lukashenka and limited but overwhelmingly negative coverage of the opposition. The print media showed greater variation in tone and coverage but still provided more extensive attention to the president (OSCE 2004d). Available reports on elections in other countries offer similar judgments on biased media coverage. While the media does not directly coerce voters to support specific parties or candidates, manipulation of the media can influence the outcomes of an election by limiting access or overexposing contestants outside of the norms of free and fair competition.

While interference in the free and fair conduct of elections prior to election day undermines the democratic quality of the contest, domestic and international observers, as well as scholars, have focused most of their attention on election day activities. Efforts to influence how, or whether, voters cast their ballots, how those ballots are tallied, and how data from polling stations are translated into final results are the clearest forms of fraud.

The perpetrators of fraud have developed many techniques to successfully commit vote theft and limit detection. To increase support for a candidate or party, ballots could be added to the box, voters could be coerced to support a candidate or party, election results could be reworked outside the polling station, or cast ballots could be exchanged for forged ballots. To decrease support for an opponent, ballots could be spoiled, invalidated, or destroyed, and voters could be coerced to stay away from the polls or to shift their vote to another candidate (Argersinger 1985–1986; Sobyanin and Sukhovolskiy 1995; Schedler 2002). Many of the alleged techniques used to alter the vote show remarkable creativity and coordination: the use of disappearing ink to invalidate ballots (Charter 2004), voter "carousels,"[7] bussing voters to multiple precincts, and abusing the mobile ballot box.[8]

Election reports produced by OSCE observer teams illustrate the extensive nature of manipulation and fraud in post-Soviet elections.[9] Observers noted media bias in forty-six of fifty-four total elections; voter list problems, improper or unequal campaigning, and voter coercion in forty-three; protocol tampering in thirty-nine; ballot tampering or ballot-box stuffing in thirty-seven; electoral commission bias in thirty-five; inconsistent ballot access or registration in twenty, and inconsistent ballot invalidation in seventeen. Manipulation and fraud generally favored the incumbent regime. While this summary does not distinguish between high- or low- intensity activities, OSCE reports illustrate that illicit activities are pervasive.

Careful evaluation of each report provides a more nuanced view of the intensity and scope of misdeeds. For example, the OSCE report from Azerbaijan's 2000 parliamentary election details unsophisticated ballot-box stuffing, with stacks of ballots illegally placed in the ballot box, and lights turned off during the counting process to facilitate fraud. By contrast, reports from Kazakhstan comment on potential problems emanating from the use of electronic voting machines that are not independently certified and discuss protocol tampering rather than more direct ballot-box stuffing to alter results. These two examples illustrate the challenges of comparing election quality based on the reports. While many elections produce evidence of manipulation and fraud, the frequency and intensity of activities varies.

Some reports, such as those for elections in Russia (1996 and 1999) and Ukraine (1998) identified a moderate number of problems. In contrast to some scholarship on the 1996 Russian presidential election (Mikhailov 1999; 2000), the OSCE report does not indicate the presence of widespread falsification or alterations of protocols. Rather, the final reports on Russia's 1996 presidential and 1999 parliamentary elections are positive, noting localized problems with administration and unequal media access and campaign conditions. Similarly, the report on Ukraine's 1998 parliamentary election identifies significant issues but more limited evidence of manipulation and fraud. In nine elections (Estonia (1999 parliamentary), Latvia (2002 and 2006 parliamentary), Lithuania (1996 parliamentary), Moldova (1996 presidential, 1998 and 2001 parliamentary), and Ukraine (2006 and 2007 parliamentary) few violations to international standards are reported.

International observer reports remain a valuable source of information about the quality of elections. However, they are not the only source to consult. The following section uses several empirical tests to illustrate how data anomalies can be identified and potentially linked to systematic fraud.

ELECTION FRAUD—EMPIRICAL TESTS

Efforts to identify problematic elections using election data have focused on the detection of anomalous results that are most plausibly explained by systematic distortion of the voting record. Several approaches, with varied assumptions and methods of interacting with the data, have appeared in the literature. The first approach uses data aggregated regionally or nationally and compares the outcomes for all contestants to a set of expected outcomes (Sobyanin and Sukhovolskiy 1995). A second approach traces the movement of votes from one election to another (Myagkov and Ordeshook 2001). A third approach applies techniques from mathematics and forensic accounting to assess the distribution of digits in precinct level data, comparing them to the distribution of data anticipated by Benford's Law (Nigrini 1999; 2006; Mebane 2006). The fourth approach focuses on special precincts where particularly vulnerable voters are assigned to cast their ballots and compares the vote distribution in these precincts to standard precincts to identify anomalous results (Herron and Johnson 2008).

This section comments on all four approaches and replicates two of them using election data from several countries for the first method (Armenia [2007], Georgia [1999], Kazakhstan [2007], Russia [2004], and Ukraine [2002 and 2004]) and data from Ukraine for the second method.[10] A single test cannot adequately identify data tampering. But, a combination of several tests can reveal anomalies that speak to the issue of data quality and affect confidence in the integrity of the electoral process.

Methods of Detecting Fraud

Sobyanin and Sukhovolskiy (1995) developed the first approach to detect fraud that uses election results as the primary data source. In their analysis of early postcommunist Russian elections, Sobyanin and Sukhovolskiy proposed several simple tests of election quality. The main test involved fitting a regression line to the natural logarithm of votes received by a party as a function of the natural logarithm of that party's rank in the election. This relationship ostensibly reveals patterns produced by free and fair contests as well as compromised elections. Based on their assumptions, election fraud should produce a demonstrable "deviation from the primary rank order" (Sobyanin and Sukhovolskiy 1995, 67) manifested by a strong deviation from the regression line. Limited variance from the regression line implies freer competition; increased variance implies less freedom.

Sobyanin and Sukhovolskiy's method suffers from flaws in the assumptions, lack of attention to alternate hypotheses, and data analysis that relies on inadequately rigorous techniques to determine if the results are naturally produced. An underlying expectation in their analysis is that fair races will not be close, as a tight race can produce "suspicious" results. The authors also implicitly connect deviations from the regression line with fraud, although benign explanations may account for discrepancies observed in the data. Moreover, the detection of anomalous results relies primarily on an ocular evaluation of the figures rather than more rigorous statistical analysis. Despite these shortcomings, Sobyanin and Sukhovolskiy provided the first systematic use of election data to identify unusual patterns that plausibly could be attributed to fraud.

Myagkov and Ordeshook (2001)[11] use regional-level data from Russia and Ukraine to evaluate how votes move among parties, how turnout varies, and how turnout is related to party or candidate performance. As they noted in their article, this approach potentially suffers from problems of ecological inference. Indeed, while the method uses local-level data rather than election returns aggregated at a higher level, it is nevertheless an approach intended to assess individual voter behavior without individual voter data. Despite this problem, their efforts add another valuable test to the arsenal of fraud detection.

While the following two methods also have drawbacks, both use data aggregated at the level of the primary unit of analysis: the polling station. Since much election fraud is perpetrated at the polling station level, it is appropriate to use models that assess data aggregated at that level. The following approach applies precinct-level data to a concept from mathematics to identify implausible results. The final approach in the chapter compares results from standard precincts with those dedicated to special populations to determine if unusual discrepancies are present.

Applying Benford's Law

In 1938, Frank Benford rediscovered a pattern in the distribution of numbers that has been applied to research on data quality. Benford found that the frequency of first digits in data sets is not uniform; the number 1 is the most common first digit, with the likelihood of a digit occupying the first position declining logarithmically. His description of this phenomenon became known as Benford's Law and has been used to evaluate the accuracy of data in many disciplines, notably accounting.[12] Scholars have also extended Benford's Law to the study of election data (Mebane 2006; Nigrini 2006). Tests based on Benford's Law are particularly appropriate for finding evidence of massive data manipulation: large-scale ballot-box stuffing, alteration of results protocols, or other approaches that are likely to be extensive and coordinated.

While the application of Benford's Law to election data promises to more systematically identify anomalies in the data, there are several challenges to its use. First-digit Benford's Law tests count only digits greater than zero. However, in election returns at the precinct level, a zero for an individual party or candidate is a real outcome that could be a strong indicator of a manipulated vote. In addition to the problem of election data's lower bound, the upper bound truncates the data set. Precincts are often constrained in size by law from hundreds to a few thousand voters. This upper bound—which varies cross-nationally and within countries—affects the likelihood of certain first digits appearing in the dataset and consequently the interpretation of these data.

Concerns about the first-digit test prompted Walter Mebane (2006) to focus on other tests that flow from Benford's work, notably the second-digit test. The second-digit test is particularly tuned for manipulation of data that implies rounding up or down; more second-digit zeros and fewer second-digit nines than anticipated in Benford's ideal distribution implies rounding up. This anomaly is particularly notable in financial data. But, the second digit test is "a conditional distribution that assumes that the first digits are distributed according to (or close to) Benford's Law" (Nigrini 2005, 103). In other words, for second-digit test results to be relevant for assessing data quality, first-digit distributions should also be evaluated for their compliance with Benford's Law.

Evaluating the distribution of data for conformity with Benford's Law requires two steps. In the first step, digits must be extracted from the data; in the second step the distribution of the data must be compared to the expectations of Benford's Law. Scholars have used a chi-square test for the second stage, although potential problems with this test have been identified (Nigrini 1999). Table 9.1 shows the results of chi-square tests for precinct-level data for the main parties or candidates in elections in Armenia, Georgia, Kazakhstan, Russia, and Ukraine. The null hypothesis is that the data conform to a Benford-type distribution.

In only two cases are the national-level results statistically different from a Benford-type distribution at the .05 level: outcomes for the Communist

Table 9.1 Benford's Law First-Digit Test with National Results

Country/Election/Contestant	1st Digit Test
Armenia 2007 Armenian Revolutionary Front PR	1.300
Armenia 2007 PAP PR	7.376
Armenia 2007 RPA PR	2.595
Georgia 1999 Citizens' Union of Georgia PR	5.749
Georgia 1999 Revival PR	4.377
Kazakhstan 2007 Ak Zhol	6.935
Kazakhstan 2007 Nur-OTAN	3.051
Kazakhstan 2007 All National Social Democratic Party	15.081†
Russia 2004 Kharitonov[1]	0.254
Russia 2004 Putin	2.333
Ukraine 2002 Communist Party of Ukraine PR	11.893
Ukraine 2002 Communist Party of Ukraine SMD	34.227*
Ukraine 2002 For a United Ukraine PR	0.683
Ukraine 2002 For a United Ukraine SMD	1.235
Ukraine 2002 Our Ukraine PR	1.534
Ukraine 2002 Our Ukraine SMD	13.311
Ukraine 2004 Yanukovych	31.488*
Ukraine 2004 Yushchenko	6.753
Ukraine 2006 Bloc of Yuliya Tymoshenko	1.094
Ukraine 2006 Our Ukraine	12.295
Ukraine 2006 Party of Regions	3.149
Ukraine 2007 Bloc of Yuliya Tymoshenko	10.964
Ukraine 2007 Our Ukraine—People's Defense	15.481†
Ukraine 2007 Party of Regions	4.878

Source: Author's calculations based on data from Central Electoral Commissions in Armenia, Georgia, Kazakhstan, Russia, and Ukraine.

Note: * indicates significance at the .05 level. † indicates significance at the .10 level.

Party of Ukraine (CPU) in the nominal tier of the 2002 parliamentary elections and results for Viktor Yanukovych in the "third round" of presidential elections in 2004.[13] In two other cases, the results diverge from the expected distribution at the .10 level: Our Ukraine-People's Self-Defense (OU-PSD) in Ukraine's 2007 election and the All-National Social Democratic Party (ANSDP) in Kazakhstan's 2007 election. Second-digit tests do not support rejection of the null hypothesis in any of the cases under analysis. Given the outcomes, results from both Kazakhstan and Ukraine are worthy of further investigation.

Kazakhstan

Kazakhstan's 2007 parliamentary election produced a one-party parliament, with the propresidential Nur-OTAN party claiming all legislative seats.

Many political actors, observers, and pundits[14] praised the elections, notably President Nazarbayev (Lambroschini 2007) and observers from the Commonwealth of Independent States (TASS 2007), Shanghai Cooperation Organization (BBC 2007d), and some Western countries (BBC 2007e). But, many aspects of the election were criticized by the defeated opposition and the OSCE.

While exit polls predicted that the party of power would win the election handily,[15] data released by the Central Electoral Commission[16] suggest that Nur-OTAN's victory was buttressed by unusual results. In four precincts, Nur-OTAN received over 100 percent of the vote;[17] in 588 precincts it received all votes cast (6 percent of the 9,707 reporting precincts). Nur-OTAN received just over 2 percent of its total vote in precincts where it garnered 100 percent or more of the vote; accounting for 117,081 votes. In more than half of the reporting precincts (5,616), Nur-OTAN received 90 percent or more of the recorded votes. It received under 20 percent of the vote in fourteen precincts, with zero votes in eight precincts.

Exit polls suggested that the opposition parties ANSDP and Ak Zhol could pass the threshold. But, they exceeded the 7 percent threshold in only 2,076 (ANSDP) and 1,158 (Ak Zhol) precincts. The ANSDP received zero votes in 1,009 precincts, and Ak Zhol received zero votes in 749 precincts. In short, the anomalous findings illustrated in the comparison of Kazakhstan's results to the Benford-type distribution are further accompanied by other unusual results present in the election data.

Ukraine

Benford's Law in the Regions
In the most egregious case of manipulation and fraud to date in Ukraine, the regime-supported candidate for president, Viktor Yanukovych, claimed victory in the second round of the 2004 presidential election. International and domestic observers pointed to significant evidence of voter intimidation, ballot-box stuffing, protocol tampering, and other methods of vote theft, particularly in Yanukovych's area of strength: Ukraine's eastern and southern regions. In many of Ukraine's elections, observer and media reports have noted that the quality of election administration varies subnationally, with certain regions producing more anomalous results than others. The following analysis takes regional variation into account and assesses if anomalous results are more likely to be associated with certain areas of the country.

Testing precinct-level data against the Benford distribution does not preclude changing the level of aggregation. Table 9.2 presents significant regional results of first-digit tests for the top three parties in the 2002 and 2006 parliamentary elections, and both candidates in the 2004 repeat second round of the presidential election.[18] The results reveal interesting patterns. In most regions, the null hypothesis cannot be rejected; data statistically conform to a Benford-type distribution. Results using 2002 data in the proportional representation (PR) tier for the CPU in Dnipropetrovsk and Donetsk produce

Table 9.2 Significant Results for First-Digit Tests in Ukraine, 2002–2006

Region	2002	2004	2006
Dnipropetrovsk	CPU* (PR)		Regions*
Donetsk	CPU* (PR)	Yanukovych*	OU*
	FUU† (SMD)		
Kyiv City	OU† (PR)	Yushchenko*	BYuT*
		Yanukovych*	Regions*
			OU*
Luhansk		Yanukovych*	OU*
Odesa			BYuT*
Ternopil	FUU† (PR)		

Source: Author's calculations of data from the Central Electoral Commission of Ukraine.

Note: * indicates significance at the .05 level. † indicates significance at the .10 level.

results that exceed the critical chi-square value at the .05 level. Results for the progovernment For a United Ukraine (FUU) bloc in Donetsk's single-member district (SMD) race and Ternopil's PR race, and results for Our Ukraine (OU) in Kyiv City's PR race, exceed the critical value at the .10 level. Using data from 2006, results are significant at the .05 level for the Bloc of Yuliya Tymoshenko (BYuT) in Kyiv City and Odesa; Party of Regions in Dnipropetrovsk and Kyiv City; and OU-PSD in Donetsk, Kyiv City, and Luhansk. Presidential election data produce similar findings. Yanukovych's results in Donetsk, Kyiv City, and Luhansk, and Yushchenko's in Kyiv City exceed the critical values on the chi-square test for the first digit.

Eastern regions (Donetsk, Dnipropetrovsk, and Luhansk) figure prominently in the anomalous results. This finding is notable because it is in these regions where allegations of some of the most egregious violations of election laws—ballot-box stuffing, voter intimidation, alteration of results by complicit election commissions—are alleged to have occurred. However, a finding that the distribution of election results does not conform with Benford's Law does not prove that fraud occurred. The results in Kyiv City consistently failed to match a Benford-type distribution, yet claims of illicit activities in the capital city are scarce. While this test is a valuable tool to identify anomalous results, its findings do not demonstrate causality.

Assessing Results in Special Precincts
As noted in the previous section, election fraud may not be uniformly distributed nationally. Rather, certain locations and populations may be targeted because those regions are pivotal for the results or the populations that vote in those locations may be more vulnerable to coercion. The results of the analysis in the previous section support this observation: election data in Ukraine did not conform with a Benford-type first-digit distribution in several regions where misdeeds have been alleged.

Focusing on regional outcomes may be both scientifically and politically problematic, however. Regional analyses presume a geographic cleavage and may prompt social scientists to assume away potential problems in regions that have not typically shown anomalous results. Not only may fraud be perpetrated anywhere, but concentrating research on a particular subset of regions may raise accusations of partisanship. Lastly, while the geographic position of a precinct may provide some insight into the likelihood of fraud, especially if local political elites are suspected of pressuring election administrators into producing a particular outcome, other features may also facilitate the investigation of fraud. This section deemphasizes the search for anomalies based on geographic location and focuses on "special" precincts where the opportunity and motive for coercion is clearly present.

The designation of special precincts varies cross-nationally and sometimes within countries. Typically, special precincts are created for voters unable to cast their ballots in their "home" polling station due to hospitalization, military service, incarceration, or other obligation that requires the voter to be physically distant from the home precinct. Notably, these populations are often vulnerable to coercion due to their dependence on agents of the state to provide care, employment, protection, or some other service. While the number of voters casting ballots in these precincts is small compared to the number of voters assigned to standard precincts, data from these polling stations can provide insight into the quality of elections.

The primary expectation is that candidates or parties associated with government power—nationally or locally articulated—should perform no better in special precincts than in standard precincts when one controls for other determinants of the vote. However, markedly stronger performance by political actors whose allies exert coercive power over the voters in special precincts suggests sinister manipulation of vote outcomes. Data from Ukraine's 2002 election facilitate this analysis because the Central Electoral Commission published precinct-level protocols that provided the addresses of polling stations.[19] Ukraine permits special voting precincts for citizens who are incarcerated, hospitalized, serve in the military and on ships, and live abroad. These special precincts are the focus of the analysis.

Table 9.3 shows how results in special precincts deviate from those in all other precincts for three political parties and their candidates in both tiers of Ukraine's mixed electoral system in 2002. The results for the three main parties in these precincts are instructive. In this election, one electoral bloc, FUU, was considered to be the "party of power" and enjoyed the support of the national leadership.[20] Ukraine's regional authorities are appointed by the center, so local officials are also likely to be state agents supporting the objectives of the "party of power." The two primary opposition parties were the CPU and OU. The results on Table 9.3 show that in special precincts, FUU performed better than its grand mean. Opposition parties performed worse in special precincts, except for OU in embassy and consulate-based precincts.

Table 9.3   Deviation from Mean Levels of Support in Special Precincts, Ukraine 2002

	FUU	CPU	OU
Prison			
PR	+4.50	−1.09	−0.97
SMD	+1.86	−0.42	−0.63
Hospital			
PR	+0.57	−0.02	−0.28
SMD	+0.19	−0.10	−0.18
Ship			
PR	+1.58	−0.75	−0.90
SMD	+1.67	−0.46	−0.77
Embassy			
PR	+0.99	−0.81	+0.12
SMD	——	−0.58	+0.07

Source: Author's calculations of data from the Central Electoral Commission of Ukraine.

A deeper analysis of these data that takes into account rival hypotheses can potentially provide a more complete explanation of the discrepancies that the data reveal. The analysis herein employs Seemingly Unrelated Regression (SUR) to estimate the models. The dependent variables in the multivariate analyses are the vote outcomes of three parties, FUU, CPU, and OU in the PR and SMD components of the mixed electoral system, aggregated at the precinct level. The main explanatory variables address several possible explanations for the performance of progovernment and opposition parties: nomination patterns in SMD races (i.e., the nature of the choice set in SMD), patronage politics and the quality of competition at the district level, and variation in electoral support across regions. The model of PR performance includes candidate features of the party whose results are under analysis. The model of SMD performance also controls for features of other candidates competing in the district. The Appendix provides more details about the data and analysis.

The main variables of interest identify the type of polling station in which the vote was held. Each polling station records basic information about the vote (e.g., number of voters, votes cast for each party and candidate) and the facility (e.g., address and other identifying information) in the protocol and forwards its documents to the district electoral commission, where the results are compiled and transmitted to the Central Electoral Commission. The electronic versions of the protocols are thus formal records of the official vote tallies in the polling stations. While officials inconsistently provided information about polling stations, details about many polling stations were reported, identifying them as a club, school, prison, ship, hospital, embassy, or other structure.

Table 9.4 reports full SUR results for models of PR support. The results in Table 9.4 show the effects of candidate characteristics, region, and special precincts on PR outcomes. Having an affiliated candidate in the corresponding

Table 9.4   SUR Analysis in PR, Ukraine 2002

	FUU	CPU	OU
Constant	−2.437*	−2.849*	0.848*
	(.021)	(.017)	(.019)
Candidate	0.141*	0.054*	0.083*
	(.016)	(.001)	(.011)
Deputy	0.371*	0.168*	0.409*
	(.039)	(.016)	(.020)
High	0.494*	——	0.444*
	(.039)		(.060)
Local	0.121*	−0.093*	0.713*
	(.019)	(.031)	(.036)
North Central	0.200*	1.410*	−1.901*
	(.025)	(.017)	(.020)
Southwest	0.676*	0.890*	−0.850*
	(.041)	(.028)	(.030)
East Central	0.798*	2.464*	−3.000*
	(.027)	(.019)	(.022)
East	1.974*	2.890*	−3.366*
	(.028)	(.020)	(.023)
South	0.784*	2.296*	−2.934*
	(.025)	(.021)	(.024)
West Central	0.773*	1.393*	−0.949*
	(.025)	(.017)	(.020)
Krym	0.042	2.480*	−2.802*
	(.040)	(.027)	(.297)
Prison	3.296*	−1.215*	−0.963*
	(.240)	(.165)	(.171)
Hospital	0.338*	−0.008	−0.117*
	(.070)	(.047)	(.050)
Ship	0.892*	−1.733*	−0.536*
	(.356)	(.024)	(.254)
Embassy	1.834*	−0.501*	0.711*
	(.135)	(.092)	(.096)
RMSE	1.177	0.807	0.839
N	30449	30449	30449

Note: The dependent variable is the natural log of the ratio of the vote of party i to the vote of other parties. Standard errors are in parentheses. * indicates significance at the .05 level.

SMD race positively affects PR, reflected by the positive, significant coefficients for the variable Candidate. Candidates with parliamentary experience perform better, on average, than their counterparts without experience. The coefficients for parliamentary experience are statistically significant and positive in sign for all three parties. Candidates in national posts also benefit their parties, evidenced by the significant and positive parameter estimates. Candidates in local posts generally improve PR outcomes; coefficients are positive and significant for CPU and OU.

Regional variables also affect party performance in the expected direction; FUU receives more support, on average, in the East, East Central, and South. The CPU also garners strong support in the East, East Central, South, and Crimea, evidenced by the large positive coefficients. OU performs best in the West; negative coefficients for the regional variables reflect OU's support in the excluded category. These results conform to studies of geographic variation in party support (Craumer and Clem 1999; Birch 2000; Barrington and Herron 2004).

Coefficients for special precincts are consistently positive in sign and significant for FUU. The parameter estimate is particularly large for FUU in prisons. By contrast, coefficients for special precincts are negative in sign for the CPU, except the coefficient for hospitals, which is not statistically significant. In the OU model, parameter estimates for special precincts are negative and significant for prisons, hospitals, and ships, but not embassies. Rather, OU performs better in foreign outposts than in other polling stations situated in Ukraine. While voters on foreign soil may be state employees, they also include expatriates who may favor center-right opposition parties. These results suggest that FUU received an advantage in special precincts, even when controls for rival hypotheses are considered.[21]

Table 9.5 shows the results of SUR analysis using data from SMD. Constituency races present a particular challenge, as SUR analysis cannot accommodate missing data on values of the dependent variable. The PR race is not problematic because all parties contest every district (and thus every precinct). However, parties may or may not contest a given district race. The SMD analysis covers all districts (10,482 precincts) in which the three parties under study nominated candidates. However, this solution does not cover all possible combinations; in some districts any one of the three parties could fail to nominate a candidate, withdraw a candidate, or support another candidate. To address this problem, the analysis is repeated for all combinations of the parties. The coefficients for special precincts are reported in Table 9.5; the signs and significance levels of other coefficients are similar to those in the PR model.[22]

Few coefficients rise to statistical significance, although many are significant at the .10 level. However, the coefficients that are significant are telling: coefficients for prison precincts in the CPU equations are consistently significant and negative in sign. Further, the coefficient for ships is significant and negative for the CPU.

The analysis demonstrates that the effect of special precincts is significant and tends to benefit the party of power even when rival explanations are controlled. These results provide additional support for the hypothesis that the party of power performs better in special precincts and opposition parties worse, and fraud is a plausible explanation for this outcome.[23]

The results of this analysis provide additional insights into the quality of election data. While they cover only a small number of recorded votes, data on special precincts allow scholars to assess anomalies while controlling for rival hypotheses, an option absent in the other methods described above.

Table 9.5   SUR Analysis in SMD, Ukraine 2002

	FUU/CPU/OU			FUU/CPU		FUU/OU		CPU/OU	
	Y1	Y2	Y3	Y1	Y2	Y1	Y3	Y2	Y3
Prison	0.074	−1.274*	−0.701	0.619	−1.077*	0.774	−0.538	−1.272*	−0.701
	(.451)	(.369)	(.425)	(.429)	(.351)	(.438)	(.409)	(.370)	(.426)
Hospital	0.020	−0.175	−0.042	0.088	−0.169	0.060	−0.008	−0.181	−0.036
	(.126)	(.103)	(.118)	(.120)	(.098)	(.121)	(.113)	(.102)	(.118)
Ship	−1.040	−1.722	−0.275	−0.585	−1.560*	−1.015	1.226	−1.065	0.043
	(1.275)	(1.044)	(1.202)	(910)	(.744)	(1.312)	(.113)	(.740)	(.852)
RMSE	1.274	1.043	1.201	1.285	1.052	1.311	1.226	1.044	1.203
N	10482	10482	10482	10757	10757	11115	11115	10510	10510

Note: The dependent variable is the natural log of the ratio of the vote of party i to the vote of other parties. Standard errors are in parentheses. * indicates significance at the .05 level.

Evidence of unusual results in special precincts also conforms with a narrative about fraud that specifies the motive and opportunity for the perpetrators of fraud; other approaches are silent on this matter. But, because of the small number of votes in these precincts, only in rare cases can they be connected with changes in election outcomes.

CONCLUSION

The main question driving this chapter asked if election outcomes reported in the post-Soviet region reflect the true intentions of citizens who cast ballots. The results of the assessment are sobering: in many countries, election observers have noted significant problems with voter lists, campaign activities, voter and candidate registration, media bias, the behavior of election commissions, ballot-box stuffing, voter intimidation, and tampering with election results. Moreover, empirical analyses revealed anomalous results suggesting fraud, especially in some of Ukraine's regions and in precincts designed to accommodate vulnerable voters. Manipulation and fraud seem to be a widespread phenomenon, generally benefiting dominant politicians and parties and penalizing opposition parties.

Although the collapse of communism created new conditions for political elites, some aspects of manipulation and fraud arguably continue Soviet-era practices. The use of administrative control over electoral commissions to remove opposition candidates from the ballot is analogous to the vetting process that permitted only loyal candidates to contest seats in the communist period. Biased administrative and media coverage are also consistent with Soviet practices, even when contestation was expanded under Mikhail Gorbachev. Despite these connections, many aspects of manipulation and fraud are unique to the post-Soviet period. Because opposition movements are more robust, and elections are scrutinized by domestic and international observers, political actors adopted new techniques to control election results.

While evidence of manipulation and fraud is present in most post-Soviet elections, the scale varies from country to country and election to election. Moreover, public response to evidence of fraud varies. In some cases, the reaction to stolen elections has been limited. In other cases, evidence of fraud has galvanized the political opposition and facilitated citizen mobilization. Public protests over falsified elections have led to regime change, notably in Georgia, Kyrgyzstan, and Ukraine, but more commonly have resulted in government repression. The next chapter investigates the connection between election fraud and mobilization, evaluating the conditions that have led to postelection demonstrations and even regime change.

CHAPTER 10

ELECTION FRAUD
AND PUBLIC PROTEST

As I observed the second round of Ukraine's 2004 presidential election, it became clear that this would not be an ordinary post-Soviet campaign featuring evidence of corruption, with the opposition crying foul but ultimately acceding to the authorities. After my return to Kyiv from observing the election in the south, I milled about the city's center with thousands of Ukrainian citizens who were occupying the main square to challenge results that provisionally declared the proregime candidate, Viktor Yanukovych, to be the winner. I spoke with many protesters, young and old, men and women, and asked them why they had taken to the streets. Not a single person invoked the name of the opposition candidate, Viktor Yushchenko, as their primary reason for protesting. Rather, they articulated the hope that protests would help create a "normal" country where the rule of law could prevail.

The commitment to occupy the streets can be risky; I heard several rumors that security forces were preparing to repress protesters and retake the city center. Yet, protesters continued their efforts day and night in the winter cold and ultimately succeeded: the second round was repeated with a more level playing field, and the candidate representing the corrupt status quo was defeated. First-hand experience with the Orange Revolution prompted the question driving this chapter: how do elections stimulate citizen protest?

During the Soviet era, the regime's opponents used many tools to challenge authority, including public protest. In the 1960s and 1970s, hundreds of protest events occurred, including pickets challenging dissident trials, gatherings in support of emigration for Soviet Jews, and labor strikes (Kowalewski and Schumaker 1981).[1] After Mikhail Gorbachev's elevation to the post of General Secretary, the number and intensity of protest events increased (Beissinger 1998). In 1986, Gorbachev's dismissal of the ethnically

Kazakh First Secretary of the Kazakh Republic's party organization and his replacement with an ethnic Slav prompted one of the largest protests to that point in Soviet history. While estimates vary, tens of thousands participated in the uprising, and hundreds were detained (Pannier 2006a). From 1985 to 1989, the USSR experienced at least forty-seven protests with over one hundred thousand participants, and eighty-four with over ten thousand participants. Most of these demonstrations were associated with demands for increased autonomy or independence and primarily took place in the South Caucasus and Baltic republics (Roeder 1991). Elections, however, did not inspire public demonstrations. They instead provided a new opportunity for citizens to oppose the status quo.

Since the USSR's collapse, however, thousands of disgruntled citizens have taken to the streets, challenging the outcomes of allegedly fraudulent elections. This chapter assesses when election protests occur and what characteristics have contributed to successful and unsuccessful outcomes.[2] The first section outlines the literature on contentious politics, focusing on how fraudulent elections may be used as a signal to mobilize citizens. The second section uses daily protest data from one hundred elections to evaluate how post-Soviet experiences comply with or diverge from explanations of protest behavior. The third section assesses successful and unsuccessful protest events more deeply, focusing on characteristics that led to the "Colored Revolutions" in Georgia, Ukraine, and Kyrgyzstan and failed electoral revolutions in Azerbaijan, Belarus, and Armenia.

THEORETICAL CONNECTIONS BETWEEN ELECTIONS AND PROTEST

Much of the existing scholarship on the connection between elections and citizen mobilization has assessed how political violence affects voter behavior during and after elections and how violence is used as a strategic tool. Scholars have noted that government often reduces repression prior to elections (Davenport 1997), while members of political minority groups, particularly losers, are more inclined to engage in protest (Anderson et al. 2005; Anderson and Mendes 2006). Postauthoritarian "founding" elections have been particularly scrutinized, with researchers associating protest likelihood with expectations about the results (Roefs, Klandermans, and Olivier 1998), or expectations about future violence stemming from election outcomes (Wantchekon 1999).

The "Colored Revolutions" in Georgia, Ukraine, and Kyrgyzstan in the mid-2000s inspired more direct investigations of the links between post-Soviet election fraud and protest. Researchers assessed the common features inspiring successful electoral revolutions (McFaul 2005; Bunce and Wolchik 2006a), causes of diffusion (Bunce and Wolchik 2006b), and the role of protesters (Tucker 2007) and elites (D'Anieri 2006a; Levitsky and Way 2006). In much of this research, elections are treated as special signals facilitating citizen mobilization.

As noted in Chapter 1, elections serve a legitimization function in democratic and authoritarian states. Although the ways that elections provide legitimacy differ across regime types, this connection makes them a potential catalyst for protest activity (Bunce and Wolchik 2006a). Moreover, unlike other forms of corruption,[3] election fraud victimizes a large group of citizens simultaneously and publicly and may affect how potential protesters weigh the costs of participation and the likelihood of success. When fraud is accompanied by deep antiregime sentiment, elections can become a signal for protest activities (Tucker 2007). But, citizens are notoriously difficult to mobilize (Lichbach 1995; 1996; Francisco 1996), and the period around elections is often peaceful.[4]

Elections and the Mobilization Process

The general literature on contentious politics draws upon several theoretical constructs to explain how and why citizens engage in protest activities. A subset of contentious politics scholarship suggests that individuals deprived of material needs, or other desired tangible or intangible goods, may accumulate grievances that are ultimately expressed through public protest.[5] This approach implies that higher levels of grievances should be accompanied by more intense protest activity.[6]

Other scholars argue that political culture plays a critical role in determining the likelihood of protest. Past protest activity may be a key indicator of the likelihood of future protests. Not only do past protests suggest cultural permission for these actions, but political activists accumulate material and symbolic resources that can be instrumental in staging future demonstrations. While the approach is not fully deterministic, it suggests that the frequency, size, or modes of past protest drive subsequent actions.[7]

Extensive scholarship has also applied collective action theory to mobilization. Protest is driven not solely by citizen grievances in this approach but rather by the ability of dissident leaders to overcome the impediments to collective action. Citizens may not join in public protest, even though successful protest may lead to a public good, because they have a strong incentive to "free ride" on others. By participating in protests, citizens put their own well-being at risk. If others are willing to incur the risk, individuals have strong motivation to reap the benefits without paying the costs. The task for opposition leaders is to reduce the perceived costs of protesting and enhance the perceived benefits. Even with reduced costs and increased incentives, the proportion of the population actively participating in protest activity does not rise above 5 percent (Lichbach 1995a).

Mark Lichbach (1995b; 1996) presents four groups of mobilization solutions (market, community, contract, and hierarchy) and argues that at least two must be present for collective action to occur. Market and community solutions are the most prevalent in post-Soviet protests.[8] Market solutions are largely unplanned and economic and aim to lower participation costs, increase benefits and resources, and facilitate adaptation to government repression. For example, strong organizational capacity and a supply chain kept protesters in Kyiv's center well fed and warm in the face of outdoor actions in the winter cold. These accommodations lowered the costs associated with demonstrating.

Community solutions provide a different source of motivation than pecuniary self-interest, drawing instead upon associations, such as ideological or ethnic ties, that induce cooperation among potential protesters. The connections can be informal or they can be driven by formal organizations such as political parties or interest groups. The tactics most regularly used in the community solution are leveraging common knowledge, overcoming mutual ignorance, and stressing common values. To continue the example from Ukraine, while protest was not solely connected with Ukrainian national identity and residence in the western part of the country, this community was instrumental in driving the protest movement. The "Orange" identity was replicated all over the country, with orange banners, ribbons, and window displays symbolically linking citizens together.

Several activities on the part of government can provide evidence that the electoral process has been compromised and signal dissident leaders to mobilize. The disqualification of opposition candidates, limits to opposition media access, lack of cooperation with domestic or international observer organizations, delays in the vote count, discrepancies between exit polls or parallel vote counts and official results, and media or observer reports of improper influence on voters suggest improprieties and can induce mobilization efforts. The most significant rallying event is the failure of opposition candidates to perform well in elections, especially when the opposition seems to enjoy widespread public support.

Strong, identifiable opposition leadership can translate circumstantial evidence of fraud into mobilizing signals. Domestic opposition can be bolstered by media coverage, even if much of the media is state controlled. International actors also play a role, especially when observers note fraudulent practices. As the stakes of the election outcomes are portrayed as high, and as citizens can be nationally engaged in protest activities, the likelihood of successful mobilization should increase.

Massive fraud reduces costs of protest because all citizens simultaneously experience the act of corruption, generating a perception that punishment in response to protest could be more diffuse (Tucker 2007). Moreover, perceptions that the regime is vulnerable or unwilling to coordinate massive repression against protesters can embolden opposition leaders and grassroots activists (Lichbach 1987). As citizens perceive the costs of protest to be low and the probability of success high, they are more likely to participate and potentially reach a "tipping point" that leads to massive mobilization (D'Anieri 2006).

Based on the conditions for mobilization noted above, protest events following elections should be most common in semiauthoritarian states and less common in the most democratic and most authoritarian societies. In the most democratic societies, election administration should be reasonably competent and unbiased, undermining the demand for protest actions. In the most authoritarian societies, elections are likely to be perceived as unfair, creating a motive for mobilization. However, authoritarian states limit avenues for the expression of dissenting ideas[9] and maintain high costs for public protest.

In semiauthoritarian societies, election fraud is more likely to be present and serve as a catalyst for protest, and the risk of harsh repression is likely to be perceived as lower than in fully authoritarian societies. Thus the motive for protest and opportunities to overcome collective action problems are more likely to be found in semiauthoritarian systems. The following section addresses this expectation and also assesses the connection between Soviet-era and post-Soviet protest activities.

ANALYSIS USING DAILY PROTEST DATA

Elections are mobilizing events. Parties organize rallies for partisan supporters, and government agencies and civil society generally work to get out the vote. This analysis focuses on demonstrations prompted by perceptions that elections are unfair, using data on daily protest activities gathered from wire service reports. The dataset includes protests about election fraud, fair elections, minority enfranchisement, or protests against canceled elections and excludes standard rallies for politicians unless the character of those events is decidedly focused on election quality.[10] After presenting data from one hundred elections across the region, this section presents a more detailed discussion of the factors characterizing successful and unsuccessful protests.

Regime Type and Protest Frequency

Table 10.1 categorizes elections by regime type and the size of the largest protest event for the elections under analysis.[11] Eighteen elections took place in countries deemed "free" by Freedom House, forty-two in countries labeled "partly free," and forty in countries labeled "not free." In fifty-nine elections, no protest activities were reported. In twenty-six elections the largest protest ranged from 1 to 4,999 participants, and in fifteen elections, the largest protest included over 5,000 participants.

Protest activities tended to be short term; in only a few cases were protests sustained over several days or weeks. Extended protests ended most often with government repression through violence, detentions, states of emergency, or opposition surrender. Fifteen elections provide examples of sustained protest:[12] Armenia (1996, February 2003, 2007, and 2008), Azerbaijan (2003 and 2005), Belarus (2004 and 2006), Georgia (2003 and January 2008),[13] Kyrgyzstan (2000, March 2005, and 2007), Russia (2007), and Ukraine (2004). In three cases, large-scale sustained protest led to regime change: Georgia (2003), Ukraine (2004), and Kyrgyzstan (2005).

Based on this initial assessment of the data, protest frequency seems to be greater in semiauthoritarian societies than in democracies; large-scale

Table 10.1   Comparison of Election Protests by Regime Type

	No Protest Activity	Protests 1>4,999	Protests >5,000	Total
Free	14 (78%)	4 (22%)	0 (0%)	18
Partly Free	22 (52%)	9 (21%)	11 (26%)	42
Not Free	23 (58%)	13 (33%)	4 (10%)	40
Total Elections[1]				100

Sources: See the appendix for a detailed list of sources.

Note: Table entries denote the size of the largest election protest.

mobilization seems to be more prevalent in semiauthoritarian societies than in autocracies. In partly free societies, 48 percent of all elections met some protest activity; 26 percent of elections inspired large protests. By contrast, only 22 percent of elections held in democracies were accompanied by election-related protests. Two of these protests, in Latvia (1993) and Ukraine (2006), attracted approximately three thousand to four thousand participants. But, the remaining events had at most a few hundred protesters. In authoritarian countries, elections were accompanied by some protest activity 43 percent of the time, but only 10 percent of the protests were large.

These data provide insights into some of the proposed explanations for protest initiation. If grievances were the primary factor driving election protest, one would expect protest frequency to be highest in countries with the most problematic electoral practices. Demand might be especially acute if those societies shared a border with neighbors enjoying free and fair elections. But, the number and size of protests tends to be smaller in authoritarian societies.

By contrast, some of the protest data comply with cultural or historical explanations. If prior protest activity reveals cultural conditioning or the development of material and technical capacity over time, public demonstrations should be more common in republics where populations engaged in active protests during the Soviet period. In the 1960s and 1970s, Lithuanians and Ukrainians were the most vocal national groups.[14] During the Gorbachev era, many protests took place in the Baltics, South Caucasus, and Ukraine, while protest activity in Central Asia and the remaining European republics was nearly absent (Roeder 1991).[15] In the post-Soviet period, major protests following questionable elections occurred in the South Caucasus and Ukraine, but also in states with limited or no Soviet-era experience with large protests: Belarus and Kyrgyzstan. Although some regions with histories of protest activity experienced election protests, many poor-quality elections in these regions were accompanied by limited or no protest action.

Successful Election Protests

While some scholars have credited the postcommunist region with a wave of electoral revolutions,[16] successful election protests are rare events. Michael McFaul (2005) has identified several characteristics that these revolutions have shared, notably an unpopular reigning chief executive with divided elite supporters, an organized opposition with the capacity to mobilize large groups of protesters, media access to express nonregime viewpoints, and clear evidence of fraud. In addition, successful protests seem to feature security services unwilling to preempt public meetings and harshly repress citizens,[17] technical capacity built partly by assistance from abroad,[18] support from other political institutions such as local government and the courts, and an acceptable exit opportunity for the outgoing leadership (D'Anieri 2006). This section discusses the presence or absence of these features in three notable successes, the "Colored Revolutions."

Georgia 2003

As the Republic of Georgia approached the 2003 parliamentary election, opposition leaders joined forces to challenge the incumbent president, Eduard Shevardnadze. Shevardnadze returned to Georgia in the early 1990s, forging a resolution to the civil war sparked by ousted President Zviad Gamsakhurdia's policies. Initially viewed as a potential savior, Shevardnadze became increasingly authoritarian in style after failed assassination attempts. Moreover, Shevardnadze was unable to solve Georgia's most serious challenges: separatist and irredentist threats, economic and energy problems, and widespread corruption.

In the year leading up to the 2003 parliamentary election, Shevardnadze's party, the Citizens Union of Georgia (CUG) performed poorly in local elections, revealing potential weakness in the upcoming election. CUG joined forces with other parties in an effort to boost its popularity (RFE/RL Caucasus Report 2003d). The opposition also united, coalescing into two main parties (RFE/RL Caucasus Report 2003b).

The potential for fraud loomed over election preparations, especially as problems with voter lists were discovered; entire apartment blocks were missing from the rolls while names of the dead remained on lists (RFE/RL Caucasus Report 2003d). The possibility of fraud failed to mobilize citizens. Instead, the signal inspiring opposition leaders to organize protest, and thousands of Georgian citizens to take to the streets, was a delayed vote count.

Although Shevardnadze stated that the election was the most free and transparent in Georgian history, evidence of fraud emerged, especially discrepancies between official results, exit polls, and parallel vote counts. While official results identified CUG as the winner, the opposition argued that the party led by Mikheil Saakashvili had been victorious (RFE/RL Caucasus Report 2003a). International organizations echoed the opposition's skepticism in the results, noting that the elections did not meet international standards (OSCE 2004b).

After the November 2 election, Mikheil Saakashvili, Zurab Zhvania, and Nino Burjanadze, the main opposition leaders, joined forces to protest the results. Saakashvili was more confrontational, demanding that his party be recognized as winner, while the others called for new elections. As opposition leaders announced the formation of a Resistance Front to mobilize the population, around three thousand citizens took to the streets in Tbilisi on November 4 to challenge the pace of ballot counting. By November 6, protests began to expand, with ten thousand protesters occupying Tbilisi's main square. Tbilisi remained the focal point of protests, and the size of protests stabilized in the subsequent days, with most protest events garnering around three thousand participants. After failed talks between government and opposition forces on November 9, Saakashvili called for mass protests. The following day, officials admitted that revotes would need to take place in 27 precincts due to improprieties. Despite the government's willingness to admit errors and repeat voting in some districts, protest events continued daily.

On November 22, Saakashvili and his supporters stormed the parliament building, disrupting the parliamentary session and chasing Shevardnadze from the premises. Shevardnadze prepared to declare a state of emergency as the opposition stated that it was taking control of government. On November 23, Shevardnadze resigned and the Rose Revolution triumphed (RFE/RL Caucasus Report 2003c). Over fifty thousand Georgians gathered on November 25 to celebrate the ouster of Shevardnadze's regime.

The Rose Revolution matches the characteristics outlined for successful electoral revolutions. Shevardnadze was unpopular, evidenced in part by his party's poor showing in local elections. While the opposition did not contest seats under a single banner, it united behind Saakashvili in the postelection protest, even though all of the leaders did not agree on tactics. The opposition proved to be capable of mobilizing supporters and received technical assistance in preparations for protest from Serbia's Otpor group (Beissinger 2007). Independent media outlets provided citizens with information about evidence of fraud, including observer critiques and the parallel vote count. The judiciary sided with the protesters' contention that the election was falsified, and security services proved unwilling or unable to harshly repress protesters.

Ukraine 2004

As the 2004 presidential election approached, opposition members warned of the potential for fraud benefiting progovernment candidates. These allegations were not new, as opposition leaders and Ukrainian nongovernmental organizations had accused the government of preelectoral manipulation and vote theft in earlier elections. Moreover, Ukrainian citizens had mobilized in past efforts to challenge President Leonid Kuchma's corrupt regime, most notably in the "Ukraine without Kuchma" movement that conducted public protests in spring 2000. The effort to oust Kuchma lost momentum but was instrumental in laying the groundwork for the opposition to once again take to the streets in 2004.

As the 2004 presidential election approached, Kuchma anointed a successor, Viktor Yanukovych, to contest for the office of president. Yanukovych was perceived by many in the Ukrainian opposition as a candidate who could win only through the use of massive electoral fraud. The opposition portrayed Yanukovych as an intellectually challenged, corrupt thug, but most media coverage favored him, as did the incumbent administration (Melnichuk 2004).

A student-led movement, Pora, based on and trained by successful movements in Serbia and Georgia, threatened massive protests if Yanukovych were to steal the election. Yushchenko's strength in public opinion polls, and the coverage of Yushchenko's poisoning by what was later determined to be dioxin, exposed Yanukovych's vulnerability. Russian President Vladimir Putin twice visited Ukraine to support Yanukovych's sinking campaign, but Russian interference further galvanized the opposition.

After the first round held on October 31, Pora quickly mobilized students into the streets of L'viv and Kyiv to protest alleged falsification in favor of Yanukovych. A few days later, on November 6, fifty thousand Yushchenko supporters gathered in Kyiv to denounce election fraud (Ukrainian News Agency 2004). The rally was not challenged by municipal or national authorities. As preparations for the second round moved forward, allegations of fraud increasingly circulated in the Ukrainian and international press.

After the second round of balloting on November 21 yielded a Yanukovych victory that domestic and international observers credited to massive fraud, tens of thousands of protesters across the country went to the streets. On November 22, more than twenty thousand protesters mobilized in Kyiv, L'viv, Ternopil, Vinnytsa, and Ivano-Frankivsk, and smaller protests occurred in other parts of the country. Over the next few days, the protests converged on Kyiv, where hundreds of thousands demonstrated and set up a permanent protest site with the approval of Kyiv's mayor. Negotiations between the opposition and government, buttressed by judicial decisions, eventually set a repeat second round for late December. Around five thousand protesters continued to occupy Independence Square around the clock until the results on December 26 showed that Yushchenko was the winner.

Over the course of the election campaign, all of the ingredients for successful postelection protest were put in place. The regime was widely seen as corrupt and vulnerable, and it egregiously violated principles of free and fair elections. While the progovernment media favored Yanukovych, the independent media provided evidence of fraud and live coverage of protest activities. The opposition had a clear leader in Viktor Yushchenko, and Yushchenko's cause engaged other prominent regime opponents. The willingness of competitors in the opposition to unite under one banner, accompanied by Russian involvement in favor of Yanukovych, showed that the stakes were high.

As protest continued, the unwillingness of the government to repress became clearer. Defections by security services and prominent Ukrainians, along with judicial decisions, tipped the balance in favor of the opposition. Kuchma helped broker a compromise settlement and was rumored to have received a guarantee of immunity from prosecution for misdeeds during his tenure.

Kyrgyzstan 2005

Protest in Kyrgyzstan began before the first round of the parliamentary election on February 27, 2005, when several opposition candidates were omitted from the ballot. The People's Movement of Kyrgyzstan and a youth organization, KelKel (modeled on Serbia's Otpor, Georgia's Kmara, and Ukraine's Pora), organized protests against election fraud (Saidazimova 2005b), and the most active protest was concentrated around major southern cities where opposition candidates had been refused registration (Saidazimova 2005a). A March 3 attack on an opposition leader and March 10 government repression in Naryn prompted an expansion of the protests (Marat 2006). Small-scale protests occurred daily in Kyrgyzstan's southern regions between the two rounds of the election.

Opposition candidates fared poorly in the second round held on March 13, and international observers declared that the election did not meet international standards. The opposition began to organize in the south, with a demonstration on March 15 attended by over ten thousand people (Saidazimova 2005c). After government troops repressed protesters on March 19 and 20, protests became increasingly violent.

While the capital city of Bishkek had been relatively calm, around a thousand people demonstrated on March 23 and were repressed by government security services. The next day, fifteen thousand to twenty thousand protesters took to the streets, calling for President Askar Akayev's ouster. They ultimately attacked the office of the presidential administration, looting government offices and businesses associated with President Akayev and his inner circle on March 25 (Marat 2006). A few days later, Akayev resigned, and the interim government began organizing new elections.

Kyrgyzstan's "Tulip Revolution" combined election fraud with growing frustration about economic inequalities and disparities in access to power between those in the south and those in the north. The failure to register southern opposition candidates, and the success of progovernment candidates, reinforced the unfairness of the election. Opposition protests throughout the election period shed light on improper electoral practices, with allegations of fraud supported by international organization reports. Protests that began in the south spread across the country, eventually capturing the capital city and leading to the ouster of the incumbent government. While security services attempted to disperse some protests, as the protests grew in the capital city the appetite for repression subsided. Kyrgyzstan's mobilization was also sustained—lasting for thirty days—longer than all events except Ukraine's Orange Revolution.

Failed Election Protests

The "Colored Revolutions" of 2003–2005 received significant international media attention and were credited with inspiring electoral revolts elsewhere in the world. However, protest movements rarely succeed in overturning questionable results and ousting corrupt rulers. More typically, the opposition is not well organized, it lacks access to the media, or protesters face the likelihood of harsh government repression. In addition, in the wake of post-Soviet electoral revolutions, government actors adapted to the successful tactics of protesters, creating conditions that have undermined subsequent successes. This section assesses how three large-scale movements failed to meet the conditions for successful protest.

Azerbaijan 2005

The temporal proximity of Azerbaijan's 2005 parliamentary election to the "Orange" and "Tulip" Revolutions raised expectations of international attention, as well as the potential for a showdown between the opposition and government. President Ilham Aliyev attempted to preempt opposition claims of improper procedures by issuing a decree in May 2005 that outlined new regulations for election administration, threatened officials with punishment for violation of the rules, and announced the use of exit polls. Aliyev suggested that a "post-Soviet mentality" among unprofessional officials at the lower levels of administration caused past problems; the decree was designed to alleviate those problems (Fuller 2005).

Months before Azerbaijan's 2005 parliamentary polls, opposition parties began public demonstrations demanding free and fair elections. In August, the police challenged opposition rallies in several cities (Abbasov and Ismailova 2005). Demonstrations continued, with the first large rally in early September involving approximately twenty thousand people. Additional protests in September and October were met with police repression. Members of the opposition, especially the leadership, were threatened, as officials claimed that the opposition was planning a coup (Interfax 2005b; Sultanova 2005a; 2005b; BBC 2005c). Two opposition figures in exile, Rasul Guliyev and Ayaz Mutalibov, registered to participate in the election, but Guliyev's attempt to return to Azerbaijan in mid-October failed. The dismissal of high-ranking officials in October raised questions about disputes among the ruling elite and the potential for discord to expand (Ismayilov 2005b).

The November 6 election produced a substantial victory for progovernment candidates. Exit polls diverged from official results, but only in a handful of constituencies (Ismayilova 2005). Due to disputed procedures and results, new elections were announced in ten districts. While the OSCE's report indicated that the election did not meet democratic standards, some opposition activists claimed that international reaction was not adequately negative.[19]

Authorities permitted some postelection protests but responded to unofficial demonstrations with harsh repression. A rally on November 26 was dispersed by police armed with truncheons and water cannons after opposition members attempted to create a more permanent protest site (Sultanova 2005b). While the opposition attempted to sustain protest, attendance dropped and street demonstrations ceased.

Azerbaijan's 2005 parliamentary election provided an early replication test for the "Colored Revolutions." President Aliyev's May decree responded to international concerns about the quality of election administration and could be interpreted as a symbolic gesture to undermine opposition criticisms of electoral processes. Further, the invalidation of some election results implied that government was concerned about conducting fair elections, and this action was praised by international actors. While Azerbaijan featured a potentially divided government elite, evidenced by the dismissal of high-ranking officials, any apparent divisions did not undermine the resolve of security services to repress protesters. Moreover, although the opposition gained some media access, prominent members of the opposition were able to register as candidates, and some protests were permitted, the major opposition groups failed to unite and were unable to mobilize citizens after harsh repression was used.

The conduct of the 2005 parliamentary election in Azerbaijan provides some evidence of government adaptation to the lessons of the "Colored Revolutions." By creating some avenues for citizens to air grievances but preventing the opposition from galvanizing adequate support to sustain large protests over time, government reduced the potential benefits of participation in public protest and sent signals that costs for unauthorized protest would be high.

Belarus 2006

While Belarus had experienced mass protests prior to the 2006 presidential election, none had directly followed elections (Agence France Presse 2006). However, as the election approached, the opposition gave signals of its intent to protest (Associated Press 2006a), and the government sent signals of its readiness to repress.[20] Beginning on election night, around ten thousand protesters occupied the main square of the capital, Minsk. The opposition held large demonstrations with approximately five thousand activists on March 20 and 21. By March 22, the participation level had dropped to around fifteen hundred participants, with a smaller contingent of protesters numbering in the hundreds occupying Minsk's central square overnight. Faced with extremely cold temperatures and government intimidation, the protesters declined in number day by day.

During the first few days following the election, protesters were not directly challenged on the square, although oppositionists were arrested elsewhere. After five days of protest, police led a crackdown, clearing the main square and arresting activists (RIA Novosti 2006). Following these detentions, two competing opposition leaders (Alyaksandr Milinkevich and Alyaksandr

Kozulin) staged demonstrations. Kozulin's protest march led to many arrests and injuries and exposed significant differences among opposition leaders, especially regarding tactics (Kashin, Kudashkina, and Goncharova 2006). Following these protests, regime opponents held a small demonstration on the eve of the presidential inauguration, but it was broken up by authorities.

While the election was condemned by international organizations for failing to meet democratic standards, opposition protesters were inhibited from sustaining their actions. The media was strictly controlled by the government, and the opposition had limited means to communicate with the public. The supply lines for Belarusan protesters were poor, and weather conditions were a significant impediment to street protests. Not only did the opposition fail to have a single charismatic leader, but it was divided on how to conduct protest activities.

Moreover, despite his reputation outside of Belarus, President Lukashenka enjoyed support among many Belarusans (Marples 2006). Security services were willing to crack down on regime opponents and signaled this willingness prior to the election. As in Azerbaijan, the successful "Colored Revolutions" affected regime tactics, undermining the opposition's momentum.

Armenia 2008

Armenia's 2008 presidential contest was contentious, pitting the prime minister, Serzh Sarkisian, against several opponents. The most notable challenger was the former president, Levon Ter-Petrossian. Sarkisian enjoyed the support of outgoing President Robert Kocharian, who was vacating the post due to term limits. Prior to the election, Ter-Petrossian alleged that fraud would be used to prevent his victory and that his supporters would take to the streets if the election were stolen. He rallied around fifty thousand supporters in the capital city three days before the election to express opposition to possible fraud.

On the day after the election, observers from the OSCE, European Parliament, and Council of Europe announced that the election was "mostly in line" with international standards, although they documented many problems with the conduct of the campaign as well as the casting, counting, and compiling process (OSCE 2008c).[21] When the preliminary results indicated that Sarkisian had secured 53 percent of the vote and a first-round victory, Ter-Petrossian's supporters took to the streets. For over a week after the election, more than twenty thousand citizens rallied for Ter-Petrossian, alleging that fraud elevated Sarkisian over the 50 percent mark and demanding a second round contest between the two candidates. Protesters set up camp on Yerevan's main square. Increasingly, Armenian authorities challenged the protesters, accusing some of plans for violence, and arresting organizers.

On March 1, after several days of sustained demonstrations, Armenia's government declared a state of emergency, dispersing protesters with tear gas and batons and detaining many regime opponents. News reports indicated that eight people were killed and 131 injured in the violence (Demourian

2008). After the state of emergency expired, some Ter-Petrossian supporters renewed protests, but these events failed to reach preclampdown levels in scope or intensity. To avoid violating the law and experiencing repression, the opposition loosely organized small "political walks" around the main square of Yerevan.

The failure of Armenia's opposition protesters to force a second-round contest between Sarkisian and Ter-Petrossian was due to several factors. While Ter-Petrossian was able to rally large numbers of protesters to the streets, he was not the leader of a unified opposition, and his demands were tainted by his own actions as president. Ter-Petrossian himself had cracked down on protesters alleging falsification when he was president in 1996 (Demourian 1996). Moreover, in the 2008 election, international organizations suggested that the election was reasonably fair; no evidence of large-scale falsification was presented. Government also showed its willingness to crack down on the opposition by harshly repressing protesters and declaring a state of emergency (Chupryna 2008). While protests continued after the state of emergency was lifted, the opposition's goal of ousting Sarkisian failed when he was confirmed as president.

CONCLUSION

Because elections influence who wields power, their results can provoke strong responses. When the process is viewed as unfair or the outcome as unfavorable, public reaction can be especially dramatic. The "Colored Revolutions" in Georgia, Ukraine, and Kyrgyzstan exemplify the dramatic quality of postelection protests, although the outcomes were unusual. While falsified elections provide a strong signal for regime opponents and potentially provide tools to overcome collective action problems, this chapter illustrated that the costs of protest are often high and the probability of success is often low.

The assessment of election protest in this chapter favored an explanation treating the mobilization process as a collective action problem. Simply depriving citizens of free and fair elections does not generate protest; elections in authoritarian states produced limited protest activity. Past protest experience bore some relationship with more recent activity, as many countries with a Soviet-era history of demonstrations also witnessed significant post-Soviet protest events. But, past protest experience does not fully explain why protests occur.

Protest activities viewed through the lens of collective action provide insight into why mobilization often fails. Indeed, the underlying assumption of this approach is that mobilizing citizens is difficult. Citizens are more likely to demonstrate when they have confidence that participation will be free of punishment and success is possible. Several features reduce the costs of participation and increase the likelihood of success: the presence of an unpopular executive, divisions among the elite that are manifested by ancillary institutional support for the opposition, security services unwilling to harshly repress citizens, an organized opposition that has accessed international technical support and is capable of mobilizing citizens, media coverage, and clear evidence of fraud. The absence of these features, along with regime adaptation to protest tactics, undermined opposition efforts to overturn compromised elections.

CONCLUSION

The evolution of elections and democracy in post-Soviet Eastern Europe and Eurasia features remarkable progress and stunning reversals. At the end of 1991, the Soviet Union's collapse introduced fifteen newly independent states with little experience in managing competitive politics and elections. While Estonia and Latvia initially stumbled in efforts to address integration of the Russophone population, all three Baltic states moved steadily toward free elections and democratic decision making. Their successes were capped off by accession to the European Union less than fifteen years after the USSR's demise.

Other post-Soviet countries developed the foundations for democratic politics, although their ultimate fates have yet to be determined. Three countries—Georgia, Moldova, and Ukraine—have demonstrated potential for free electoral practices and democratic governance. But, all three countries are situated at critical points in their transitions where they could move toward democracy or authoritarianism.

After the Rose Revolution in 2003, Georgia seemed to be a promising case for democratic development. But, the president's increasingly undemocratic behavior, exemplified by the closure of an opposition television station, harsh repression of antigovernment protesters, and elections that continued to evidence manipulation and fraud, suggest that the Rose Revolution's potential to initiate progress toward democracy dissipated. The threat to Georgian democracy was further exacerbated by Russia's August 2008 invasion of Georgian territory. While the Russian government claimed that its intervention was intended to protect the population of South Ossetia, it revealed other motives by asserting that Georgia's president should be replaced (Kramer, Barnard, and Chivers 2008).

Moldova's multiparty elections have featured genuine competition, but the quality of recent elections has deteriorated. Government efforts to enhance the country's appeal for admission to the European Union have not been enthusiastically welcomed in the West. Moldova's deep poverty, corruption, and tense relations with Russia create a potentially lethal mix undermining future democratic developments.

After more than a decade of corrupt semiauthoritarian politics, Ukraine's 2004 Orange Revolution created an opportunity for increased pluralism and genuine democracy. Discord among political elites, as well as the divided nature of Ukraine's politics, has generated an unstable political environment. But, Ukraine's advances are also clear: following the falsified presidential election that mobilized Ukrainian citizens to take to the streets, Ukraine has conducted two free and fair parliamentary elections. Competing forces battle for control, but political life is more transparent and open than under the previous regime. But like Georgia and Moldova, Ukraine's movement toward democracy is not guaranteed, and a return to more authoritarian practices is not out of the question.

While some post-Soviet states never developed even rudimentary democratic institutions (Tajikistan, Turkmenistan, and Uzbekistan), the region more typically features interrupted or failed transitions. Armenia and Azerbaijan showed limited movement toward democracy, but their ongoing fight over Karabakh, repression of the political opposition, and poor quality elections place these countries among the region's many semiauthoritarian regimes. Two Central Asian states also evidenced elements of democracy that failed to take hold. Kyrgyzstan featured a relatively free press and rudimentary pluralism in the early 1990s, but creeping authoritarianism and deep corruption chipped away at this progress. Similarly, Kazakhstan showed some signs of contested policy making in the early post-Soviet period, but the political opposition was quickly restricted. Belarus' initial flirtation with pluralism was also short-lived. After the 1994 presidential election and subsequent referendums, Belarus descended into dictatorship.

Russia's democratic reversal carries the most significant implications for the region's future development. While Russia's politics in the 1990s were not fully democratic—President Yeltsin's erratic rule, political corruption, oligarchic influences, and the war in Chechnya undermined Russia's nascent democracy—Russia featured a free press, competitive multiparty politics, and improving electoral practices. After Vladimir Putin's elevation to the presidency, his policies undermined the foundation of competitive politics that had grown in the 1990s. While Putin's efforts to centralize decision making also addressed many ills of the Yeltsin era and introduced greater political stability, they curtailed opportunities for Russian citizens to influence political life.

Russia's attitudes toward its neighbors' political agendas will significantly influence the future of elections and democracy in the post-Soviet region. The Putin administration's approach to its neighbors particularly underscores Russia's antipathy toward the accession of post-Soviet states to European institutions, and democratic electoral practices are a prerequisite for European integration. Personnel movement in the executive branch, with Dmitriy Medvedev's selection as president and Putin's move to the prime minister's seat, do not augur change in this orientation. Russia's August 2008 invasion of Georgia may herald an even more aggressive policy toward countries that defy its preferences, imperiling prospects for democratic advances in the region.

The remainder of this final chapter revisits the issues addressed in the book: election rule design, citizen decision making, political party activities, impediments to free elections, and the influences underlying the conduct of elections. It summarizes each chapter's findings, discusses unanswered questions, and outlines an agenda for future research.

INHERITANCE VERSUS AGENCY

The first chapter noted that an ongoing controversy in the study of the region relates to the effect of the communist legacy on the behavior of citizens and political elites. While particularly virulent in the 1990s, the debate about whether individuals are anchored to different values and norms imposed by decades of communist rule (and perhaps centuries of collectivism) or behave as self-interested actors is directly relevant for the study of elections.[1]

Cultural explanations of political processes in the former Soviet region sometimes refer to historic governance patterns as predictive; notably a preference for strong rulers. Post-Soviet variation is consequently explained by years of Soviet experience:[2] the Baltic states, Moldova, and parts of Ukraine were not subjected to as many years of Soviet rule as their counterparts, and their more democratic post-Soviet experience may be explained by this political history. Yet, after brief post-WWI experiments with democracy, authoritarian regimes took hold in the Baltics prior to Soviet capture. Similarly, Moldova and western Ukraine were controlled by regimes that became authoritarian in the interwar period. While the historical legacy includes brief periods of semidemocratic governance, these regions did not have long-standing democratic traditions interrupted by Soviet occupation.[3]

These societies also represent varied cultural traditions; the titular nationalities of the Baltic states and Moldova are not Slavic, but Ukrainians are. The dominant religion is not Orthodoxy in the Baltics, but it is in Moldova and Ukraine. While none of the traditionally Islamic societies in the post-Soviet region has become democratic, citizens of these states are not immune to democratic impulses, evidenced by public protest against corrupt rulers, efforts to create opposition parties, and attempts to develop a free media. Traditions influence individual attitudes and behavior, but they are not deterministic.

History and cultural traditions do not determine political outcomes, but elements of the Soviet institutional and behavioral legacy affect post-Soviet politics. As noted in Chapter 1, the Soviet experience could manifest itself in the persistence of formal institutional rules or informal norms. Indeed, analyses in several chapters found aspects of behavior that could be attributed to inherited conditions, values, and habits. Many post-Soviet states shared the following characteristics:

- Soviet-era institutional rules persisted, at least in the early postcommunist period.
- Soviet-era elites retained high-level posts.
- Leaders use elections as a tool for citizen mobilization and elite recruitment, even when the process is undemocratic.

- Parties-of-power dominate the state apparatus, and influence nomination procedures and election outcomes through the use of administrative resources.
- Voters socialized earlier in the Soviet period tend to be more likely to vote and support communist successor parties.
- Regimes persistently invoke the rhetoric of democracy, amid malfunctioning institutions and false pluralism, to justify authoritarian policies.

Despite these connections to the symbols and behaviors of the Soviet era, political actors also defy the conventions of the communist period:

- Elites pay close attention to election rules as vehicles to generate preferred political outcomes, and they regularly modify them. This behavior suggests that the rules matter, even in nondemocratic societies.
- Voters do not monolithically come to the polls out of habituation, but abstain in large numbers. Indeed, voters show sophistication in their decisions, demonstrating a tendency to come to the polls when they are dissatisfied and when the stakes of the votes are higher.
- Despite the inchoate nature of the party systems, voters also show an ability to distinguish their preferences among major parties.
- Politicians have developed new ways to falsify elections, adopting techniques that were not available or necessary in most of the Soviet era.
- Citizens respond to falsification but are most likely to mobilize when the costs of protest are reduced and the likelihood of success is perceived as higher. Large-scale mobilization is not limited to societies that showed the highest levels of activism in the Soviet period.

The Soviet Union's formal institutional legacy has been far less robust than informal norms, a point illustrated throughout the book.

FINDINGS

The book began with definitions of terminology central to the analysis, covering the meaning of elections in democratic and nondemocratic societies. The first chapter also outlined competing approaches to explaining political phenomena in the region, focusing on the role of Soviet institutional and behavioral legacies, and the competing paradigm of rational decision making.

Chapter 2 outlined the foundation of the Soviet legacy by describing electoral practices in three distinct periods of Soviet rule. The first era, during Bolshevik consolidation, featured decentralized procedures and restricted suffrage. The second era, the longest and arguably quintessential period, was characterized by centralized rules, an emphasis on full citizen participation, and no voter choice at the polls. The third era, coinciding with the reform period prior to Soviet collapse, provided limited choice through expanded contestation. While Soviet elections were never free and fair, they served as a mechanism for citizen mobilization and elite recruitment.

The analysis of election rule design and reform in Chapter 3 explored the robustness of Soviet institutional forms. In initial elections, many Soviet-era rules were retained. But, they have not persisted and instead have been replaced by a wide array of election systems. Election rules have been dynamic, and political actors have regularly modified all aspects of them. The case studies of election rule reform in Russia and Ukraine identified some elements common in successful and unsuccessful redesign efforts. Political actors, especially those occupying veto points, perceived advantages that would accrue by changing the rules. In the case of Russia, the president and his team ultimately preferred a form of proportional representation that would facilitate centralization of power. Coupled with a 7 percent threshold and restrictive rules for party registration, Russia's new election rules allowed President Putin's preferred party to consolidate its dominant position, while local politicians, independents, and the foundering rightist opposition were squeezed out of competition. Similar rules prevailed in Ukraine when President Kuchma packaged them as part of broader institutional reform. His position on proportional representation changed when he could use it as a negotiating tool to gain support on constitutional changes. His short-term aims were thwarted when election rule changes were approved but constitutional revisions failed. In both cases, elites understood the power of election rules to shape political competition and used extraordinary events to muster support and propel election system change.

Chapter 4 investigated the consequences of elections, assessing how institutional rules and social cleavages impact the number of political parties. The analysis accounted for the conditions of postcommunism in two ways. First, a cross-national analysis of elections in democratic societies over several decades assessed how the history of communist rule affected party systems. Institutional rules showed a consistent effect on party systems, while social cleavages and the postcommunist legacy demonstrated less robust effects. Second, an analysis restricted to post-Soviet countries evaluated the effects of institutions, cleavages, and regime type. Regime type played the dominant role in this analysis, encompassing institutional effects. An in-depth discussion of the effects of majoritarian, proportional, and mixed rules across post-Soviet space supplemented the cross-national analysis. This discussion illustrated how the rules produced expected effects in some cases, but in other cases regimes distorted the effective number of parties by artificially inflating or constricting the number of parties. Institutional rules indeed induce expected behaviors, but their effects are substantially mitigated by regime interference in the political process.

Chapter 5 explored why post-Soviet citizens vote. After the first era of elections ended in the 1920s, the Soviet leadership focused on enhancing turnout to affirm its democratic credentials, manage citizen mobilization, and help detect potential malcontents. In the USSR's waning years, the obligatory essence of elections evaporated, but turnout remained high. With the advent of fifteen newly independent states, turnout varied from the absurd heights of Turkmenistan's reportedly near-perfect participation to less than a quarter of citizens in Latvia's 2007 referendum. Based on scholarship explaining turnout, the analysis addressed how citizen attitudes about economic conditions and the relative importance of the vote affected the likelihood of participation. The initial investigation assessed individual-level attitudes, using survey data from the first decade of postcommunism. This analysis showed that attitudes about economic conditions and democracy, age, and education level particularly influenced the decision to vote, although these variables exhibited cross-national and temporal variation in their effects. The next investigation assessed aggregate-level turnout data and found that elections for the most important institutions tended to induce more citizens to cast ballots. This effect was robust even when authoritarian systems were removed from the analysis. Some regimes attempt to manipulate election turnout as did Soviet elites, but citizens often make decisions about participation that reflect their perceptions of well-being and the relevance of the vote at hand.

Chapter 6 turned to a deeper exploration of political parties. The chapter assessed elite supply of parties by comparing the relative levels of party system volatility across many countries and illustrated how political competition is stabilizing. It included definitions of party families operating across the region and distinguished these groups by their functions in the party system. The chapter turned to citizen demand for parties, analyzing support for political parties using survey data. While the data were confined to the early postcommunist period, they illustrated the emerging connections between citizens and parties based on attitudes about the economy and democracy, as well as demographic features. Citizens socialized earlier in the Soviet period showed persistent support for parties of the left, while opposition parties drew support from more educated populations. Faced with many, sometimes ambiguous, choices, post-Soviet citizens often displayed coherent decision making in party support.

Referendums have proved to be a popular method to make policy and test public support, and Chapter 7 investigated how elites have used these votes. The Soviet Union's leadership did not call referendums until the very end of the communist period. In the post-Soviet era, dozens of referendums have been held to approve or change constitutions, extend presidential rule, gauge citizen support for accession to international organizations, and ask various policy questions. Most referendums have been designed by the elites in power, and the leadership has often controlled the voting process to ensure success. Nevertheless, some votes have been genuinely democratic and have afforded citizens the opportunity to directly influence policy.

Chapter 8 outlined the mechanisms for administering and overseeing election processes. The first section compared election commission guidelines across the region and illustrated how administrators interfere in the election process in many post-Soviet states. The second section addressed the role of the courts in adjudicating election disputes, outlining how the judiciary has made important rulings on election rule design, ballot access, campaign violations, election commission actions, and allegations of fraud. The final section discussed the role of domestic and international observer missions as essential actors in assessing the quality of elections. The chapter served as a bridge to the final two analytical chapters, which more directly explored election quality and its consequences.

The quality of elections has received increased scrutiny in the political science literature recently, and Chapter 9 demonstrated some approaches to assessing the impact of manipulation and fraud. Because most Soviet-era elections offered no competition on the ballot, many forms of fraud were not needed to ensure victory by regime supporters. In the post-Soviet era of increased competition, politicians developed new techniques to legally and illegally increase the likelihood of victory. After reviewing the tools available to the perpetrators of fraud, the analytical section of the chapter sought to identify results most plausibly explained by fraud. The analysis used a technique derived from Benford's Law and showed that anomalous results were present in some areas where fraud had been alleged by international observers. A subsequent investigation of votes in special precincts extended this analysis and found evidence suggesting falsification. The chapter's analysis implies that scholars must use caution when assessing election results in the region given the possibility that fraud may distort reported vote outcomes.

Evidence of fraud in post-Soviet elections has inspired citizens to take action. Chapter 10 addressed the dynamics of citizen mobilization in response to allegations of falsification. After outlining explanations of protest based on relative deprivation, political culture, and collective action, the chapter presented daily protest data from election periods across the post-Soviet region. Democratic societies produce limited demand for protest, as the election processes are generally of high quality; authoritarian societies may be characterized by unfair elections but also feature high costs of protest. Countries between democracy and authoritarianism are the most likely to produce poor quality elections and perceptions of acceptable costs for protesting. The chapter explored election protests, noting that the presence of unpopular executives, divided elites, an organized opposition, media access, ambivalent security services, support from competing institutional bodies, and clear evidence of fraud contributed to the success of the "Colored Revolutions." The absence of many of these features characterized prominent failures. The experience of election protest in the region follows the basic contours of the argument based on collective action, although some societies with histories of Soviet-era protest also witnessed large-scale citizen mobilization.

FUTURE RESEARCH

One goal of this book was to comprehensively address the major issues of electoral politics across the post-Soviet region. Inevitably, my analysis omitted many important issues due to data availability and space constraints. These absent issues constitute a research agenda for future investigation.

While some scholars have explored regional elections (Moraski 2003; 2006; Golosov 2003a; 2003b), this book focused on national elections. Local and municipal contests are rich environments to test propositions generally evaluated at the national level, however, and these elections and referendums have significantly impacted political life. For example, gubernatorial elections in Russia, prior to their cancellation under President Putin, helped local elites to create fiefdoms and pursue independent policies. As noted in Chapter 6, local elections helped to briefly unify Moldova's democratic opposition. Votes in contested regions such as Abkhazia and South Ossetia (Georgia), Crimea (Ukraine), and Transnistria (Moldova), have played a prominent role defining political competition with the center. Moreover, local-level politics may interact with national politics, and measuring the scope and substance of this interaction is an important area for research.

While Chapter 1 noted that campaign regulations constitute an important category of election rules, later chapters did not deeply explore them. Yet, determining how candidates and parties attempt to mobilize voters, and what approaches are successful, is an open question. The media has covered the influence of imported foreign campaign advisers and campaign tactics, especially during the 1996 Russian presidential election, but no systematic analysis has addressed the effectiveness of various campaign tactics on the behavior of post-Soviet voters.

Similarly, the media has been a subject of analysis,[4] but its role in campaigns has been under-studied. The media is a major player in elections, as the amount and tenor of coverage can influence outcomes. The impact of television, radio, print, and Internet media on election campaigns and outcomes is an open area of inquiry.

Scholars have extensively explored parties and party systems in the post-Soviet region but have not investigated the growth and development of party organizations. Indeed, organizations may be the key to understanding parties (Schlesinger 1991), and they are also connected to party system institutionalization (Mainwaring and Scully 1995). Post-Soviet parties are generally treated as abstract objects; informed research on how organizational capacity affects party behavior would fill gaps in this literature.

While the election literature has investigated how some political institutions interact—notably assessing coattail effects and how the proximity of elections for different offices affect outcomes—other important institutional interactions have been neglected. As noted in Chapter 8, judicial and administrative bodies can substantially influence the competitive environment, determining who may vote and contest seats as well as adjudicating disputes about the propriety of the vote. A more thorough investigation of courts and election commissions will fill gaps in our understanding of how electoral institutions structure competition.

The effect of technology on voting is a burgeoning research area,[5] and changes to balloting methods are infiltrating the region. Estonia was an early adopter of new technologies; after a pilot project in the 2005 local elections, e-voting was successfully incorporated into the 2007 national parliamentary election. Estonian politicians are discussing further innovations, exploring the use of mobile phones for voting. Other countries have begun implementing electronic balloting (e.g., Kazakhstan), and still others have incorporated computerized systems to transmit data in the aggregation process (e.g., Ukraine). While most post-Soviet states still use paper ballots and hand counts, the continued adoption of advanced technologies will generate new questions about the election process.

This book applied many of the major questions in the electoral studies literature to the post-Soviet states, but countless opportunities for further study and refinement exist. While the postcommunist region was marginalized for many years, incorporating the states of the former USSR into broader comparative analysis provides additional insights into our growing knowledge about election rules and their consequences.

CONCLUSION

The disintegration of the Soviet Union and its empire at the beginning of the twentieth century's final decade heralded an unprecedented shift in world politics. In the early 1990s, liberal democracy seemed to have triumphed, although developments in many corners of the globe foreshadowed a more complicated future. Democratic regimes successfully consolidated in the Baltic states and made faltering progress in Georgia, Moldova, and Ukraine. The failure of democratic transition and consolidation in many former Soviet territories generated seemingly stable semiauthoritarian—or fully authoritarian—regimes. The most consistently authoritarian systems, Belarus, Tajikistan, Turkmenistan, and Uzbekistan, made little progress in developing open, pluralistic politics. The remaining states of the former USSR—Armenia, Azerbaijan, Kazakhstan, Kyrgyzstan, and Russia—illustrated best the ebbs and flows of democratization, with authoritarianism punctuated by elements of more democratic politics. Some of these "grey area" countries were generally more authoritarian in practice, while others showed signs, albeit briefly, of the potential for democratic transition and consolidation to triumph.

All of the former Soviet states—democratic and authoritarian—have held elections. The quality of elections, and their purpose in political life, has varied cross-nationally and temporally. In more democratic societies, elections serve as a vehicle for politicians to vie for positions of power and for citizens to hold officials accountable. In less democratic societies, elections facilitate elite recruitment, mobilize populations to demonstrate regime support, and provide the illusion of democracy. In all cases, elections matter. But, the goals and objectives of staging public votes vary. Political elites recognize the power of elections as instruments of functioning or ersatz democracy, and for this reason the status of elections and democracy in the region is likely to remain contested and ambiguous.

APPENDIX

CHAPTER 1 NOTES

Chapter 1 discussed assessments from elections missions dispatched by the Organization for Security and Cooperation in Europe (OSCE). The fifty-four cases included thirty-three parliamentary elections (Armenia 1999, 2003, 2007; Azerbaijan 1995, 2000, 2005; Belarus 2000, 2003; Estonia 1999; Georgia 1999, 2003, 2004; Kazakhstan 1999, 2004, 2007; Kyrgyzstan 2000, 2005, 2007; Latvia 1998, 2002, 2006; Lithuania 1996; Moldova 1998, 2001, 2005; Russia 1999, 2003; Tajikistan 2000, 2005; Ukraine 1998, 2002, 2006, 2007) and twenty-one presidential elections (Armenia 1996, 1998, 2003, 2008; Azerbaijan 1998, 2003; Belarus 2001; Georgia 2000, 2004, 2008; Kazakhstan 2000, 2005; Kyrgyzstan 2000, 2005; Moldova 1996; Russia 1996, 2000, 2004; Tajikistan 2006; Ukraine 1999, 2004).

CHAPTER 4 NOTES

Chapter 4 assessed determinants of the effective number of parties using a cross-national time-series dataset developed by Matt Golder (2005) and an expanded subset of the data focusing on the post-Soviet states. Because full election results are unavailable for many countries, the dependent variable was the effective number of legislative parties rather than the effective number of electoral parties. The latter is arguably more desirable because it focuses on political parties that contest seats. However, the effective number of legislative parties, which incorporates institutional filtering into the calculation, is a suitable proxy, and the measures are highly correlated (the correlation coefficient is 0.82).

Models 1a and 1b were evaluated with Ordinary Least Squares, including only the most recent election. Models 2a and 2b used panel-corrected standard errors and included all elections.[1] However, as recent research notes, the accuracy of panel-corrected standard errors can be affected by the number of elections in each country under analysis (Clark and Golder 2006). To account for this challenge, the data were reanalyzed using robust standard errors, clustering by country. The results of this analysis produced substantively similar results for Model 2a. In the analysis of Model 2b, only majoritarian rules were statistically significant. The coefficient for concurrent elections was significant at the 0.10 level (0.06), and the coefficients for the natural log of assembly size and effective number of ethnic groups were just beyond the 0.10 level. The parameter estimate for postcommunist states was not statistically significant. These results provide additional support to the argument that institutional rules affect the party system and suggest that contextual features may be weaker determinants of the effective number of parties, as noted in the chapter.

The analysis included the following elections: Armenia (1995, 1999, 2003, 2007), Azerbaijan (1995, 2000, 2005), Belarus (1995, 2000, 2004), Estonia (1992, 1995, 1999, 2003, 2007), Georgia (1992, 1995, 2003), Kazakhstan (1994, 1995, 1999, 2004, 2007), Kyrgyzstan (1995, 2000), Latvia (1993, 1995, 1998, 2002, 2006), Lithuania (1992, 1996, 2000, 2004), Moldova (1994, 1998, 2001, 2005), Russia (1993, 1995, 1999, 2003), Tajikistan (1995, 2000, 2005), Ukraine (1994, 1998, 2002, 2006), and Uzbekistan (2004). I based the values of the effective number of parties on my own calculations.[2]

Freedom House scores distinguished each country's democratic qualities at the time of every election. To check the consistency of Freedom House scores, I also conducted an analysis using Polity IV scores. Because Polity IV scores do not cover elections after 2004, nine cases were excluded. In the replication of Model 4, the results are substantively similar: higher levels of democracy yield more parties. In the replication of Model 6, however, majoritarian systems are significant and negative in sign at the 0.10 level (0.059), and the level of democracy is not significant. This result could be associated with the Polity dataset's different emphasis (Gleditsch and Ward 1997), the effect of missing cases, or the more robust effect of institutional features.

CHAPTER 5 NOTES

Vote Intention Data

The analysis of voter intentions to participate in elections included data from two publicly available datasets: the Central and Eastern Eurobarometer (CEEURO) and the Comparative Study of Electoral Systems (CSES). CEEURO was a series of nationally representative surveys conducted in postcommunist states from 1990 to 1997. The investigators included respondents above age fifteen in the dataset; respondents who were not of voting age were excluded from the analysis. The trend dataset, from which the variables were extracted, included questions with similar wording posed over several countries and time periods.

Two questions identified respondents who planned to participate in elections. In the 1992 version of the survey, respondents were asked directly if they planned to participate in the next election by voting.[3] In most versions of the survey, respondents were asked to identify their "vote intention" or their "vote intention inclined to."[4] This question includes responses of those who did not plan to vote or who planned to spoil their ballot. The latter group of respondents was included among likely nonparticipants.

Responses to questions covering individual financial expectations served as proxies for prospective and retrospective economic attitudes.[5] The CEEURO survey asked respondents about their satisfaction with the development of democracy[6] across time and countries. Questions about the frequency of political discussions and left-right placement were posed only in 1992; they were included in some versions of the analysis.[7] Demographic variables such as age, gender, and education were included in all countries and years. Demographic factors were coded consistently with the original dataset: age as a continuous variable, gender as dichotomous, and education as ordinal.

CSES provides individual- and district-level data on elections held from 2001 to 2006 and includes many post-Soviet states. The questions were more consistently posed in the CSES project, but nevertheless the survey features some cross-national and temporal inconsistencies.

Responses to questions A2028 "did respondent cast a ballot" and B3004_1 "did respondent cast ballot—current election" served as the dependent variable. Answers to question A3023 "economy change" were a proxy for prospective economic evaluations in Module 1 countries. The question was not available in Module 2. Attitudes about democracy were derived from responses to question A3001 "satisfaction with democratic process" and B3012 "satisfaction with democracy." As in the CEEURO data, education was coded as an ordinal variable, although it had more categories in the CSES dataset.

The dependent variable was the likelihood of abstention (intent to abstain was coded as a one; intent to vote was coded as a zero). The intent to abstain included all respondents who indicated that they did not vote and those who said they voted but did not indicate a vote choice.[8] The coding yielded the following interpretations for the coefficients in the multivariate analysis (the coefficient sign is in parentheses):

- Prospective Economic Assessments (+) = As economic assessments worsen, the likelihood of nonvoting increases.
- Retrospective Economic Assessments (+) = As economic assessments worsen, the likelihood of nonvoting increases.
- Satisfaction with Democracy (+) = As dissatisfaction with democracy increases, the likelihood of nonvoting increases.
- Age (+) = At higher ages, the likelihood of nonvoting increases.[9]
- Gender (+) = Women are more likely to abstain.
- Education (+) = As level of education increases, the likelihood of nonvoting increases.
- Urban Residence (+) = City dwellers are more likely to abstain. Urban residence included citizens residing in cities or suburbs.

Data from election years were assessed using probit (Armenia 1995, 1996; Belarus 1994, 1995, 2001; Estonia 1992, 1995; Georgia 1992, 1995; Kazakhstan 1994, 1995; Kyrgyzstan 2005; Latvia 1995; Lithuania 1992, 1997, 1997; Russia 1995, 1996, 1999, 2000, 2004; Ukraine 1994, 1998).

Turnout Data

The nongovernmental organization International IDEA (http://www.idea .int) provides a detailed database on turnout, but it does not cover all post-Soviet votes. Data from central electoral commissions across the region, research organizations (Eurasianet, Freedom House, University of Essex), and media sources (Agence France Presse, Associated Press, Baltic News Service, BBC, Interfax, Komsomolskaya Pravda, Radio Free Europe/Radio Liberty, Reuters, and TASS) supplemented IDEA's database. In some cases, turnout data were reported inconsistently, although the deviation from source to source was typically small. The differences may be attributable to reports using early returns rather than the final results, variation in how turnout was calculated,[10] or reporting errors. Because of population and economic data availability, the analysis includes elections held through the end of 2006.

All models were assessed using panel corrected standard errors. But, as noted in the discussion of Chapter 4's data analysis, panel corrected standard errors are sensitive to the number of cases in each country. A replication of the analysis using robust standard errors and clustering by country produced statistically and substantively similar results. While the results were generally robust, some discrepancies emerged. In Model 3a, coefficients for referendum voting, simultaneous elections, and GDP were not statistically significant. In Model 4b, coefficients for simultaneous elections, effective number of parties, and ethnicity were significant. Additional replications replacing Freedom House scores with Polity IV data, including a measure of presidential strength, and replacing IDEA data with turnout figures reported from alternate sources, generated statistically and substantively similar results.

CHAPTER 6 NOTES

Volatility and Replacement Scores

Similar to the turnout analysis, data about election performance was constructed from several sources, including: central electoral commissions across the region, research organizations (Eurasianet, Freedom House, University of Essex), and media sources (Agence France Presse, Associated Press, Baltic News Service, BBC, Interfax, Komsomolskaya Pravda, Radio Free Europe/ Radio Liberty, Reuters, and TASS).

The assessment of party system stability relied upon two measures: volatility and replacement. The former measure is based on the work of Mogens Pedersen (1979) for whom the index is named. The data used in Chapter 6 followed Roberts and Wibbels' explanation for calculating the index (1999;

576 footnote 2). Instead of including only continuous parties in the calculation (i.e., those that contested elections at times t and $t + 1$), these calculations included all parties contesting election t and election $t + 1$.

While widespread in the electoral studies literature, volatility scores have some shortcomings (Birch 2001). Most notably, changes in aggregate performance may not reflect underlying changes to the electorate's beliefs but rather a change in the choice set or the composition of the citizens who cast ballots. Sarah Birch (2001) proposed an additional index—replacement scores—that assesses the votes accumulated by new entrants in each election.

To calculate both volatility and replacement scores, researchers require complete voting results and information about party system development. Incomplete and inconsistent information is a common problem in the post-Soviet states, however. Reconstruction the complicated "family trees" of many parties presented significant challenges. Determining what is a "continuous party" from one election to another is often difficult; the names change regularly, but personnel resources move from one organization to the next. On one hand, counting new labels as new parties is sensible, as voters may not be fully aware of behind-the-scenes machinations. But, this approach risks coding as "new" parties that have changed labels with the full knowledge of the electorate.

The chapter's coding draws upon several sources to best ascertain which parties were reasonably considered to be successors of earlier political groups. But, given the lack of adequate information about all of these organizations, volatility and replacement scores may be overstated. Using alternate coding, in which party organization with different names were treated as new entrants, replacement values were generally higher than the results reported in the chapter.

The electoral rules also created coding challenges. Ukraine's move from a majority-runoff to a mixed, and finally to a pure proportional representation (PR) system is illustrative. In calculating scores for the 1994 and 1998 elections, when Ukraine abandoned majority-runoff and adopted a mixed system, which tiers are comparable? The majoritarian system in 1994 did not offer voters the choice of all parties in each district, as did 1998's PR tier of the mixed system. Because of this choice-set variation across the country, 1994 data do not provide a true assessment of parties' national popularity. In addition, assessing these scores in mixed electoral systems is problematic. Party-affiliated candidates contest not only the PR tier but also the majoritarian tier. However, complete data for party affiliations is not always available.

Because the chapter's main concern is the development of parties, and the party list is the primary tier for party-based competition, the calculations rely upon PR data when they are available. The dataset includes national-level data for majoritarian systems, even though the choice set and mechanisms of voting do not provide voters with a full range of choices in each district. While the dynamics of ballot access, campaigning, and voting in majoritarian, proportional representation, and mixed systems differ, the results are treated as equivalent for this analysis.

Armenia

The following groups are considered to be continuous:

* Armenian National Movement, Liberal Democratic Party, Republican Party, Christian Democratic Union, Union of Intellectuals, Social Democratic Party and Republic Bloc;
* Republican Party, People's Party of Armenia, and Unity Bloc;
* Union of Communist and Socialist Parties, and Union of Industrialists and Women; Dignified Future Party and Dignity, Democracy, Motherland Bloc.

The following parties are treated as new:

1999: Law and Unity, Rule of Law Party, Worthy Future, Mighty Fatherland Party, Freedom, Union of Communists and Socialists Election Bloc, and Homeland Bloc
2003: United Labor Party, Liberal Democratic Union of Armenia, and People's Party[11]
2007: Prosperous Armenia, Heritage, New Times, Alliance, and Impeachment Alliance

Estonia

Following scholarship on Baltic party systems (Pettai and Kreuzer 1999; Birch 2001), the following groups are considered to be continuous:

* Left Alternative and Justice Alliance;
* Secure Home and Coalition Party–Rural Union;
* Popular Front, Estonian Center Party, and Estonian Entrepreneurs Party;
* Estonian Green Party and Fourth Power;
* Our Home is Estonia and Russian Party.

The following parties are treated as new:

1995: Estonian Reform Party, Right Wingers, Our Home is Estonia, Future Estonia, Better Estonia/Estonian Citizen, and Estonian Peasants Party
1999: Estonian Christian People's Union and Progressive Party
2003: Res Publica and Independence Party
2007: Estonian Greens

Georgia

Georgia presents a peculiar challenge for calculating party system evolution. Only seat distributions were available for 1992. In 1995 and 1999, partial voting data were available for fifty-three and thirty-three parties and blocs, respectively. The 2003 election was complicated by partial court invalidation, with new elections held in 2004. Given these challenges, volatility calculations begin with the second and third elections. The following parties are treated as new:

1995: Citizens Union of Georgia, Socialist Party of Georgia, Bloc of the Union of Georgian Reformers/National Agreement, Tanadgoma, United Republican Party, Progress Bloc, State Legal Unity, and thirty-nine others
1999: Georgian Labour Party, People's Party Didgori, and twenty-six others
2003: National Movement, Tavisupleba—Gamsakhurdia, and Ertroba Bloc
2008: Christian Democratic Alliance, Political Union of Citizens—Georgian Policy, Political Union—Georgian Sportsmen's Union, National Party of Radical Democrats, Our Country, and Targamadze-Christian Democrats

Kazakhstan

Kazakhstan's data were also incomplete; only seat distributions were available for 1994 and 1995. Nur-OTAN is considered to be a successor of the People's Union of Kazakhstan (SNEK) and OTAN. The following parties are treated as new:

1999: Agrarian Party of Kazakhstan, Civic Party, People's Cooperative Party, Azamat, Alash, Revival, and Labor Party
2004: Ak Zhol, Asar, Democratic Party, Auyl Social Democratic Party, Party of Patriots, and Rukhaniyat Party
2007: National Social Democratic Party

Latvia

The following combinations are considered to be continuous (Pettai and Kreuzer 1999; Birch 2001):

- Latvian Farmer's Union, Latvian Christian Democratic Union, and United List of the Latvian Farmer's Union, Latvian Christian Democratic Union, and Latgale Democratic Party;
- Latvian National Independence Movement and Green List, Latvian National Conservative Party, and Latvian Green Party.

The following parties are treated as new:

1995: Popular Movement for Latvia—Zigerist's Party, Latvian National Democratic Party, Political Union of Economists, Latvian Party of Russian Citizens, Union of the Indigent and Latvian Independence Party, and Democratic Party.
1998: Latvian Revival Party, People's Party, Latvian Social Democratic Alliance, New Party, Helsinki 86, People's Assembly Freedom, Conservative Party,

Social Democratic Women's Organization, Mara's Land, National Progress Party, and Latvian National Reform Party.

2002: New Era, Union of Social Democrats, Light of Latgale, Social Democratic Welfare Party, Political Alliance—The Center, Russian Party, Latvian Party, Freedom Party, Progressive Center Party, and United Republican Party of Latvia.

2006: Motherland, All for Latvia, and New Democrats.

Lithuania

Lithuania's coding follows existing research on its party system (Pettai and Kreuzer 1999). The following groups are considered to be continuous:

- Sajudis and Homeland Union–Lithuanian Conservatives;
- Polish Union and Electoral Action of Lithuanian Poles;
- Christian Democratic Party, Union of Political Prisoners and Deportees, and Democratic Party;
- Parties that participated in broad blocs such as the Brazauskas Social Democratic Coalition (2000) and For Order and Justice (2004).

The following parties are treated as new:

1996: Women's Party, Peasant's Party, Alliance of Lithuanian National Minorities, Union of Russians, Party of the Economy, Social Justice Union, Socialist Party, Republican Party, Party of Life's Logic, and People's Party

2000: Moderate Conservatives' Union, Freedom Union, and Moderate Christian Democratic Union

2004: Christian Conservative Social Union

Moldova

Coding decisions for Moldova's party system follow existing classifications (Birch 2001, and Adept [http://www.parties.e-democracy.md]). The following groups are considered to be continuous:

- Bloc of Peasants and Intellectuals, Alliance of Democratic Forces, Party of Democratic Forces, and Party of Reform;
- Christian Democratic People's Front, Ecological Party Green Alliance, and the Electoral Bloc—Democratic Convention;
- Electoral Bloc of Moldovan Democrats, Democratic Party, and the Electoral Bloc for a Democratic and Prosperous Moldova;
- Association of Women of Moldova and the Social Democratic Bloc, Social Democratic Electoral Bloc Hope, and Social Democratic Party;
- Republican Party, Party of Socialists, and Electoral Bloc Edinstvo;
- Socialist Party Unity Movement Bloc and Braghis Alliance.

The following parties are treated as new:

1998: Party of Communists, Party of Social and Economic Justice, Christian Democratic Union, and United Party of Labor
2001: Electoral Bloc Native Land, Alliance of Lawyers and Economists, For Order and Justice, Democratic Agrarian Party, Republican Social Movement Ravnopravie, and Christian Democratic Peasant Party

Russia

Based on information from various sources (Birch [2001], Korgunyuk [1999], and Part Archive [http://www.indem.ru/pa98/]), the following groups are treated as continuous:

- Russia's Choice, Democratic Choice of Russia–United Democrats, and Union of Right Forces;
- Congress of Russian Communities, and the Congress of Russian Communities and Boldyrev Movement;
- Liberal Democratic Party of Russia and Zhirinovskiy Bloc;
- Bloc of Ivan Rybkin and Socialist Party of Russia;
- Yedinstvo, Fatherland–All Russia, and United Russia;
- Party of Pensioners, Russian Party of Life, and Just Russia.

The following parties are treated as new:

1995: Bloc of Ivan Rybkin, Communists-Working Russia-for the USSR, Congress of Russian Communities, Our Home is Russia, Power to the People, Social Democrats, Union of Labor, Party of Worker Self-Government, and twenty-eight others
1999: Party of Peace and Unity, Unity, Fatherland–All Russia, Party of Pensioners, Conservative Movement of Russia, Stalinist Bloc, Peace-Labor-May, Bloc of Nikolayev and Fyodorov, Spiritual Heritage, Russian Party for the Defense of Women, Movement in Defense of the Army, For Citizens' Dignity, Russian Deed, Party of the People, and Socialist Party (Bryntsalov)
2003: Party of Life, Unification, For Holy Russia, Rus', New Course—Automotive Russia, People's Republican Party, Greens, True Patriots of Russia, People's Party, Great Russia—Eurasian Union, SLON, Motherland, Russian Constitutional Democratic Party, and Development of Entrepreneurship
2007: Citizen's Power, Party of Social Justice, and Patriots of Russia

Ukraine

Party histories are drawn from Birch (2001), party Web sites, and the media (i.e., http://www.brama.com/ua-gov/pol-detl.html). The following combinations are considered to be continuous:

- Socialist and Peasant Party (although they contested some elections separately);
- Bloc of Nataliya Vitrenko and Progressive Socialist Party;
- For a United Ukraine and its component parts (including the Party of Regions);
- Republican Party, Ukrainian Conservative Republican Party. and National Front;
- Party of Economic Rebirth and Bloc of Democratic Parties;
- Socialist Nationalist Party and Menshe Sliv;
- Ukrainian Christian Democratic Party, Christian Popular Party, and Forward, Ukraine.

For purposes of replacement scores, Our Ukraine and the Bloc of Yuliya Tymoshenko are considered to be new parties in 2002, although they are arguably continuous with parties that balloted in 2002 and earlier. The following parties are treated as new:

1998: Progressive Socialist Party, People's Democratic Party, Agrarian Party, Reforms and Order, European Choice, Party of the Defenders of the Motherland, Hromada, and eleven other parties

2002: Bloc of Yuliya Tymoshenko, People's Movement of Ukraine, and nineteen other parties

2006: Pora, Lytvyn Bloc, and thirty other parties

2007: Svoboda and 8 other parties

Party Support

Similar to the analysis of vote abstention in Chapter 5, models of party support rely on CEEURO and CSES data. The leading political parties are coded independently; minor parties are relegated to a residual "other" category.

Several independent variables are coded in the same manner as in the analysis from Chapter 5: satisfaction with democracy, evaluations of economic conditions, gender, education, and age.[12] Income is also included, coded as an ordinal variable with values from one to the highest value (varying from country to country). The use of many independent variables generated a missing data problem because some respondents did not provide answers. While multiple imputation has been proposed as a solution to missing data (Honaker et al. 2001), it is not employed here.

The models of respondent support for political parties were assessed with multinomial logit, with the communist successor party and the party of power as comparison categories in separate analyses. Some scholars have noted that multinomial logit analysis suffers from several shortcomings, notably its assumption of the independence of irrelevant alternatives (Alvarez and Nagler 1998). However, subsequent assessments of multiparty competition have used multinomial logit (Brader and Tucker 2001).

Chapter 8 Notes

Chapter 8 presented data on electoral commission performance collected and coded by Sarah Birch and her research assistants at the University of Essex. The elections include Armenia (1999, 2003), Azerbaijan (1995, 2000), Belarus (2000, 2004), Estonia (1995, 1999), Georgia (1999, 2003), Kazakhstan (2004), Kyrgyzstan (2000, 2005), Latvia (1998, 2002), Lithuania (1996), Moldova (2001, 2005), Russia (1999, 2003), Tajikistan (2000, 2005), Ukraine (1998, 2002), and Uzbekistan (1999, 2004). Each question was coded on a five point scale, with one representing the fewest problems and five representing significant problems. The question categories were these:

1) Were major contestants banned, or did they have their applications to contest the elections refused in (evident) violation of the law?
2) Were significant sections of the citizenry refused registration or misregistered in (evident) violation of the law?
3) Did the state hinder the "level playing field" by obstructing free and fair voting?
4) In practice, were international and domestic observers allowed to observe the campaign, polling, vote counting, and tabulation?
5) How does the report describe the probity of the election overall?

Chapter 9 Notes

Benford's Law

To conduct the Benford's Law analysis, I used the program Datas to extract the first and second digits from entries with at least two digits.[13] The samples' distributions were compared with the Benford distribution using a chi-square test. As noted in the chapter, rejection of the null hypothesis does not demonstrate that fraud was perpetrated, but rather that the results are anomalous and worthy of additional investigation.

Special Precinct Analysis

Data from Ukraine's Central Electoral Commission permitted the coding of special precincts in the 2002 election (available online at http://195.230.157.53/pls/vd2002/webproc0v). The CEC electronically published protocols for 32,790 of the 33,113 precincts, and the protocols included information about precinct locations. The level of detail varied from district to district, with some regions providing more information about the location of polling stations than others.

Prisons. Prison precincts were identified by various terms in Ukrainian and Russian, including *vypravna koloniya* and *ispravitel'naya koloniya*, as well as acronyms such as "VK" and "IK." The dataset includes forty-eight polling stations coded as penitentiaries.

Military. While some areas of Ukraine (e.g., Sevastopol) are more likely to have military voters, none of the precincts provided enough information to conclude that voters were in military service. But, many ships served as polling stations; voters casting ballots in these stations were likely to be members of the merchant marine or navy. The dataset includes thirty-seven ships.

Hospitals. Hospital precincts included Ukrainian and Russian terms such as: *likarnya*, *poliklinika*, *roddom*, and *dispenser* for general treatment, as well as special treatment facilities (e.g., treatment centers for tuberculosis or cancer patients). The dataset includes 360 patient-care facilities.

Foreign. Precinct-level protocols labeled embassies, consulates, and foreign missions. These polling stations serve Ukrainian expatriates as well as state employees stationed abroad. The dataset includes eighty-nine foreign diplomatic posts.

Although some observers reported that the number of voters casting ballots in special polling stations approached 5 percent, the dataset includes results for only 0.7 percent of SMD voters and 0.6 percent of PR voters in special polling stations. This discrepancy is likely due to the inconsistent record-keeping of local electoral commissions. The potential gap between the actual number of special precincts and the coding raises a methodological question. If the precincts coded as special precincts are only a subset of the population, is the "sample" adequately representative?

It is possible that the sample is not random. If government officials selectively reported outcomes, the state is likely to withhold the most unflattering data. Thus, available data would be biased downward. Under this assumption, the estimates might understate the effects of special precincts. Another possibility is that, instead of being unreported in the data, unlabeled special precincts may be included incorrectly among "standard" precincts. If these mislabeled precincts are biased toward progovernment forces, the estimates would understate the effects of these precincts. If their results are no different from standard precincts, the estimates would overstate the effects of special precincts. Based on the analysis of the data, however, it seems more likely that the uncoded special precincts would provide support to the hypotheses.

Seemingly Unrelated Regression

Scholars have noted that the use of standard ordinary least squares (OLS) to assess outcomes in multiparty elections generates two problems: OLS may produce nonsensical predictions, since the distribution of the dependent variable is typically bound by zero and one (or 100 percent), and the performance of a given party is not independent of other parties' performance. Seemingly unrelated regression (SUR) analysis addresses these technical problems (Katz and King 1999; Tomz, Tucker, and Wittenberg 2002).

To accommodate SUR analysis, the variables were transformed by cal-culating the natural log of each party's vote relative to all other parties that contested in the precinct. The category of "Other" includes all parties or can-didates not associated with the three parties under analysis: FUU, CPU, and OU. The analysis of single-member district (SMD) races was more complex than the analysis of PR. When analyzing data with SUR, one cannot have missing data on values of the dependent variable. The PR race presented no complications, because it had a single national district: all parties contested PR in every district (and thus every precinct). However, parties may or may not contest any given district race. The SMD analysis thus covered districts (10,482 precincts) in which the three parties nominated candidates. This solution does not encompass all possible combinations, however. In some districts, any one of the three parties could fail to nominate a candidate, with-draw a candidate, or support another candidate. The analysis was replicated for all combinations of the parties; the signs and significance levels of other coefficients are similar to those in the PR model. Explanatory variables cover-ing alternate hypotheses were coded in the following way:

1) *Choice Set*: Each precinct where a candidate affiliated with the party in question appeared on the ballot was coded "one."

2) *Candidate Quality*: The following variables controlled for parliamentary experience and national-level or local-level positions: FUU Parliament, FUU National, FUU Local, CPU Parliament, CPU Local, OU Parliament, OU National, and OU Local. Based on candidate biographies published by the Central Electoral Commission, candidates who served in the national Rada from 1994 to 2002, occupied a national government post, and served as a local mayor or member of a local assembly or served in another executive position were coded "one" for the relevant variable.

3) *Region*: The regional variable divided Ukraine into eight distinct areas to maximize the number of regions while harnessing the benefits of clus-tering regions with similar demographic, historical, and other features into macroregional units (Barrington and Herron 2004). The regions were: East (Donetsk, Luhansk), East Central (Kharkiv, Zaporizhzhia, Dnipropetrovsk), Krym (Crimea and Sevastopol), South (Kherson, Mikolayiv and Odesa), North Central (Chernihiv, Sumy, Poltava, Cherkasy, Kirovohrad, Kyiv City and Oblast), West Central (Khmelnytskyi, Zhytomyr, Vinnytsa, Rivne, Volyn), West (Ivano-Frankivsk, L'viv, Ternopil) and Southwest (Chernivtsi, Zakarpatia). The analysis excluded the West to prevent perfect collinearity.

CHAPTER 10 NOTES

The data for Table 10.1 and many of the details describing protest size in the six short case studies were collected by searching Lexis-Nexis wire service databases for entries about election-related protests in each country. Searches generally began thirty days prior to the election and continued for thirty days after the election. The database includes material from Agence France Presse, Arminfo (an Armenian news agency), Associated Press, Baltic News Service, British Broadcasting Corporation, Deutsche Presse Agentur, Interfax, Nezavisimaya Gazeta, Radio Free Europe, RIA Novosti, *St. Petersburg* (Russia) *Times*, TASS, United Press International, Voice of America, and Xinhua.

Notes

Preface

1. Poll results are available at: http://www.pravda.com.ua/ru/news/2007/12/7/67961.htm (accessed December 8, 2007).
2. Medvedev's pending nomination for president was announced by Putin and representatives of United Russia on the previous day (December 10, 2007).
3. The Constituent Assembly elections in 1917, and elections in the short-lived democratic republics in the South Caucasus (1918–1921), featured multiple parties. But, this experience was limited in duration and ultimately unsuccessful.

Chapter 1

1. See Arendt (1951) and Friedrich and Brzezinski (1956) for classic treatments of totalitarianism.
2. While elections are the *primary* tool in democratic politics to assess preferences, encourage efficacy, confer legitimacy, hold leaders accountable, and encourage politicians to organize and govern effectively, they are not the only tool that accomplishes th*ese ta*sks. Public opinion polls provide insight into preferences, although they do not precipitate change in leadership like elections. A well-developed civil society may spark citizen participation, generate feelings of efficacy, and facilitate accountability. Efforts to overcome collective action problems in the legislative process may encourage politicians to organize with or without fully competitive elections.
3. Riker's (1982a) classic on social choice theory compares the expectations of populist and liberal interpretations of democracy, rejecting the populist view as untenable.
4. A referendum refers to a public vote on policy called by government, while an initiative is called by citizens. I also include public initiatives under the label "referendum" in this book.
5. Some research indicates that voters in the post-Soviet region are developing clear views on policy and are able to differentiate among parties (Miller et al. 2000; Miller and Klobucar 2000; Brader and Tucker 2001). But, candidates often benefit from ambiguity, or "fuzziness," and may use vaguely developed platforms to their advantage in electoral campaigns (Franklin 1991; Rose, Tikhomorov, and Mishler 1997; Rose, Munro, and White 2001).

6. Brady (2000) defines these terms in an unpublished discussion of the contested U.S. presidential election in 2000.

7. Some scholars have argued that public participation in farcical Soviet elections underscored citizens' acceptance of the contradictions—or "illegitimacy"—of the Soviet system (Zaslavsky and Brym 1978, 371). Nevertheless, holding elections allows even authoritarian societies to participate in the international conversation about what constitutes democratic political practices and to gain leverage in international negotiations. For example, Kazakhstan's rhetoric about the 2007 parliamentary election was part of a successful campaign to gain the OSCE presidency in 2010.

8. The Gorbachev era's introduction of competitive races could have increased the system's legitimacy. Instead, reforms undermined citizen and elite confidence in the regime.

9. Carson (1955, 12) calls elections "laboratories of citizenship."

10. Nove (1968) suggests that mobilizing the population to achieve economic goals is facilitated by proper training and preparation for mass efforts. Elections serve this training function.

11. Elections help not only to foster citizenship but to identify malcontents. In two notable studies, Gilison (1968) and Jacobs (1970) assess dissent based on data about voters casting "against all" ballots and voter abstention. Zaslavsky and Brym (1978) suggest that these studies underestimate dissent. Karklins (1986) later evaluated nonvoting through surveys of émigrés, noting that abstention was a purposeful political act.

12. Wright (1961) addresses the relative commitment of the West to free and fair elections in light of Cold War politics.

13. Universal suffrage was not always a Soviet value, however. In early Soviet elections, certain economic and political classes were purposely excluded to cleanse society of negative influences (Teper 1932, Carson 1955).

14. While the demographic distribution of deputies closely followed the regions they purportedly represented, reelection favored candidates who were "older, better educated, belong[ed] to major nationality groups, and [were] male party members who occupy powerful commanding positions in the bureaucratic apparatus" (Hill 1973, 208).

15. The "third wave" of democratization is a construct popularized by Huntington's (1991) book of the same name. He argues that, beginning with the American and French revolutions of the eighteenth century, human societies have witnessed three "waves" in which large numbers of sovereign states abandoned authoritarianism for democracy. See Diamond (1996), Carothers (2002), and Levitsky and Way (2002) for details on democratization and a discussion of whether or not the third wave has ended.

16. See Dahl (1971) and Schmitter and Karl (1991) for other definitions of democracy.

17. For an assessment of democracy in the region that connects success with past habits and practices, see Bendersky (2005).

18. In 1997, Heydar Aliyev challenged the fit of democracy to contemporary Azerbaijan, noting that democracy is "not an apple you buy at the market and bring back home" (*Azerbaijan International* 1997). Specific comments from the other leaders may be found in the following sources: Akayev (Beshimov 2004); Berdymukhammedov (RFE/RL 2007c); Karimov (RFE/RL 2005b); Nazarbayev (MacWilliam 2005); and Niyazov (CBS News 2004).

19. Freedom House is a nongovernmental organization that assesses "freedom" in an annual survey. The organization uses expert assessments of political rights and civil liberties to generate a score ranging from 1 (free) to 7 (not free). Freedom House also reports a composite score for each country, dividing the world into three categories: Free, Partly Free, and Not Free.

20. Baltic independence movements used many issues, such as the environment and opposition to nuclear power, to advocate for local autonomy and build the case for independence. See, for example, Peterson (1993).

21. Latvia experienced a decline in political rights during 2007 due to political scandals.

22. Many organizations sponsor election observation missions. Among them are the United States–based National Democratic Institute and International Republican Institute, the European Parliament, and the Commonwealth of Independent States.

23. See the Appendix for a list of the fifty-four elections included in this discussion.

24. "International standards" for elections is a loose term but typically includes agreements such as the UN Charter, Declaration on Human Rights, several UN General Assembly resolutions, Statute of the Council of Europe, Protocol to the Convention for the Protection of Human Rights and Fundamental Freedoms, Document of the Copenhagen Meeting of the Conference of the Human Dimension of the CSCE, and the Inter-Parliamentary Union's Declaration of Criteria for Free and Fair Elections. See *Association of Central and Eastern European Election Officials* (n.d.) for more details.

25. Readers should not infer from this observation that the Soviet experience was perfectly uniform. Institutionally, for example, Russia was set apart from other republics. Unlike its fourteen union-republic neighbors, Russia did not have its own party or planning apparatus. In addition, policies addressing ethnic diversity in the assignment to leadership posts changed over time.

26. Also see Jowitt (1996).

27. Bunce (1995) rejects the notion that the debate is between area specialists and comparativists, as implied by Schmitter and Karl (1994; 1995). She suggests (1995, 470) that Schmitter and Karl's characterization of "area studies" as the other side of the debate implies that area specialists are not interested in theory, know only a single case and assume it is unique, isolate themselves from others in political science, and eschew general theory for explanations that are country specific. Rather, Bunce argues, the debate is about research methods and the equivalence of cases. Even if Bunce's intention was to limit the debate to narrow methodological issues, the exchange became a part of the broader discussion of epistemology and the qualitative-quantitative divide.

28. This debate missed an important point: methods and theoretical ideas from other disciplines regularly permeated the thin barriers of Soviet area studies (Fleron and Hoffman 1993).

29. Rhetorical claims about the alleged insensitivity of the "other side" in the debate have extended the controversy into the twenty-first century. For example, Graham and Kantor (2007) argue that area studies is not "soft" despite criticisms from social scientists. Yet they do not specify the criticisms of the area studies approach nor do they name specific research in which these claims are leveled.

30. See Djilas (1958) for a classic critique of the double standards in communist systems.

31. Some scholars have suggested that pre-Soviet legacies may influence contemporary attitudes and behavior as well (Roper and Fesnic 2003; Bennich-Bjorkman

2007). This observation begs the question: how far back in time must one trace the "legacy" before the core influences are uncovered?

TABLE 1.2

1. The table does not include by-elections.
2. Planned, but not completed, at the time the book was written.
3. Elections to Belarus' Republic Council were held from September 13-December 13, 2000 and August 18-November 18, 2004. These elections are indirect (representatives are selected by local government organs) and are not reported on the table.
4. Planned, but not completed, at the time the book was written.
5. Elections to Kazakhstan's Senate were held on September 17, 1999, and August 19, 2005. These elections are indirect and are not reported on the table.
6. Planned, but not completed, at the time the book was written.
7. Planned, but not completed, at the time the book was written.
8. Planned, but not completed, at the time the book was written.

CHAPTER 2

1. Carson (1955) divides Soviet elections into two eras. I extend his approach until the collapse of the USSR.
2. See Carson (1955) and Marsh (2001) for more information about pre-Soviet elections.
3. In the *Manifesto of the Communist Party*, Marx and Engels note that bourgeois institutions of property, education, and family life are designed to maintain exploitation. Lenin, in *State and Revolution*, calls for destruction of bourgeois institutions because they serve oppressing classes. Both works are available at http://www.marxists.org.
4. The theoretical basis for work emphasizing the centralized nature of the Soviet Union can be found in Popper (1945), Arendt (1951), and Friedrich and Brzezinski (1956).
5. Many scholars suggest that the centralized model of Soviet governance broke down during or shortly after the Stalin era (Fleron and Hoffman 1993).
6. Known then as Petrograd.
7. For example, the Russian Republic's 1918 Constitution detailed election procedures, including apportionment and extension of the franchise. See Teper (1932) and Carson (1955) for more discussion of local variation.
8. Carson (1955, 16) notes that in Penza, one delegate represented two hundred voters in unions and industry and one delegate represented a thousand voters outside of organizations.
9. The interview was transcribed from *Pravda* and published online at: http://www.marxists.org/reference/archive/stalin/works/1936/03/01.htm. Carson (1955) notes that real election contests were anticipated at this time, but security services stifled these reforms.
10. Put another way, by 1961, over 6 percent of the population worked in election administration (Gilison 1968).
11. The material in this paragraph was drawn from a photocopy of a Commission on Security and Cooperation in Europe report, dated March 20, 1989.

Chapter 3

1. By contrast, Mozaffar and Schedler (2002) emphasize a wide range of electoral governance issues, categorize rules differently, and include additional laws and regulations that fall beyond the scope of this analysis.

2. For example, the provision of free advertising and access to national-level televised debates likely encouraged party formation in Russia's 1995 campaign. The party Pamfilova-Gurov-Lysenko was not competitive for party list seats, but its inclusion on the ballot provided advantages to its namesakes in their SMD campaigns.

3. Duverger (1954) introduced these concepts, and his work serves as the foundation for the study of electoral institutions and their effects.

4. Kingdon's (1995) book on the policy process outlines how political entrepreneurs seek out opportunities to enact the policies they advocate.

5. Researchers must consider how the political environment affects the available choices for election rule design; a complete menu of options is not always politically feasible. Further, the environment surrounding initial choice and subsequent reform may differ, influencing the process and outcome of reform efforts. While scores of international experts weighed in on initial election rule design, their input was often solicited after crucial design decisions had been made (Birch et al. 2002).

6. As Birch et al (2002) note, a combination of self-interest and normatively driven influences may affect political actors' decisions.

7. Estonia and Moldova allocate seats nationally on a closed list; Latvia favors regional allocation with preference votes.

8. STV allocates seats in multimember districts based on ballots in which voters rank-order their choices. Reilly (2001) describes STV in detail.

9. Massicotte and Blais (1999), Shugart and Wattenberg (2001), and Ferrara, Herron, and Nishikawa (2005) discuss the development of mixed electoral systems.

10. Gorbachev was made president by the legislature.

11. Frye (1997) provides an index of presidential strength that was subsequently updated by Frye, Hellman, and Tucker (2000). Rankings are based on the latter. Azerbaijan was not included in data but would be rated above the median. Azerbaijan's president has the right of legislative initiative, appoints or dismisses the prime minister (with legislative approval), oversees the cabinet, calls referendums, issues decrees, but may be dismissed by the combined efforts of the legislature and Constitutional Court.

12. Minor variation in presidential election rules includes a two-thirds majority requirement for first round victories in Azerbaijan that was eliminated in 2002 constitutional changes, and a qualified majority for first round victory in Lithuania (contingent on at least 50 percent turnout).

13. Uzbekistan's 2003 election law retains negative voting for parliament.

14. The relative stability of presidential election rules compared to legislative rules is in part due to the greater variation in rules available to select legislatures.

15. Changes to campaign regulations have been less significant and are not featured here.

16. In 1992, Georgia's PR allocation rules were complex. Voters provided an ordinal preference for parties. Parties earned 5 points for each first preference, 3 points for each second preference, and 2 points for each third preference. The overall point total was divided by the number of mandates to identify the quota. Each

party's point total was divided by the quota and it received the number of seats corresponding to the integer. Remaining seats were transferred to a compensatory list where they were distributed via D'Hondt.

17. Kyrgyzstan instituted controversial regional thresholds in addition to its national threshold, in contrast to other post-Soviet PR systems.

18. Interview by the author with Viktor Sheynis (October 1999), and Sheynis (1999).

19. McFaul (1999, 41) discusses Viktor Sheynis' observation that Yeltsin was especially swayed by arguments emphasizing how mixed electoral rules could benefit Yeltsin's allies. An alternate account suggests that Yeltsin was swayed by more politically altruistic motives, approving PR to give his opponents an incentive to use elections rather than extraconstitutional means to advocate for their interests (Aron 2000). McFaul's account is supported by the author's personal interview with Viktor Sheynis (October 1999) and Sheynis' (1999) book.

20. Presidential representative Aleksandr Kotenkov indicated that President Yeltsin wanted to eliminate the PR tier, replacing it with a "more democratic" single-member district system. According to Kotenkov, the disproportionate results from 1995's PR race justified this change (RFE/RL 1998).

21. In a *Washington Post* piece, McFaul notes that "Putin advisers speak openly about eliminating proportional representation from the Duma electoral law" (McFaul 2000).

22. Annual Address to the Federal Assembly, April 26, 2007, http://www.kremlin .ru/appears/2007/04/26/1156_type63372type63374type82634_125339 .shtml (accessed September 5, 2007).

23. Personal conversation with the author (June 6, 2005).

24. The OSCE election observation mission was canceled after the organization asserted that the Russian government was intentionally delaying visas for its limited delegation. The organizations Transparency International and Golos alleged improper influence by government officials and outright fraud (Reuters 2007). The Council of Europe, EU, and several spokespersons from various governments also challenged the fairness of the polls (Levy 2007).

25. For a detailed discussion of this and other key events in Ukrainian politics during the 1990s and 2000s, see chapter 4 of D'Anieri (2006b).

26. As in Russia, legislators from various political forces who occupied majoritarian seats opposed the PR system more vigorously than those in PR seats.

27. The division among deputies based on seat mandate is due, in part, to the distribution of majoritarian deputies among party factions. Some progovernment factions were disproportionately populated by SMD deputies (such as Labor Ukraine, Regional Rebirth, and Solidarity). Conversely, some opposition factions had more members elected to PR seats (such as the Communist Party, Rukh, and the Socialist Party). This calculation does not include deputies who replaced outgoing members of parliament, because they likely face different incentives.

28. The president's representative to parliament stated that Kuchma could not sign the bill due to its violations of the constitution and because changes would give power not to "the people, but to parties and party organizations" (Verkhovna Rada 2001).

29. Regional Rebirth disbanded and new factions emerged, including Regions and Democratic Union. Both of the new factions opposed the draft law, with all but one deputy in each faction failing to cast a vote. Labor Ukraine and Solidarity continued to oppose institutional reform. The People's Democratic Party

remained split, but fewer deputies supported change than in the January vote. The Party of Greens also split on this vote; a majority of members supported change. The only major change in support came from the Social Democratic Party of Ukraine (United), which moved from strong opposition to support.

30. The intervening election, changes in faction identities, and individual deputy movement among factions complicates comparison of the 2004 vote with votes in 2001.

31. Fatherland, associated with Yuliya Tymoshenko, was characterized at this time as a more "pragmatic," oligarch-driven faction. Beginning in 2001, it "developed into one of Kuchma's most ardent opponents" (Whitmore 2004, 96). Consequently, it is not listed among the opposition factions here.

32. During negotiations over the contested 2004 presidential election, Kuchma's allies secured changes to presidential powers that were enacted in 2006. While the election rule reform saga ended with constitutional reform's failure, many provisions were later adopted when exogenous events provided an opportunity to secure concessions from opponents.

TABLE 3.3

1. In both 2001 votes, the Socialist faction was combined with the Peasant faction.

CHAPTER 4

1. In this chapter's analysis, political parties are defined abstractly; any political group that contests an election is included. A more detailed assessment of political parties is available in Chapter 6, which discusses post-Soviet parties' organizational forms and functions.

2. The effective number of parties specifically refers to an index of party performance, weighted either by votes or seats received: $1 / \Sigma p_i^2$, where p is the proportion of votes or seats. The index is calculated by assessing values for all parties (i). It is called the Laakso-Taagepera index after its creators (Laakso and Taagepera 1979).

3. Lijphart (1994) labels this barrier for entry into parliament the "effective threshold" and estimates its value as the percentage of $75 / (M+1)$, where M is the district magnitude.

4. The first decision—whether or not to vote—is left to Chapter 5.

5. Further, because majority support guarantees victory, candidates and their parties are confronted by strong incentives to build a platform that has broad appeal and leads to majority support. A politically extreme ideology or platform is, by definition, unlikely to garner majority support, so political actors in plurality systems have an incentive to stake out positions that will be attractive to the median voter. As Grofman (2004) notes, however, Downs' (1957) median voter theorem rests on several assumptions, the violation of which can undermine the applicability of this prediction.

6. Scholars have noted that many SMD plurality systems do not produce two-party competition, especially at the national level (Rae 1967; Taagepera and Shugart 1989; Gaines 1999). Duvergerian logic predicts two-party competition at the

district level; it does not indicate that the two parties in competition must be the same in all districts.

7. E.g., Cain (1978) and Cox (1997).

8. For various approaches to understanding "exceptions" to Duverger's Law, see Rae (1967), Taagepera and Shugart (1989), Chhibber and Kollman (1998), Gaines (1999), and Diwakar (2007).

9. See Cox (1997) for more about strategic voting and entry in PR systems.

10. A point supported by subsequent investigation (Mair 1993).

11. The analysis covers parliamentary elections only, as the election rules for presidents do not vary adequately across post-Soviet space.

12. Nishikawa and Herron (2004) structure the analysis differently, but the rank ordering in this chapter follows their logic.

13. Data on ethnicity are transformed into an "effective number of ethnic groups" using the Laakso-Taagepera index.

14. Parties most closely associated with the chief executive.

15. Postcommunist states in the Golder dataset include: Albania, Armenia, Bulgaria, Croatia, Czech Republic or Czechoslovakia (1992), Estonia, Hungary, Latvia, Lithuania, Macedonia, Moldova, Mongolia, Romania, Russia, Slovakia, Slovenia, and Ukraine. If it is a relevant contributor to behavior, the postcommunist "syndrome" should be observed in all of these cases, albeit to varying degrees.

16. To maintain a parallel analysis of models using interregional and intraregional data, the analysis includes a majoritarian variable that combines SMD plurality and SMD majority runoff. Only one post-Soviet election used pure plurality rules (Azerbaijan's 2005 election). It is not possible to disentangle the effect of the political institution from the country or election effect. However, a separate analysis isolating plurality and majoritarian rules revealed similar results. Coefficients for majority-runoff elections were significant and negative; plurality rules were not statistically significant.

17. The data are from Clark and Golder (2006) with the addition of variables and cases not included in the original dataset.

18. See the Appendix for more details.

19. The comparison category is proportional electoral systems. An additional analysis eliminating nonlist PR systems (e.g., STV) from the comparison category produced similar results, with one exception. Postcommunist was not significant in model 4 with this specification, suggesting some ambiguity in the effect of postcommunism on these results. However, a significant number of observations were lost (the N for respecified model 4 was 490).

20. Clark and Whittrock (2005) find that executive strength also exerts a mitigating effect on the number of parties. Their logic is similar to the effect that this chapter assesses via regime type.

21. The variable for concurrent presidential elections is absent from these models because post-Soviet states hold nonconcurrent elections. The only exception was the 1992 presidential election in Estonia that was held concurrently with the founding parliamentary election.

22. Freedom House scores are coded in reverse; more freedom (democracy) yields a lower score. A negative sign means that as democracy levels increase (the score decreases), more political parties are likely to gain seats.

23. Moreover, some association exists between regime type and electoral rules. While some authoritarian regimes use mixed and PR systems, majoritarian rules are

more commonly employed in post-Soviet countries with dubious democratic credentials.

24. Affiliation classifications are based on Eurasianet (2005) http://www.eurasianet .org/azerbaijan/map/. The data are preliminary but include details from all districts. Other analysis in the chapter is based on Kara (2007), who reports official final results aggregated nationally (and without information on how independent candidates lean). The effective number of parties using these data is 2.66.

25. Taagepera and Shugart (1989) note that plurality systems in the United States produced a mean number of competitive parties slightly under two in the twentieth century (1.81 for the House of Representatives and 1.91 for the Senate). The United Kingdom, Canada, and India produced more parties than the United States over several elections. New Zealand produced the largest number of competitive parties among plurality systems, with an average of 2.56 competitive parties from 1972–1993.

26. However, the plurality rule requires the winner to receive at least 33 percent of the vote.

27. Mongolia's Freedom House ratings in 2007 were 2 for political rights and 2 for civil liberties, classifying it as "free."

28. While parliament consisted of 450 seats in Ukraine's 1994 election, many positions remained unfilled due to the combination of a majority requirement in both rounds of the election and the use of negative ballots (Bojcun 1994).

29. According to article 58 in the law "O Vyborakh v Respublike Kazakhstana," "42 deputies of the Supreme Soviet are elected according to a state list of candidates for deputy in the Supreme Soviet, formed by the president of Kazakhstan."

30. Members of the Senate were appointed by local legislatures and the president.

31. Second-round presidential elections have been held several times, including Armenia 1998, 2003; Belarus 1994; Lithuania 1998, 2002, 2004; Moldova 1996; Ukraine 1994, 1999, 2004; and Russia 1996.

32. Preexisting multiparty competition was absent, given the longstanding Soviet ban on competitors to the Communist Party. Efforts to constrain civil society until the Gorbachev period also restricted the number of organized political forces emerging from the communist era.

33. This argument was particularly prevalent in Ukraine during the debate over election rule reform in the early 2000s (Herron 2007). Moreover, some research has suggested that closed-list PR produces less perceived corruption than other rules (Chang and Golden 2007), while other work has suggested that it is more corruptible (Persson, Tabellini, and Trebbi 2003; Kunicova and Rose-Ackerman 2005).

34. The main Kyrgyz opposition party, Ata-Meken, received 8 percent of the overall vote but failed to pass the regional threshold. Several opposition parties failed to pass the threshold or gain registration in Russia.

35. Russia and Ukraine equally divided seats between the majoritarian (225 seats) and PR tiers (225 seats). Lithuania allocates 71 majoritarian and 70 proportional seats.

36. 100 majoritarian and 25 PR seats in 1995 and 2000.

37. 67 majoritarian and 10 PR seats in 1999 and 2004.

38. 45 majoritarian and 15 PR seats in 2000.

39. 41 majoritarian and 22 PR seats in 2000 and 2005.

40. The index is calculated by subtracting the proportion of seats from votes and dividing by 2 (Lijphart 1994).

41. See Moser (1999) for more discussion of the disproportional results in Russia.
42. For example, in 1993, deviation was 0.11 in PR and 0.09 in SMD. In 1999 deviation was 0.16 in PR and 0.12 in SMD.

Chapter 5

1. Saakashvili emerged as the main opposition figure and sole viable candidate in the special election to succeed discredited former President Eduard Shevardnadze.
2. Alvarez, Bailey, and Katz (2007) show that individual- and aggregate-level turnout analyses may produce different results.
3. See White (1990) for a detailed account of the Congress of People's Deputies election.
4. Mean international turnout was 68 percent in the 1980s, falling to around 64 percent in the 1990s and beyond. See also International IDEA (2007) http://www.idea.int/vt/findings.cfm.
5. Lower turnout could reflect a real decline in citizen participation or better data reporting by authorities.
6. Scholars have debated the effect of race on turnout in the United States. Some report race's independent effects, while others suggest that it is confounded with class- and region-based effects (Abramson and Claggett 1991). Recent studies have found conditional effects in race's influence on turnout (Barreto, Segura, and Woods 2004; Griffin and Keane 2006). The dynamics of racial politics in the United States differ from those elsewhere in the world, however, and the generalizability of these findings has not been fully evaluated.
7. Norris (2000) notes that early research found women less likely to participate than men, but contemporary data suggests that participation rates often do not differ statistically by gender.
8. Some literature argues that parties of the left traditionally receive support from lower or working classes, a group that also tends to abstain more than voters in other classes (see, for example, Pacek and Radcliffe (2003) for a brief discussion).
9. Some research has found that registration requirements undermine participation among voters with lower levels of education (Wolfinger and Rosenstone 1972), although this finding has been disputed (Nagler 1991).
10. The approach has been modified over time to emphasize the possibility of regret (Ferejohn and Fiorina 1974) or mixed strategies (Grofman 1979) as catalysts for participation.
11. See Aldrich (1993) for a review of the problems related to the calculus of voting. In much of the early empirical literature assessing the calculus of voting, the assessment of cost was downplayed or ignored because its role was viewed as marginal (Sigelman and Berry 1982).
12. See Blais (2006) for a review of the empirical literature on turnout.
13. For example, researchers commonly include party system variables, typically the effective number of parties, to account for the influence of political competition on participation. Contestation by a high number of parties could enhance turnout because voters have a wide range of choices, and many groups actively attempt to mobilize voters. Alternatively, more fragmented party systems could depress turnout because they are more likely to yield coalition governments, reducing the direct impact of the voters' decisions on policy-making outcomes

(Blais 2006). In addition, due to higher payoffs for sincere votes, proportional representation systems may generate incentives for participation. But accountability mechanisms are indirect, potentially undermining the incentives for voter participation (Ladner and Milner 1999).

14. Rules that punish citizens for not voting also provide strong incentives for participation (Blais et al 2003; cited in Blais 2006).

15. Jackman (1987) includes presidential elections for France and the United States, but focuses on parliamentary elections.

16. See Kostadinova and Power (2007) for an analysis of postcommunist Europe and Latin America, and Kuenzi and Lambright (2001) for an analysis of Africa. Researchers also have investigated other institutional rules affecting access, such as registration requirements (Rosenstone and Wolfinger 1978), voting age, the days elections are held, the existence of special precincts, and the accessibility of precinct locations (Blais 2006).

17. More homogeneity may increase turnout due to socialization and pressures. But, less homogeneity may lead to greater turnout due to resource allocation issues (i.e., more parliamentary seats for a party associated with a specific group will yield more resources vis-à-vis other groups).

18. For more information about the surveys, please consult the Appendix.

19. This measure includes all respondents who indicated that they did not vote or did not indicate a vote choice. The survey data generally understate actual abstention rates, consistent with respondents' tendencies elsewhere in the world (Anderson and Silver 1986; Silver, Anderson, and Abramson 1986). However, exceptions exist. Self-reported intent to abstain is higher than the actual abstention rate in Belarus (1996) and Kazakhstan (1994). For Russia's 2000 survey, this category includes all nonrespondents. (No respondents indicated that they abstained, but 289 did not respond. Other nonrespondents were dropped from the analysis.)

20. Questions oriented toward assessing general economic conditions were not available.

21. The individual-level analysis permits an assessment of socioeconomic effects on the propensity to vote but not a direct assessment of voter beliefs about the likelihood of casting a decisive vote, the level of disappointment they might experience if their candidate lost, their duty to participate in the process, or other factors that directly speak to the rational choice explanation of turnout. This is a common challenge for empirical analyses of turnout.

22. In two-round parliamentary elections, the analysis includes only the first round because the second round may not involve voters in all districts. In two-round presidential elections, the analysis includes data from the decisive second round.

23. Frye (1997) addresses the relative power of presidents. Ishiyama and Kennedy (2001) analyze how presidential power affects party system development, suggesting that powerful presidents exert a weaker role than commonly thought.

24. Because the analytical technique does not allow two observations from the same country to occupy the same time point, the more "important" election is given precedence.

25. The analysis does not include variables that cannot be measured across all of the election types (some institutional features of parliamentary elections and the closeness of elections are not measurable in the context of referendums).

26. Further, authoritarian states are more likely to emphasize the presidential polls and referendums about presidential power as events showcasing support for the leader. This emphasis, in turn, encourages officials to report high turnout levels.

Thus, incentives exist for voters to participate when strong presidents are elected (relative to weaker parliaments) and for officials to enhance turnout data. Regardless of the mechanism by which turnout is enhanced, the results conform with expectations.

CHAPTER 6

1. Schattschneider (1942) famously notes that "democracy is unthinkable save in terms of parties."
2. See Herron (2002a; 2002 b), Whitmore (2004), and Thames (2007) for discussions of factions in Ukraine. Faction formation issues are similar across the region.
3. Some scholarship has linked the behavior of political parties to the mechanisms of their birth, growth, and development, including the expansion of suffrage, political modernization, and legislative cycling. While a full review is beyond the scope of this book, see Katz and Mair (1995) for an account of the origins and functions of four party types and Aldrich (1995) for an argument connecting the emergence of parties to collective action problems.
4. Janda (1980, 5) notes that parties are *organizations that pursue a goal of placing their avowed representatives in government positions* (emphasis in original). Sartori (1976, 64) also states that a party is "any group that presents at election, and is capable of placing through elections, candidates for public office."
5. Belarus prohibits the president from being a party member. The Russian law notes that the president may suspend membership while in office. Estonia's statute indicates that the president must suspend activities.
6. See similar assessments of other party systems in the Baltics (Pettai and Kreuzer 1999) and Russia (Korgunyuk 1999).
7. Figure 6.1 was compiled from profiles about Moldovan parties from the organization ADEPT. The information is available online at: http://www.parties.e-democracy.md/en/parties/. Last accessed December 11, 2007.
8. The Social Liberal Union was founded in 2001 on the basis of the National Liberal Party and the For Order and Justice Party.
9. Popular Movement for Latvia (Zigerist's Party).
10. The Brazauskas Social Democratic Coalition.
11. Bloc of Ivan Rybkin, Bloc of Stanislav Govorukhin, Pamfilova-Gurov-Lysenko, Tikhonov-Tupolev-Tikhonov, Bloc of Andrey Nikolayev and Svyatoslav Fyodorov, and the Zhirinovskiy Bloc (LDPR in 1999). Blocs were eliminated when the new election law took effect in 2007.
12. Most notably, the Bloc of Yuliya Tymoshenko and the Bloc of Volodymyr Lytvyn, but also the Bloc of Yuriy Karamzin, Bloc of Kostenko and Plyuchsh, Bloc of Borys Oliynyk and Mykhail Syrota, Bloc of Evgen Marchuk, and Bloc of Lyudmila Suprun.
13. Other Moldovan blocs include: Socialist Party/Unity Movement Bloc, Bloc of Peasants and Intellectuals, Electoral Bloc Faith and Justice, Electoral Bloc–Democratic Convention of Moldova, Electoral Bloc for a Democratic and Prosperous Moldova, and Social Democratic Electoral Bloc Hope.
14. Republic Bloc, Unity Bloc, Justice Bloc, and Homeland Bloc.
15. Pro Patria and Res Publica.

16. Peace Bloc, October 11 Bloc, Unity Bloc, Bloc–United Communist Party and Social Democrats, Bloc of 21st Century–Konstantine Gamsakhurdia Society–United Georgia, Bloc of United Georgian Reforms and National Agreement, Bloc For Life, Progress Bloc, Way of Zviad—Voice of a Nation Bloc, Christian Democracy-European Choice Bloc, and Bloc of Economic Revival.

17. Latvian Way and Latvia First; United List of the Latvian Farmers' Union, Latvian Christian Democratic Union, and Democratic Party of Latgale; Latvian National Conservative Party and Latvian Green Party; and Union of Labor Party, Latvian Christian Democratic Union, and Latvian Green Party.

18. Brazauskas Social Democratic Coalition, For Order and Justice.

19. Zhirinovskiy Bloc and Motherland Party blocs were eliminated for the 2007 election.

20. Our Ukraine–People's Self Defense, People's Opposition Bloc of Nataliya Vitrenko (which included the Progressive Socialist Party of Ukraine), and For a United Ukraine.

21. The Bloc of Yuliya Tymoshenko and Our Ukraine had a contentious relationship that undermined effective governance, especially after the 2007 parliamentary election.

22. See the Appendix for more detail.

23. See, for example, Grzymala-Busse (2002) and Ishiyama (1996; 1997; 1999).

24. For example, in Latvia, Moldova, Russia, and Ukraine.

25. See Radio Free Europe/Radio Liberty (2008a): http://www.rferl.org/specials/kazakhelections/parties.asp.

26. For a discussion of machine politics in post-Soviet space, see D'Anieri (2006).

27. The European Institute on the Media has conducted studies of media activity in postcommunist elections, assessing coverage of government and the opposition on television, on radio, and in print. In the past, it published these reports on its Web site, but the Web site was dormant at the time this manuscript was completed.

28. This seat total is based solely on official affiliation. If one were to count unofficially affiliated candidates, the seat total would be higher.

29. The Armenian Revolutionary Federation is not included as an opposition party. While it claims to be an opposition force, its status is dubious, as it has participated in government. See Abrahamyan (2008).

30. The United Democratic Forces is a bloc of parties supporting the opposition politician Alyaksandr Milinkevich.

31. Other Russia, a political group formed in 2006 and associated with Garri Kasparov, Mikhail Kasyanov, and Eduard Limonov, has not been granted party status.

32. Shveda (2001) includes a discussion of Ukraine's oligarchic parties.

33. In 1999, the Liberal Democratic Party of Russia was removed from the party list ballot. Using ancillary party organizations registered by family members, Vladimir Zhirinovskiy was able to register the Zhirinovskiy Bloc and run on its party list in 1999. Creating supplementary parties allowed Zhirinovskiy to hedge his bets and gain ballot access after he was initially denied.

34. For example, in Ukraine's 2004 presidential election, I encountered local precinct commissions whose leaderships claimed to be representing Viktor Yanukovych. I questioned them about their affiliations and discovered that most were not officially representing Yanukovych but one of the many minor candidates that had contested the first round unsuccessfully. Their support of these minor

candidates was a fiction; the minor candidates were a vehicle to stack commissions with partisan supporters.

35. All Ukrainian Hromada is quite similar in name to Hromada, the party of jailed former Prime Minister Pavlo Lazarenko. The KUCHMA Bloc did not have the former Ukrainian president on its list but invoked his name as an acronym.

36. Early voting behavior research focused on intensive studies of bellwether communities to unearth the determinants of voting, focusing on membership in various social groups (Berelson et al. 1954; Lazarsfeld et al. 1968).

37. In Campbell et al. (1960), voting behavior research shifted from group membership to long-term psychological connections with parties.

38. Rather than accepting the notion of party identification as a long-term psychological attachment, Morris Fiorina (1981, 247) suggests that party support results from a "running tally of retrospective evaluations of party promises and performance."

39. The exception to this generalization is the Communist Party of the Russian Federation.

40. These datasets cover a large number of post-Soviet countries but relatively few election years. Moreover, the data focus on the mid-late 1990s; no comparable data from the 2000s are publicly available. See the Appendix for details.

TABLE 6.2

1. The parties of power in this analysis are: Republic Bloc (Armenia), Citizens Union of Georgia, People's Union of Kazakhstan, and Our Home is Russia.

TABLE 6.3

1. The main opposition parties in this analysis are: National Democratic Union (Armenia), Belarusan Popular Front, Pro Patria (Estonia), National Democratic Party (Georgia), Democratic Party (Kazakhstan), Latvian Way, Homeland Union (Lithuania), Yabloko (Russia), and People's Rukh (Ukraine).

TABLE 6.4

1. The main opposition parties in this analysis are National Democratic Union (Armenia), National Democratic Party (Georgia), Democratic Party (Kazakhstan), and Yabloko (Russia).

TABLE 6.5

1. In this analysis, Russia's party of power is Unity and its major opposition party is Yabloko. In Ukraine, the party of power is the People's Democratic Party and the main opposition is People's Rukh.

CHAPTER 7

1. Following several scholars in the literature (e.g., Butler and Ranney 1978), I use the plural form "referendums" rather than "referenda."

2. Butler and Ranney (1978) summarize the arguments supporting the democratic qualities of referendums. Qvortrup (2000) challenges this assessment.
3. This issue is addressed in Butler and Ranney (1978), Lijphart (1984), Mendelsohn and Parkin (2001), Scarrow (2001), and Setala (2006).
4. Butler and Ranney (1978), Budge (1996), Bowler and Donovan (1998), and Lupia and Matsusaka (2004) discuss voter competence issues.
5. Suksi (1993) finds that national referendums are permitted in 53 percent of countries surveyed. The ACE Project (2008) reports similar findings, with 59 percent of surveyed countries having mandated referendums on some issues, 53 percent allowing optional referendums, and 26 percent allowing citizen initiatives. http://aceproject.org/epic-en/dd (accessed on June 3, 2008).
6. While the analysis includes only national-level referendums, many subnational units in the region have held policy votes.
7. Whether they produce binding or consultative decisions (Setala 2006).
8. Whether or not the process is controlled by political elites (Smith 1976; Qvortrup 2000).
9. The legal foundation of the referendum, and whether or not it was binding or consultative, was unclear (Venice Commission 2000). Because of this ambiguity, and the fact that it was never implemented, it is coded as consultative.
10. Smith (1976, 6) notes that the dimension of control must be "construed as an expression of manifest intention, apart from the particular issue and irrespective of the actual result."
11. Smith (1976, 6) indicates that "in general . . . it can be assumed that strong control will only be associated with referenda that have foreseeable results in favour of the governing authority."
12. While international organizations did not officially monitor the referendum, the vote was held concurrently with a parliamentary election that received scrutiny. The parliamentary election evidenced significant issues associated with manipulation and fraud.
13. One could also code by the proportion of questions that fall into particular categories, but a more refined measure is not necessary for this analysis.
14. Another example of coding challenges is presented by Russia's 1993 referendum on confidence in President Yeltsin. While the referendum was initiated by Yeltsin, he conceded to the wording preferred by parliament. In this case, the content is coded as uncontrolled (to account for the role of parliament) and prohegemonic.
15. This count is based on questions asked, not referendums held. For example, a referendum posing a policy question and constitutional reform question simultaneously is listed in both categories in this paragraph.
16. The four countries that do not call for referendums to change all or part of the constitution are Georgia, Russia, Turkmenistan, and Uzbekistan. The Georgian constitution envisions constitutional changes enacted through parliament (Article 102), although citizens may initiate efforts to change the constitution. Russia's constitution allocates the power of amendment to national and regional legislative assemblies or to a Constitutional Assembly (Articles 134–137). The Khalk Maslikhaty is given the power to approve constitutional changes in Turkmenistan (Article 113). Uzbekistan's constitution gives the power to alter the constitution to the legislature (Articles 127–128).
17. See Central Electoral Commission of Azerbaijan (2007), http://www.cec.gov.az/en/common/election-referendum/2002.htm.

18. Tatyana Kvyatkovskaya, the plaintiff, won a seat in parliament as part of Naz-arbayev's OTAN Party in 1999 (Oka 2000).
19. See RFE/RL (2008b), "Results of Previous Elections and Referendums." http://www.rferl.org/specials/kyrgyzelections/pastelections.asp
20. Ibid.
21. The release of the Melnychenko tapes, allegedly containing conversations in which President Kuchma discussed a journalist who was later found murdered, demanded that officials commit election fraud, and committed other misdeeds, led to anti-Kuchma protests and helped spark the Orange Revolution four years later.
22. For an analysis of public support for the EU in the Baltic States, see Ehin (2001).
23. Lithuania scheduled a referendum in late 2008 about the status of the Ignalina nuclear plant. The referendum had not been held at the time this book was completed.
24. Both the Stalin Constitution and the 1977 Soviet Constitution authorize referendums.
25. In Russia, some politicians proposed a referendum to extend President Putin's presidency, though he rejected that option. See, for example, Gurin (2004) and Medetsky (2005).

CHAPTER 8

1. Examples of work on election administration include Pastor (1999); Mozaffar and Schedler (2002); Blais, Massicotte, and Yoshinaka (2004); Birch (2007); and Hyde (2006).
2. This quote is often attributed to Joseph Stalin and has appeared in the media all over the world. No direct evidence links the quote to any published material or speech transcripts. Indeed, most of the evidence suggests that the statement is apocryphal.
3. Oversight is the process of monitoring the behavior of the individual, group, or organization under scrutiny and potentially applying corrective action to alter behavior.
4. McCubbins and Schwartz (1984) developed the idea of fire alarm and police patrol oversight with reference to the United States Congress, although it has been applied in other contexts.
5. International observers have a more limited time commitment than domestic observers, who may be part of an ongoing effort to monitor the behavior of political elites.
6. In their report on an observation mission to the Soviet Union, representatives of the U.S. Federal Election Commission noted that "there is no hierarchical command structure from the upper level electoral commissions to the lower level ones, although there must surely be some mechanism of coordination which we were unable to discern" (Federal Election Commission 1990, 32).
7. While the official names of national-level commissions vary, they are most commonly called the Central Electoral Commission. For simplicity, I refer to national commissions using that term, although it may not accurately reflect the official title in any given state.
8. Parties are consulted on membership in Ukraine.

9. The data were coded and processed by Sarah Birch and research assistants at Essex University.

10. See Hendley (1996) for a detailed discussion of the Soviet court system.

11. Charges of partisanship by the courts are relatively common in the region. Armenia's political opposition decried the Constitutional Court's 2003 decision to validate presidential election results, arguing that the process did not comply with international norms. The opposition noted that only a political interpretation, rather than an objective legal interpretation, could have led to this outcome (BBC 2003a). In addition, the CEC alleged that local elites improperly influenced court decisions in Armenia's 1999 local elections (BBC 1999a). In Azerbaijan, the OSCE asserted that controversial registration decisions were influenced by politics and not made by an independent judiciary. The political opposition also challenged court independence (BBC 2000a), and the OSCE (2006a) noted that the courts did not follow rules of procedure and evidence. Belarus' opposition has asserted that the courts are not independent (BBC 2006b). The courts in more democratic states are not immune from criticism. The Estonian Supreme Court's ruling on a decision to ban electoral blocs in local elections prompted the court to defend its decision as purely legal and not political (Baltic News Service 2002a). After losing an appeal in court, a Latvian politician claimed that the courts were part of a "corrupt holy trinity" perverting policymaking (Baltic News Service 2006).

12. For example, the European Court of Human Rights heard *Melnychenko v. Ukraine* and issued a ruling indicating that the appellant was improperly denied the right to contest an election. Melnychenko, whose secretly recorded audio tapes implicated former President Leonid Kuchma in illegal activities, was denied registration by the CEC due to his residency abroad, although he had a valid domestic permanent residence (Goodwin-Gill 2006, 63–65). Other cases from post-Soviet states have been filed in the European Court of Human Rights. See, for example, the case of Armenia's television network A1+ (OSCE 2007a), Juri Bozko in Estonia (OSCE 1999b), or cases regarding lustration laws (Zhdanoka v. Latvia [OSCE 2007c, 5]) and language laws in Latvia (Baltic News Service, April 10, 2002).

13. Ak Zhol's leadership was likely concerned about the potential for protests if it alone gained seats in parliament. The main opposition party, Ata-Meken, failed to gain seats even after the court ruling.

14. A media report cited a slightly higher figure, 10,431 (BBC 2003d).

15. Neighboring Azerbaijan provides an additional example. In the 2003 presidential race, precinct commissions were allowed to adjudicate voter list disputes despite statutory requirements that courts manage them (OSCE 2003d, 9). Courts managed appeals of the voter list in the 2005 parliamentary election, and 14,341 voters made claims to the courts for exclusion from lists (OSCE 2006a).

16. The OSCE report does not indicate how many candidates the CEC reinstated but notes that 166 were denied and "approximately" 120 were rejected, leaving 46 cases reinstated by the CEC. The Supreme Court reinstated 2 (OSCE 2004d, 9–10).

17. Zhirinovskiy was also removed from and returned to the presidential ballot in 2000 due to questions about the veracity and completeness of financial disclosure documents (OSCE 2000h, 19–20).

18. Insulting the president can lead to more serious punishment. A human rights activist was sentenced to two years in prison for offensive comments (Associated Press October 23, 2006).

19. See Bjornlund (2004) for a detailed discussion of the differences among the terms election "election supervision," "election monitoring," and "election observation." Also see Padilla and Houppert (1993), Beigbeder (1994), and Bjornlund (2004) for a history of election observation.

20. Carothers (1997, 18) notes that many smaller organizations that send observers often focus on election day activities and send less-experienced professionals "who stay for only a short time around election day are unlikely to see beyond the obvious."

21. Hyde (2006), however, notes that in Armenia's 2003 presidential election, short-term observer placement approximated random selection.

22. Anecdotally, I encountered overlap in observation and lack of coordination among observer groups on the ground in several election observation experiences.

23. Mendelson (2001) underscores the problem of preliminary reports with reference to Russian elections.

24. For a discussion of parallel vote counts, see Garber and Cowan (1993).

25. For example, representatives from the Committee of Voters of Ukraine received credentials to observe the 2002 election as members of the media.

26. Alexei Borodavkin, Russia's representative to the OSCE, criticized the organization for double standards. He contrasted the OSCE's decision not to observe Estonia's election with its actions in Serbia (Interfax 2007).

CHAPTER 9

1. Elklit and Svennson (1997, 38) note that "irregularities on polling day seriously threaten freedom and fairness only to the extent that they are extensive, systematic, or decisive in a close race."

2. I thank Valentin Mikhailov for this observation.

3. Pressure is not limited to state employers. Private enterprises may also attempt to influence employee voting.

4. As an election observer in Ukraine's 2002 parliamentary election, I received credible testimony from another observer who allegedly witnessed hospital staff instructing voters to choose the progovernment candidate.

5. For examples of pressure in Russia's 2007 parliamentary election, see Solovyov (2007) and Vakhonicheva (2007).

6. Approximately 30 ballots in one polling station were reviewed because they included stray marks outside the boxes provided for candidates. In many cases, voters wrote additional comments or crossed off the opponent's name. Questionable ballots that could reasonably be interpreted as pro-Yanukovych were admitted by a majority vote of the precinct commission. Analogous ballots that favored Yushchenko were dismissed. Yushchenko supporters on the commission and other domestic observers protested these decisions, but they were upheld.

7. "Carousels" are a procedure in which voters remove blank ballots, complete them under the scrutiny of a partisan activist, and then provide completed ballots to another voter who subsequently takes blank ballots from the station to continue the process. See OSCE (2003b) for a description of the process in Armenia.

8. As an international observer for Ukraine's 2002 parliamentary election, I witnessed questionable use of the mobile ballot box. Based on inquiries directed to the chairman of a precinct commission, I was told that the mobile ballot box had been dispatched to a local psychiatric hospital to collect 296 votes. The precinct chairman provided documents ostensibly demonstrating that patients had requested the box, but the documents were patient lists signed by physicians. My observation team visited the hospital and inquired about the box with staff and patients. We received contradictory information about whether or not it had been in the hospital. Upon returning to the precinct, we were told that the box had returned and had been dispatched to another voter's home, rendering it unavailable for inspection.

9. Because the sample is limited to elections where the OSCE completed final reports, selection bias may undermine the generalizability of these observations. The OSCE does not tend to send full missions to countries with adequate election processes or to those with the worst records. For example, Turkmenistan and Uzbekistan are excluded from this discussion because full observation missions were not staged in those countries for any election. This selection mechanism in deployment decisions censors the observations by eliminating cases on the extreme ends of the spectrum.

10. The analysis includes these elections largely because appropriate precinct-level or territorial-level data are available.

11. Also see Myagkov, Ordeshook, and Shakin (2005; 2007).

12. See Hill (1998) and Nigrini (1999; 2006) for applications of Benford's Law.

13. The "third round" of the presidential election occurred after the second-round runoff was deemed fraudulent, prompting massive protests and the "Orange Revolution." The third round repeated the runoff between the progovernment candidate Viktor Yanukovych and the opposition candidate Viktor Yushchenko. Unfortunately, data for the second round are unavailable.

14. For example, Ariel Cohen (2007) of the Heritage Foundation wrote a positive appraisal of the election in the *Washington Times*. While his commentary acknowledged vote fraud of "about 10 percent," Cohen concluded that the election was "relatively clean."

15. Exit polls suggested that Nur-OTAN's vote was inflated (Ivanova 2007).

16. For precinct-level results, see Central Electoral Commission of the Republic of Kazakhstan (2008). http://election.kz/portal/page?_pageid=73,473388&_dad=portal&_schema=PORTAL. Last accessed on March 10, 2008.

17. In one precinct in Karasai, the ruling party received 615 votes although the results indicate that only 62 voters turned out to cast ballots. This could be a typographical error, or an egregious effort to inflate results for Nur-OTAN.

18. The second-digit test was not significant in any region for any party.

19. The data used in this analysis were compiled from electronic versions of precinct-level protocols provided by the Ukrainian Central Electoral Commission (2002) available online at: http://195.230.157.53/pls/vd2002/webproc0v). The CEC reported that Ukrainian citizens cast ballots in 33,113 polling stations; the data set includes 32,790 precincts. In some cases, data are only reported for one of the PR or SMD ballots in a precinct, however, creating variation in the total number of PR and SMD precinct results.

20. This observation does not rule out the possibility that other parties may commit fraud. Local control of election commissions could allow parties in the opposition or propresidential camp to systematically influence precinct level results.

21. This assumption is complicated by the "selection mechanism" for voters in some special precincts. Voters casting ballots in special precincts may not match the overall distribution of voters based on demographic factors or party support. While military voters or those in the foreign service may be more likely to support the president than the general population, no clear evidence suggests that sick or incarcerated voters should be more likely to support the president's party.

22. Because expatriates voted in two precincts whose choice sets did not match the criteria, embassy precincts are excluded.

23. A parallel analysis using OLS produced similar results (Herron and Johnson 2008).

TABLE 9.1

1. Russia's results were derived from detailed territorial election commission results reported in percentage terms, with the total number of voters in each territory. The analysis includes 2,761 TIK results.

CHAPTER 10

1. The size and cause of protest events varied, but some were large and directly related to Soviet political institutions. In 1978, for example, the debate over language issues in local constitutions mobilized thousands of protesters in Georgia (Beissinger 1998).

2. The stated goals of protesters vary, rendering the definition of "successful" and "unsuccessful" protest challenging. In the analysis, a successful protest results in candidate reinstatement, a repeat of the disputed election, or annulment of election results. Unsuccessful protests may end with repression or simple attrition of protesters, but the initial election outcome is certified and stands.

3. For a primer on post-Soviet corruption, see Karklins (2005) and Ledeneva (2006).

4. Francisco and Herron (2006) note that elections do not consistently produce large-scale demonstrations or protest activity. In their assessment of West European states, elections did not send more powerful mobilization signals to European citizens than other rallying events. Moreover, in the analysis discussed later in this chapter, over half of the elections surveyed were accompanied by no reported protest activity.

5. See, for example, Gurr (1970).

6. This assertion follows Ekiert and Kubik (1998). They acknowledged that this formulation assesses general feelings of deprivation rather than *relative* deprivation, as many proponents of the theory suggest.

7. Ekiert and Kubik (1998) note that past protest activity is connected with later protest activity, but better explains the methods of subsequent protests rather than their scale.

8. Contract solutions involve the creation of a strong "us" versus "them" sentiment in which individuals monitor each other for signs of disloyalty or defection to the other side. Hierarchy solutions use preexisting organizations to mobilize.

9. Kowalewski and Schumaker (1981) note that in more open societies, protest groups and governments attempt to convince third parties to support their cause. In more authoritarian societies, participation by third parties is actively

discouraged by the state apparatus, restricting the conflict to protesters and the government.

10. The analysis does not include the Tajik Civil War as a postelection protest, although it was, in part, sparked by the 1991 presidential results.

11. See the Appendix for more information about the data used on Table 10.1 and in the case studies.

12. In this analysis, protest activity is considered to be sustained when three events occur within one week.

13. Protest activity in 2007 led to an early presidential election in 2008. However, an election was not the catalyst for this protest.

14. Kowalewski and Schumaker (1981, 63) indicate that 88 percent of protest activities were designed to achieve specific goals for the group initiating the protest, rather than more diffuse outcomes. Religious organizations advocating free religious expression were prominent among these groups, as were nationally or ethnically based groups.

15. Ukrainians led all ethnic groups from 1987–1992 in the number of ethnonationalist protests, with 782, followed by Armenians, (546), Georgians (394), and Lithuanians (325) (Beissinger 2002, 210–11).

16. Successful electoral protests are not as common as some scholars have suggested. While Bunce and Wolchik (2006a) note the strong connection between regime change and election protest, they only include twenty elections that "allow for the possibility of turnover" and do not fully account for failed efforts.

17. Francisco (1996), D'Anieri (2006), and Levitsky and Way (2006) note the important role of security services in determining the fate of public protest.

18. Assistance includes the diffusion of ideas from comparable groups in other postcommunist states, as well as support from independent organizations and foreign governments (Bunce and Wolchik 2006a; 2006b). In a personal conversation with a leader of the Ukrainian youth group Pora that organized the protests in Kyiv during the Orange Revolution, I was told about the group's contact with other organizations abroad to gain and disseminate technical expertise on mobilization. Personal conversation, March 22, 2006.

19. In particular, the U.S. government response was interpreted as displaying a double standard. Due to its praise of court decisions vacating election results in ten districts and recommendation that the opposition contest by-elections in those districts, the United States was accused by some in the opposition of "selling out" in Azerbaijan while it had supported opposition claims in Georgia and Ukraine (Ismayilov 2005a).

20. Belarusan government officials attempted to increase the costs of protest significantly. They alleged that the opposition was planning to commit fraud (BBC 2006a) and stage a coup (Associated Press 2006b), signaling that they were treating the opposition as a threat to state security. Moreover, officials indicated that protesters would be considered terrorists (Deutsche Presse Agentur 2006).

21. However, the report has been criticized, even by OSCE observers, for spinning the election too positively (de Pourbaix-Lundlin and Eorsi 2008).

TABLE 10.1

1. The total includes election periods. In some cases, the election period includes two elections.

CONCLUSION

1. Clark's (2002) book on the study of postcommunist states addresses both traditions, noting that conditions are appropriate in some states to apply rational choice approaches.
2. The cultural inheritance is often traced back well beyond the Soviet period.
3. The brief tenure (1918–1921) of republics in the South Caucasus did not provide a substantial democratic foundation either.
4. See, for example, the work of Ellen Mickiewicz (1997; 2006).
5. See, for example, Herron and Sekhon (2003), Knack and Kropf (2003), and Tomz and van Houweling (2003).

APPENDIX

1. The xtpcse command in Stata.
2. In some cases, there are minor discrepancies between my calculations and the Golder data.
3. Trend 30 on Table 3 (Reif et al. 2004).
4. Trends 31 and 32 on Table 3 (Reif et al. 2004).
5. Trends 8 and 9 on Table 3 (Reif et al. 2004).
6. Trend 14 on Table 3 (Reif et al. 2004).
7. Engagement in other forms of democratic political participation was associated with a greater propensity to vote in Lithuania. Left-right placement was not significant.
8. In Russia's 2000 survey, no respondents indicated that they abstained (an implausible result). The 289 nonrespondents were included as nonvoters.
9. At this time, no sizable age cohorts were socialized outside of the communist experience (i.e., in 1996, eighteen-year-olds were thirteen when the USSR collapsed). Using a continuous variable should capture the depth of experience in the Soviet system.
10. Calculations based on overall participation including invalid votes, or only valid votes, produce slightly different results.
11. This party differs from the People's Party of Armenia.
12. The analysis of Estonia and Latvia also included a variable for Russian ethnicity because of their particularly contentious ethnic politics. The variable was not statistically significant.
13. Datas is a series of Excel macros developed by Mark Nigrini.

REFERENCES

BOOKS, JOURNAL ARTICLES, AND WORKING PAPERS

Abramson, Paul R., and William Claggett. 1991. Racial differences in self-reported turnout in the 1988 presidential election. *Journal of Politics* 53 (1): 186–97.

Aldrich, John. 1993. Rational choice and turnout. *American Journal of Political Science* 37 (1): 246–78.

———. 1995. *Why parties? The origin and transformation of political parties in America.* Chicago: University of Chicago Press.

Alvarez, R. M., Delia Bailey, and Jonathan N. Katz. 2007. *The effect of voter identification laws on turnout.* Social Science Working Paper 1267. California Institute of Technology.

Alvarez, R. M., and Jonathan Nagler. 1998. When politics and models collide: Estimating models of multiparty elections. *American Journal of Political Science* 42 (1): 55–96.

Amorim Neto, Octavio, and Gary W. Cox. 1997. Electoral institutions, cleavage structures, and the number of parties. *American Journal of Political Science* 41 (1): 140–74.

Anderson, Barbara A., and Brian D. Silver. 1986. Measurement and mismeasurement of the validity of the self-reported vote. *American Journal of Political Science* 30 (4): 771–85.

Anderson, Christopher J., Andre Blais, Shaun Bowler, Todd Donovan, and Ola Listhaug. 2005. *Losers' consent: Elections and democratic legitimacy.* Oxford: Oxford University Press.

Anderson, Christopher J., and Silvia M. Mendes. 2006. Learning to lose: Election outcomes, democratic experience, and political protest potential. *British Journal of Political Science* 36 (1): 91–111.

Andrews, Josephine T., and Robert W. Jackman. 2005. Strategic fools: Electoral rule choice under extreme uncertainty. *Electoral Studies* 24 (1): 65–84.

Arendt, Hannah. 1951. *The origins of totalitarianism.* New York: Harcourt, Brace.

Argersinger, Peter H. 1985–1986. New perspectives on election fraud in the gilded age. *Political Science Quarterly* 100 (4): 669–87.

Aron, Leon. 2000. *Yeltsin: A revolutionary life.* New York: St. Martin's Press.

Barreto, Matt A., Gary M. Segura, and Nathan D. Woods. 2004. The mobilizing effect of majority-minority districts on Latino turnout. *American Political Science Review* 98 (1): 65–75.

Barrington, Lowell W. 1995. The domestic and international consequences of citizenship in the Soviet successor states. *Europe-Asia Studies* 47 (5): 731–64.

Barrington, Lowell W., and Erik S. Herron. 2004. One Ukraine or many?? Regionalism in Ukraine and its political consequences. *Nationalities Papers* 32:53–86.

Barrington, Lowell W., Erik S. Herron, and Brian D. Silver. 2003. The motherland is calling: Views of homeland among Russians in the near abroad. *World Politics* 55 (2): 290–313.

Bawn, Kathleen. 1993. The logic of institutional preferences: German electoral law as a social choice outcome. *American Journal of Political Science* 37 (4): 965–89.

Beetham, David. 2005. Freedom as the foundation. In *Assessing the quality of democracy*, ed. Larry Diamond and Leonardo Morlino. Baltimore: Johns Hopkins University Press.

Beigbeder, Yves. 1994. *International monitoring of plebiscites, referenda and national elections*. Boston: Martinus Nijhoff Publishers.

Beissinger, Mark R. 2002. *Nationalist mobilization and the collapse of the Soviet state*. Cambridge: Cambridge University Press.

———. 1998. Nationalist violence and the state: Political authority and contentious repertoires in the former USSR. *Comparative Politics* 30 (4): 401–22.

———. 2007. Structure and example in modular political phenomena: The diffusion of Bulldozer/Rose/Orange/Tulip Revolutions. *Perspectives on Politics* 5 (2): 259–76.

Bennich-Bjorkman, Li. 2007. The cultural roots of Estonia's successful transition: How historical legacies shaped the 1990s. *East European Politics and Societies* 21 (2): 316–47.

Benoit, Kenneth. 2004. Models of electoral system change. *Electoral Studies* 23: 363–89.

———. 2007. Electoral laws as political consequences: Explaining the origins and change of electoral institutions. *Annual Review of Political Science* 10:363–90.

Benoit, Kenneth, and Jacqueline Hayden. 2004. Institutional change and persistence: The origins and evolution of Poland's electoral system, 1989–1999. *Journal of Politics* 66 (2): 396–427.

Benoit, Kenneth, and John W. Schiemann. 2001. Institutional choice in new democracies: Bargaining over Hungary's 1989 electoral law. *Journal of Theoretical Politics* 13(2):159–88.

Bensel, Richard F. 2004. *The American ballot box in the mid-nineteenth century*. New York: Cambridge University Press.

Berelson, Bernard R., Paul F. Lazarsfeld, and William N. McPhee. 1954. *Voting*. Chicago: Chicago University Press.

Bielasiak, Jack. 2002. The institutionalization of electoral and party systems in post-communist states. *Comparative Politics* 35:189–210.

Birch, Sarah. 1995. Electoral behaviour in Western Ukraine in national elections and referendum, 1989–1991. *Europe-Asia Studies* 47 (7): 1145–76.

———. 2000. *Elections and democratization in Ukraine*. New York: St. Martin's Press.

———. 2001. Electoral systems and party system stability in post-communist Europe. Paper presented at the American Political Science Association Conference, September 2001.

———. 2007. Electoral systems and electoral misconduct. *Comparative Political Studies* 40(12):1533–66.

Birch, Sarah, Frances Millard, Marina Popescu, and Kieran Williams. 2002. *Embodying democracy: Electoral system design in post-communist Europe*. Houndmills, UK: Palgrave Macmillan.

Bjornlund, Eric C. 2004. *Beyond free and fair: Monitoring elections and building democracy*. Washington, DC: Woodrow Wilson Center Press.

Blais, Andre. 2006. What affects voter turnout? *Annual Review of Political Science* 9:111–25.

Blais, Andre, Louis Massicotte, and Antoine Yoshinaka. 2004. *Establishing the rules of the game: Election laws in democracies*. Toronto: University of Toronto Press.

Boix, Carles. 1999. Setting the rules of the game: The choice of electoral systems in advanced democracies. *American Political Science Review* 93 (3): 609–24.

Bojcun, Marko. 1995. The Ukrainian parliamentary elections in March-April 1994. *Europe-Asia Studies* 47 (2): 229–49.

Bollen, Kenneth A. 1980. Issues in the comparative measurement of political democracy. *American Sociological Review* 45 (2): 370–90.

———. 1993. Liberal democracy: Validity and method factors in cross-national measures. *American Journal of Political Science* 37 (4): 1207–30.

Bollen, Kenneth A., and Pamela Paxton. 2000. Subjective measures of liberal democracy. *Comparative Political Studies* 33 (1): 58–86.

Borders, Karl. 1929. Local autonomy in Russian village life under the Soviets. *Social Forces* 7 (3): 409–14.

Bowler, Shaun, and Todd Donovan. 1998. *Demanding choices: Opinion, voting, and direct democracy*. Ann Arbor: University of Michigan Press.

Boylan, Scott P. 1998. The status of judicial reform in Russia. *American University International Law Review* 13:1327.

Brader, Ted, and Joshua A. Tucker. 2001. The emergence of mass partisanship in Russia, 1993–1996. *American Journal of Political Science* 45 (1): 69–83.

Brady, Henry E., and Cynthia S. Kaplan. 1994. Eastern Europe and the former Soviet Union. In *Referendums around the world*, ed. Ian Budge and Austin Ranney. Washington, DC: American Enterprise Institute.

Brunner, Georg. 1990. Elections in the Soviet Union. In *Elections in socialist states*, ed. Robert K. Furtak. New York: Harvester Wheatsheaf.

Budge, Ian. 1996. *The new challenge of direct democracy*. Cambridge: Polity Press.

Bunce, Valerie. 1995a. Paper curtains and paper tigers. *Slavic Review* 54 (4): 979–87.

———. 1995b. Should transitologists be grounded? *Slavic Review* 54 (1): 111–27.

Bunce, Valerie J., and Sharon L. Wolchik. 2006a. Favorable conditions and electoral revolutions. *Journal of Democracy* 17 (4): 5–18.

———. 2006b. International diffusion and postcommunist electoral revolutions. *Communist and Post-Communist Studies* 39:283–304.

Butler, David, and Austin Ranney. 1978. *Referendums: A comparative study of practice and theory*. Washington, DC: American Enterprise Institute.

Cain, Bruce E. 1978. Strategic voting in Britain. *American Journal of Political Science* 22 (3): 639–55.

Callahan, William A., and Duncan McCargo. 1996. Vote-buying in Thailand's northeast: The July 1995 general election. *Asian Survey* 36 (4): 376–92.

Campbell, Angus, Philip E. Converse, Warren E. Miller, and Donald E. Stokes. 1960. *The American voter*. Chicago: Chicago University Press.

Campbell, Tracy. 2005. *Deliver the vote: A history of election fraud, an American political tradition (1742–2004)*. New York: Carroll and Graf.

Carnaghan, Ellen. 2007. Do Russians dislike democracy? *PS: Political Science & Politics* 40 (1): 61–66.

Carothers, Thomas. 2002. The end of the transition paradigm. *Journal of Democracy* 13 (1): 5–21.

———. 1997. The observers observed. *Journal of Democracy* 8 (3): 17–31.

Carson Jr., George B. 1955. *Electoral practices in the USSR*. New York: Frederick A. Praeger.

Chang, Eric C. C., and Miriam Golden. 2007. Electoral systems, district magnitude, and corruption. *British Journal of Political Science* 37 (1): 115–37.

Chaturvedi, Ashish. 2005. Rigging elections with violence. *Public Choice* 125: 189–202.

Chhibber, Pradeep, and Ken Kollman. 1998. Party aggregation and the number of parties in India and the United States. *American Political Science Review* 92 (2): 329–42.

Chiesa, Giuletto. 1993. *Transition to democracy: Political change in the Soviet Union, 1987–1991.* Hanover: University Press of New England.

Clark, Terry D. 2002. *Beyond post-communist studies: Political science and the new democracies of Europe.* Armonk, NY: M. E. Sharpe.

Clark, Terry D., and Jill N. Wittrock. 2005. Presidentialism and the effect of electoral law in postcommunist systems: Regime type matters. *Comparative Political Studies* 38 (2): 171–88.

Clark, William R., and Matt Golder. 2006. Rehabilitating Duverger's theory: Testing the mechanical and strategic modifying effects of electoral laws. *Comparative Political Studies* 39 (6): 679–708.

Collier, David, and Steven Levitsky. 1997. Democracy with adjectives: Conceptual innovation in comparative research. *World Politics* 49 (3): 430–51.

Colomer, Josep. 2005. It's the parties that choose the electoral systems (or Duverger's law upside down). *Political Studies* 53 (1): 1–21.

Colton, Timothy J. 2000. *Transitional citizens: Voters and what influences them in the new Russia.* Cambridge: Harvard University Press.

Colton, Timothy J., and Michael McFaul. 2003. Russian democracy under Putin. *Problems of Post-Communism* 50 (4): 12–21.

Cox, Gary W. 1997. *Making votes count: Strategic coordination in the world's electoral systems.* Cambridge: Cambridge University Press.

Cox, Gary W., and J. M. Kousser. 1981. Turnout and rural corruption: New York as a test case. *American Journal of Political Science* 25 (4): 646–63.

Cox, Homersham. 1868. *Antient parliamentary elections.* Repr., London: Longmans, Green, 2005.

Cox, Karen, and Len Schoppa. 2002. Interaction effects in mixed-member electoral systems: Theory and evidence from Germany, Japan and Italy. *Comparative Political Studies* 35 (9): 1027–53.

Craumer, Peter R., and James I. Clem. 1999. Ukraine's emerging electoral geography: A regional analysis of the 1998 parliamentary elections. *Post-Soviet Geography and Economics* 40:1–26.

D'Anieri, Paul. 2006a. Explaining the success and failure of post-communist revolutions. *Communist and Post-Communist Studies* 39:331–50.

———. 2006b. *Understanding Ukrainian politics: Power, politics, and institutional design.* Armonk, NY: M. E. Sharpe.

Dahl, Robert. 1971. *Polyarchy: Participation and opposition.* New Haven, CT: Yale University Press.

Dando, William A. 1966. A map of the election to the Russian constituent assembly of 1917. *Slavic Review* 25 (2): 314–19.

Davenport, Christian. 1997. From ballots to bullets: An empirical assessment of how national elections influence state uses of political repression. *Electoral Studies* 16 (4): 517–40.

Dawisha, Karen. 2000. The unintended consequences of electoral reform. Working Paper, Johns Hopkins School of Advanced International Studies.

DeBardeleben, Joan. 2003. Fiscal federalism and how Russians vote. *Europe-Asia Studies* 55 (3): 339–63.

Diamond, Larry J. 1996. Is the third wave over? *Journal of Democracy* 7 (3): 20–37.

Diwakar, Rekha. 2007. Duverger's law and the size of the Indian party system. *Party Politics* 13 (5): 539–61.

Djilas, Milovan. 1958. *The new class: An analysis of the communist system*. London: Thames and Hudson.

Duverger, Maurice. 1954. *Political parties, their organization and activity in the modern state*. New York: Harper and Row.

Duverger, Maurice. 1954. *Political parties, their organization and activity in the modern state*. New York: Wiley.

Easter, Gerald. 2000. *Reconstructing the state: Personal networks and elite identity in Soviet Russia*. Cambridge: Cambridge University Press.

Ehin, Piret. 2001. Determinants of public support for EU membership: Data from the Baltic countries. *European Journal of Political Research*. 40:31–56.

Ekiert, Grzegorz, and Jan Kubik. 1998. Contentious politics in new democracies: East Germany, Hungary, Poland, and Slovakia, 1989–93. *World Politics* 50 (4): 547–81.

Eldersveld, Samuel. 1982. *Political parties in American society*. New York: Basic Books.

Elklit, Jorgen, and Palle Svensson. 1997. What makes elections free and fair? *Journal of Democracy* 8 (3): 32–46.

Elster, Jon, Claus Offe, and Ulrich K. Pruess. 1998. *Institutional design in postcommunist societies: Rebuilding the ship at sea*. Cambridge: Cambridge University Press.

Fainsod, Merle. 1965. *How Russia is ruled*. Cambridge: Harvard University Press.

Ferejohn, John A., and Morris P. Fiorina. 1974. The paradox of not voting: A decision theoretic analysis. *American Political Science Review* 68 (2): 525–36.

Ferrara, Federico, and Erik S. Herron. 2005. Going it alone? Strategic entry under mixed electoral rules. *American Journal of Political Science* 49 (1): 16–31.

Ferrara, Federico, Erik S. Herron, and Misa Nishikawa. 2005. *Mixed electoral systems: Contamination and its consequences*. New York: Palgrave.

Figes, Orlando. 1988. The village and volost Soviet elections of 1919. *Soviet Studies* 40 (1): 21–45.

Fiorina, Morris P. 1981. *Retrospective voting in American national elections*. New Haven, CT: Yale University Press.

Fleron, Frederic J., and Erik P. Hoffman. 1993. *Post-communist studies and political science*. Boulder, CO: Westview.

Francisco, Ronald, and Erik S. Herron. 2006. Cheaters never win? Elections, fraud, and political violence. Paper presented at the Midwest Political Science Association Conference, April 2006.

Francisco, Ronald A. 1996. Coercion and protest: An empirical test in two democratic states. *American Journal of Political Science* 40 (4): 1179–1204.

Franklin, Charles H. 1991. Eschewing obfuscation? Campaigns and the perception of US Senate incumbents. *American Political Science Review* 85 (4): 1193–214.

Franklin, Mark N. 2004. *Voter turnout and the dynamics of electoral competition in established democracies.* Cambridge: Cambridge University Press.

Friedrich, Carl J., and Zbigniew K. Brzezinski. 1956. *Totalitarian dictatorship and autocracy.* Cambridge: Harvard University Press.

Frolov, Vladimir. 2005. Democracy by remote control. *Russia in Global Affairs.* http://eng.globalaffairs.ru/printver/976.html (accessed November 15, 2007).

Frye, Timothy. 1997. A politics of institutional choice: Post-communist presidencies. *Comparative Political Studies* 30 (5): 523–52.

Frye, Timothy, Joel Hellman, and Joshua Tucker. 2000. *Database on political institutions in the post-communist world.* Ohio State University.

Fukuyama, Francis. 1989. The end of history? *The National Interest* (Summer).

———. 1992. *The end of history and the last man.* New York: Free Press.

Gaines, Brian. 1999. Duverger's law and the meaning of Canadian exceptionalism. *Comparative Political Studies* 32 (7): 835–61.

Garber, Larry, and Glen Cowan. 1993. The virtues of parallel vote tabulations. *Journal of Democracy* 4 (2): 95–107.

Gerber, Alan S., Donald P. Green, and Ron Shachar. 2003. Voting may be habit-forming: Evidence from a randomized field experiment. *American Journal of Political Science* 47 (3): 540–50.

Geys, Benny. 2006. Explaining voter turnout: A review of aggregate-level research. *Electoral Studies* 25 (4): 637–63.

Gilison, Jerome M. 1968. Soviet elections as a measure of dissent: The missing one percent. *American Political Science Review* 62 (3): 814–26.

Gill, Graeme. 1991. Sources of political reform in the Soviet Union. *Studies in Comparative Communism* 24:235–57.

Gleditsch, Kristian S., and Michael D. Ward. 1997. Double take: A reexamination of democracy and autocracy in modern polities. *Journal of Conflict Resolution* 41 (3): 361–83.

Golder, Matt. 2005. Democratic electoral systems around the world, 1946–2000. *Electoral Studies* 24 (1): 103–21.

Golosov, Grigori V. 2003a. Electoral systems and party formation in Russia: A cross-regional analysis. *Comparative Political Studies* 36 (8): 912–35.

———. 2003b. The vicious circle of party underdevelopment in Russia: The regional connection. *International Political Science Review* 24 (4): 427–43.

Goodwin-Gill, Guy S. 2006. *Free and fair elections.* Geneva: Inter-Parliamentary Union.

Graham, Loren, and Jean-Michel Kantor. 2007. "Soft" area studies versus "hard" social sciences: A false opposition. *Slavic Review* 66 (1): 1–19.

Griffin, John D., and Michael Keane. 2006. Descriptive representation and the composition of African American turnout. *American Journal of Political Science* 50 (4): 998–1012.

Grofman, Bernard. 1979. Abstention in two-candidate and three-candidate elections when voters use mixed strategies. *Public Choice* 34 (2): 189–200.

———. 2004. Downs and two party convergence. *Annual Review of Political Science* 7:25–46.

Grzymala-Busse, Anna M. 2002. *Redeeming the communist past: The regeneration of communist parties in East Central Europe.* Cambridge: Cambridge University Press.

Gurr, Ted R. 1970. Sources of rebellion in Western societies: Some quantitative evidence. *Annals of the American Academy of Political Science* 391 (1): 128–44.

Hale, Henry. 2005. Why not parties? Electoral markets, party substitutes, and stalled democratization in Russia. *Comparative Politics* 37 (2): 147–66.

———. 2006. *Why not parties in Russia? Democracy, federalism, and the state.* Cambridge: Cambridge University Press.

Hendley, Kathryn. 1996. *Trying to make law matter: Legal reform and labor law in the Soviet Union.* Ann Arbor: University of Michigan Press.

Herron, Erik S. 2002a. Causes and consequences of fluid faction membership in Ukraine. *Europe-Asia Studies* 54 (4): 625–39.

———. 2002b. Electoral effects on legislative behavior in mixed-member systems: Evidence from Ukraine's Verkhovna Rada. *Legislative Studies Quarterly* 27 (3): 361–82.

———. 2002c. Mixed electoral rules and party strategies: Responses to incentives by Ukraine's Rukh and Russia's Yabloko. *Party Politics* 8 (6): 719–33.

———. 2004. Political actors, preferences and election rule re-design in Russia and Ukraine. *Democratization* 11 (2): 41–59.

———. 2007. State institutions, political context, and parliamentary election legislation in Ukraine, 2000–2006. *Journal of Communist Studies and Transition Politics* 23 (1): 57–76.

Herron, Erik S., and Paul Johnson. 2008. Fraud before the "revolution": Special precincts in Ukraine's 2002 parliamentary election. In *Aspects of the Orange Revolution III: The context and dynamics of the 2004 Ukrainian presidential elections*, ed. Ingmar Bredies, Valentin Yakushik, and Andreas Umland. Stuttgart: Ibidem-verlag.

Herron, Erik S., and Irakli Mirzashvili. 2005. "Georgians cannot help being original": The evolution of election rules in the Republic of Georgia. In *The state of law in the South Caucasus*, ed. Christopher P. M. Waters. New York: Palgrave.

Herron, Michael C., and Jasjeet S. Sekhon. 2003. Overvoting and representation: An examination of overvoted presidential ballots in Broward and Miami-Dade Counties. *Electoral Studies* 22 (1): 21–47.

Hill, Ronald J. 1972. Continuity and change in USSR Supreme Soviet elections. *British Journal of Political Science* 2 (1): 47–67.

———. 1973. Patterns of deputy selection to local soviets. *Soviet Studies* 25 (2): 196–212.

———. 1976. The CPSU in a Soviet election campaign. *Soviet Studies* 28 (4): 590–98.

Hill, T. P. 1998. The First Digit Phenomenon. *American Scientist* 86:358–63.

Honaker, James, Anne Joseph, Gary King, and Kenneth Scheve. 2001. Analyzing incomplete political science data: An alternative algorithm for multiple imputation. *American Political Science Review* 95 (1): 46–69.

Huntington, Samuel P. 1991. *The third wave: Democratization in the late twentieth century.* Norman: University of Oklahoma Press.

Hyde, Susan D. 2006. Do international election observers deter local electoral fraud? Experimental evidence from Armenian presidential elections. Paper Presented at the Annual Meeting of the International Studies Association, San Diego, California.

Ishiyama, John. 1996. Red phoenix? The communist party in post-Soviet politics. *Party Politics* 2:147–75.

———. 1997. The sickle or the rose?: Previous regime types and the evolution of the ex-communist parties in post-communist societies. *Comparative Political Studies* 30:299–330.

———. 1999. Sickles into roses: The communist successor parties and democratic consolidation in comparative perspective. *Democratization* 6:52–73.

Ishiyama, John T., and Ryan Kennedy. 2001. Mixed electoral systems, super presidentialism, candidate recruitment and political party development in Russia, Ukraine, Armenia and Kyrgyzstan. *Europe-Asia Studies* 53 (8): 1177–91.

Jackman, Robert W. 1987. Political institutions and voter turnout in the industrial democracies. *American Political Science Review* 81 (2): 405–24.

Jacobs, Everett M. 1970. Soviet local elections: What they are, and what they are not. *Soviet Studies* 22 (1): 61–76.

Janda, Kenneth. 1980. *Political parties: A cross-national survey*. New York: Free Press.

Jones Luong, Pauline. 2002. *Institutional change and political continuity in post-Soviet Central Asia*. Cambridge: Cambridge University Press.

Jones, Mark P. 1999. Electoral laws and the effective number of candidates in presidential elections. *Journal of Politics* 61 (1): 171–84.

———. 1995. *Electoral laws and the survival of presidential democracies*. South Bend: Notre Dame University Press.

Jowitt, Kenneth. 1996. Dizzy with democracy. *Problems of Post-Communism* 43 (1): 3–9.

Kara, Ahmet. 2007. The parliamentary elections in Azerbaijan, November 2005 and May 2006. *Electoral Studies* 26:721–24.

Karklins, Rasma. 1986. Soviet elections revisited: Voter abstention in noncompetitive voting. *American Political Science Review* 80 (2): 449–70.

———. 2005. *The system made me do it*. Armonk: M. E. Sharpe.

Katz, Jonathan, and Gary King. 1999. A statistical model for multiparty electoral data. *American Political Science Review* 93 (1): 15–32.

Katz, Richard S., and Peter Mair. 1995. Changing models of party organization and party democracy: The emergence of the cartel party. *Party Politics* 1 (1): 5–28.

Kiernan, Brendan, and Joseph Aistrup. 1991. The 1989 elections to the Congress of People's Deputies in Moscow. *Soviet Studies* 43 (6): 1049–64.

King, Gary, Michael Tomz, and Jason Wittenberg. 2000. Making the most of statistical analysis: Improving interpretation and presentation. *American Journal of Political Science* 44 (2): 347–61.

Kingdon, John W. 1995. *Agendas, alternatives, and public policies*. New York: Harper Collins.

Knack, Stephen, and Martha Kropf. 2003. Voided ballots in the 1996 presidential election: A county-level analysis. *Journal of Politics* 65 (3): 881–97.

Korgunyuk, Yuriy G. 1999. *Sovremennaya Rossiiskaya mnogopartiinost*. Moscow: INDEM.

Kostadinova, Tatiana. 2003. Voter turnout dynamics in post-communist Europe. *European Journal of Political Research* 42 (6): 741–59.

Kostadinova, Tatiana, and Timothy J. Power. 2007. Does democratization depress participation? Voter turnout in the Latin American and Eastern European transitional democracies. *Political Research Quarterly* 60 (3): 363–77.

Kowalewski, David, and Paul Schumaker. 1981. Protest outcomes in the Soviet Union. *The Sociological Quarterly* 22 (1): 57–68.

Kuenzi, Michelle, and Gina Lambright. 2001. Party system institutionalization in 30 African countries. *Party Politics* 7:437–68.

Kunicova, Jana, and Susan Rose-Ackerman. 2005. Electoral rules and constitutional structures as constraints on corruption. *British Journal of Political Science* 35 (4): 573–606.

Kuzio, Taras. 2001. Transition in post-communist states: Triple or quadruple? *Politics* 21 (3): 168–77.

Laakso, M., and Rein Taagepera. 1979. "Effective" number of parties: A measure with application to West Europe. *Comparative Political Studies* 12 (1): 3–27.

Ladner, A., and H. Milner. 1999. Do voters turn out more under proportional than majoritarian systems? The evidence from Swiss communal elections. *Electoral Studies* 18 (2): 235–50.

LaPalombara, Joseph, and Myron Weiner. 1966. *Political parties and political development.* Princeton, NJ: Princeton University Press.

Lazarsfeld, Paul F., Bernard Berelson, and Hazel Gaudet. 1968. *The people's choice: How the voter makes up his mind in a presidential campaign.* New York: Columbia University Press.

Ledeneva, Alena V. 2006. *How Russia really works.* Ithaca: Cornell University Press.

Lehoucq, Fabrice. 2003. Electoral fraud: Causes, types, and consequences. *Annual Review of Political Science* 6:233–56.

Lehoucq, Fabrice, and Ivan Molina. 2002. *Stuffing the ballot box: Fraud, electoral reform, and democratization in Costa Rica.* Cambridge: Cambridge University Press.

Leighley, Jan E., and Jonathan Nagler. 1992. Individual and systemic influences on turnout: Who votes? 1984. *Journal of Politics* 54 (3): 718–40.

Levitsky, Steven, and Lucan A. Way. 2006. The dynamics of autocratic coercion after the Cold War. *Communist and Post-Communist Studies* 39:387–410.

Levitsky, Steven, and Lucan A. Way. 2002. The rise of competitive authoritarianism. *Journal of Democracy* 13 (2): 51–65.

Lichbach, Mark I. 1987. Deterrence or escalation? The puzzle of aggregate studies of repression and dissent. *Journal of Conflict Resolution* 31:266–97.

———. 1995a. The 5% rule. *Rationality and Society.* 7:126.

———. 1995b. *The rebel's dilemma.* Ann Arbor: University of Michigan Press.

———. 1996. *The cooperator's dilemma.* Ann Arbor: University of Michigan Press.

Lijphart, Arend. 1984. *Democracies: Patterns of majoritarian and consensus government in twenty-one countries.* New Haven, CT: Yale University Press.

———. 1994. *Electoral systems and party systems: A study of twenty-seven democracies, 1945–1990.* Oxford: Oxford University Press.

———. 1999. *Patterns of democracy: Government forms and performance in thirty-six countries.* New Haven, CT: Yale University Press.

Lipset, Seymour M. 1960. *Political man.* New York: Doubleday.

Lipset, Seymour M., and Stein Rokkan. 1967. *Party systems and voter alignments: Cross-national perspectives.* New York: Free Press.

Lupia, Arthur, and John G. Matsusaka. 2004. Direct democracy: New approaches to old questions. *Annual Review of Political Science* 7:463–82.

Lynch, Dov. 2005. "The enemy is at the gate": Russia after Beslan. *International Affairs* 81 (1): 141–61.

Lyubarev, A. E. 2003. Golosovanie 'Protiv Vsekh': Motivy i Tendentsii. *POLIS: Politicheskie Issledovaniia,* Eastview Publications.

Mainwaring, Scott, and Timothy R. Scully. 1995. *Building democratic institutions: Party systems in Latin America.* Stanford: Stanford University Press.

Mair, Peter. 1993. Myths of electoral change and the survival of traditional parties. *European Journal of Political Research* 24 (2): 121–33.

Marat, Erica. 2006. *The tulip revolution: Kyrgyzstan one year after.* (Washington, DC: Jamestown Foundation).

Markus, Gregory B., and Philip E. Converse. 1979. A dynamic simultaneous equation model of electoral choice. *American Political Science Review* 73 (4): 1055–70.

Marples, David R. 2006. Color revolutions: The Belarus case. *Communist and Post-Communist Studies* 39:351–64.

Marsh, Christopher. 2001. *Russia at the polls: Voters, elections, and democratization.* Washington, DC: CQ Press.

Massicotte, Louis, and Andre Blais. 1999. Mixed electoral systems: A conceptual and empirical survey. *Electoral Studies* 18:341–66.

McAllister, Ian, and Stephen White. 2007. Political parties and democratic consolidation in post-communist societies. *Party Politics* 13 (2): 197–216.

McCubbins, Matthew D., and Thomas Schwartz. 1984. Congressional oversight overlooked: Police patrols versus fire alarms. *American Journal of Political Science* 28 (1): 165–79.

McFaul, Michael. 1999. Institutional design, uncertainty, and path dependency during transitions: Cases from Russia. *Constitutional Political Economy* 10:27–52.

———. 2001. Explaining party formation and nonformation in Russia. *Comparative Political Studies* 34(10):1159–87.

———. 2005. Transitions from post-communism. *Journal of Democracy* 16 (3): 5–19.

Mebane, Walter R. 2006. Election forensics: Vote counts and Benford's law. Paper presented at the 2006 Summer Meeting of the Political Methodology Society, July 2006.

Mendelsohn, Matthew, and Andrew Parkin. 2001. *Referendum democracy: Citizens, elites, and deliberation in referendum campaigns.* New York: Palgrave.

Mendelson, Sarah. 2001. Democracy assistance and Russia's transition: Between success and failure. *International Security* 25 (4): 69–103.

Mickiewicz, Ellen. 1997. *Changing channels: Television and the struggle for power in Russia.* Oxford: Oxford University Press.

———. 2006. The election news story on Russian television: A world apart from viewers. *Slavic Review* 65 (1): 1–23.

Mikhailov, Valentin V. 1999. Kolichestvo demokratii: Analiz vyborov prezidenta RF 1996 g, v regionakh. *Armageddon* 3 (1): 134–53.

———. 2000. *Osobaya zona: Vybory v Tatarstane.* Ulyanovsk: Kazan Branch of the International Assembly to Protect Rights.

Miller, Arthur H., Gwen Erb, William M. Reisinger, and Vicki L. Hesli. 2000. Emerging party systems in post-Soviet societies: Fact or fiction? *Journal of Politics* 62 (2): 455–90.

Miller, Arthur H., and Thomas F. Klobucar. 2000. The development of party identification in post-Soviet societies. *American Journal of Political Science* 44 (4): 667–85.

Mishler, William, and John P. Willerton. 2003. The dynamics of presidential popularity in post-communist Russia: Cultural imperative versus neo-institutional choice? *Journal of Politics* 65 (1): 111–41.

Moraski, Bryon J. 2003. Electoral system design in Russian oblasti and republics: A four case comparison. *Europe-Asia Studies* 55 (3): 437–68.

———. 2006. *Elections by design: Parties and patronage in Russia's regions.* DeKalb: Northern Illinois University Press.

———. 2006. Mandating party development in the Russian Federation: Effects of the 2001 party law. *Journal of Elections, Public Opinion, and Parties* 16 (3): 199–219.

———. 2007. Electoral system reform in democracy's grey zone: Lessons from Putin's Russia. *Government and Opposition* 42 (4): 536–63.

Morel, Laurence. 2001. The rise of government-initiated referendums in consolidated democracies. In *Referendum democracy: Citizens, elites, and deliberation in referendum campaigns*, ed. Matthew Mendelsohn and Andrew Parkin. New York: Palgrave.

Moser, Robert G. 1999. Electoral systems and the number of parties in postcommunist states. *World Politics* 51 (3): 359–84.

Moser, Robert G., and Ethan Scheiner. 2004. Mixed electoral systems and electoral system effects: Controlled comparison and cross-national analysis. *Electoral Studies* 23 (4): 575–99.

Moser, Robert G., and Frank Thames. 2001. Compromise amidst political conflict: The origins of Russia's mixed member system. In *Mixed-member electoral systems: The best of both worlds?*, ed. Matthew S. Shugart and Martin P. Wattenberg. Oxford: Oxford University Press.

Mote, Max E. 1965. *Soviet local and republic elections*. Stanford: The Hoover Institution on War, Revolution, and Peace.

Mozaffar, Shaheen, and Andreas Schedler. 2002. The comparative study of electoral governance—Introduction. *International Political Science Review* 23 (1): 5–27.

Mughan, A. 1981. The cross-national validity of party identification. *Political Studies* 29 (3): 365–75.

Munck, Gerardo L., and Jay Verkuilen. 2002. Conceptualizing and measuring democracy. *Comparative Political Studies* 35 (1): 5–34.

Myagkov, Mikhail, and Peter C. Ordeshook. 2001. The trail of votes in Russia's 1999 Duma and 2000 presidential elections. *Communist and Post-Communist Studies* 34 (3): 353–70.

Myagkov, Mikhail, Peter C. Ordeshook, and Dmitry Shakin. 2005. Fraud or fairytales: Russia and Ukraine's electoral experience. *Post-Soviet Affairs* 21 (2): 91–131.

———. 2007. The disappearance of fraud: The forensics of Ukraine's 2006 parliamentary elections. *Post-Soviet Affairs* 23 (3): 218–39.

Nagler, Jonathan. 1991. The effect of registration laws and education on US voter turnout. *American Political Science Review* 85 (4): 1393–405.

Nigrini, Mark J. 2006. Monitoring techniques available to the forensic accountant. *Journal of Forensic Accounting* 7 (2): 321–44.

———. 1999. The peculiar patterns of first digits. *IEEE Potentials* 24–27.

Nishikawa, Misa, and Erik S. Herron. 2004. Mixed electoral rules' impact on party systems. *Electoral Studies* 23 (4): 753–68.

Norris, Pippa. 2000. *Women's power at the ballot box*. http://ksghome.harvard.edu/~pnorris/acrobat/IDEA.pdf (accessed November 15, 2007).

Nove, Alec. 1968. *The Soviet economy*. London: Allen and Unwin.

Oka, Natsuko. 2000. The election spectacle in Kazakhstan: Transition to democracy or strengthening of an authoritarian regime? Paper presented at the Association for the Study of Nationalities Conference, New York.

Okara, Andrei. 2007. Sovereign democracy: A new Russian idea or PR project? *Russia in Global Affairs*. http://eng.globalaffairs.ru/numbers/20/1124.html (accessed December 15. 2007).

Olcott, Martha B. 1997. Democratization and the growth of political participation in Kazakhstan. In *Conflict, cleavage, and change in Central Asia and the Caucasus*, ed. Karen Dawisha and Bruce Parrott. Cambridge: Cambridge University Press.

Ordeshook, Peter C., and Olga V. Shvetsova. 1994. Ethnic heterogeneity, district magnitude, and the number of parties. *American Journal of Political Science* 38 (1): 100–123.

Pacek, Alexander C., Grigore Pop-Eleches, and Joshua A. Tucker. 2009. Disenchanted or Discerning? Turnout in Post-Communist Elections, 1990-2004. *The Journal of Politics.* forthcoming.

Pacek, Alexander C., and Benjamin Radcliffe. 2003. Voter participation and party-group fortunes in European Parliament elections, 1979–1999: A cross-national analysis. *Political Research Quarterly* 56 (1): 91–95.

Padilla, David, and Elizabeth Houppert. 1993. International election observing: Enhancing the principle of free and fair elections. *Emory International Law Review* 7:73–132.

Page, Benjamin I., and Calvin C. Jones. 1979. Reciprocal effects of policy preferences, party loyalties and the vote. *American Political Science Review* 73:1071–90.

Pastor, Robert A. 1999. The role of electoral administration in democratic transitions: Implications for policy and research. *Democratization* 6 (4): 1–27.

Pedersen, Mogens. 1979. The dynamics of European party systems: Changing patterns of electoral volatility. *European Journal of Political Research* 7:1–26.

Persson, Torsten, Guido Tabbellini, and Francesco Trebbi. 2003. Electoral rules and corruption. *Journal of the European Economic Association* 1 (4): 958–89.

Peterson, D. J. 1993. *Troubled lands: The legacy of Soviet environmental destruction.* Boulder: Westview Press.

Pettai, Vello, and Marcus Kreuzer. 1999. Party politics in the Baltic states: Social bases and institutional context. *East European Politics and Societies* 13 (1): 148–89.

Plutzer, Eric. 2002. Becoming a habitual voter: Inertia, resources, and growth in young adulthood. *American Political Science Review* 96 (1): 41–56.

Popper, Karl R. 1945. *The open society and its enemies.* London: Routledge & Sons, Ltd.

Powell, G. B. 1986. American voter turnout in comparative perspective. *American Political Science Review* 80 (1): 17–43.

Przeworski, Adam. 1991. *Democracy and the market: Political and economic reforms in Eastern Europe and Latin America.* Cambridge: Cambridge University Press.

Qvortrup, Mads. 2000. Are referendums controlled and pro-hegemonic? *Political Studies* 48:821–26.

Rae, Douglas. 1967. *The political consequences of electoral laws.* New Haven, CT: Yale University Press.

Raitviir, Tiina. 1996. *Elections in Estonia during the transition period: A comparative study (1989–1993).* Tallinn: Eesti Teaduste Akadeemia Kirjastus.

Reed, Steven R. 1991. Structure and behaviour: Extending Duverger's law to the Japanese case. *British Journal of Political Science* 29 (3): 335–56.

Reif, Karlheinz, George Cunningham, Malgorzata Kuzma, and Louis Hersom. 2004. *Central and Eastern Eurobarometer 1990–1997: Trends CEEB 1–8.* Ann Arbor: Inter-University Consortium for Political and Social Research.

Reilly, Benjamin. 2001. *Democracy in divided societies: Electoral engineering for conflict management.* Cambridge: Cambridge University Press.

Remington, Thomas F., and Steven S. Smith. 1996. Political goals, institutional context, and the choice of an electoral system. *American Journal of Political Science* 40 (4): 1253–79.

Riker, William H. 1982a. *Liberalism against populism: A confrontation between the theory of democracy and the theory of social choice.* San Francisco: W. H. Freeman.

———. 1982b. The two-party system and Duverger's law: An essay on the history of political science. *American Political Science Review.* 76 (4): 753–66.

Riker, William H., and Peter C. Ordeshook. 1968. A theory of the calculus of voting. *American Political Science Review* 62 (1): 25–42.

Roberts, Kenneth M., and Erik Wibbels. 1999. Party systems and electoral volatility in Latin America: A test of economic, institutional, and structural explanations. *American Political Science Review* 93 (3): 575–90.

Roeder, Philip G. 1989. Electoral avoidance in the Soviet Union. *Soviet Studies* 31 (3): 462–83.

———. 1991. Soviet federalism and ethnic mobilization. *World Politics* 43 (2): 196–232.

———. 1993. *Red sunset: The failure of Soviet politics.* Princeton, NJ: Princeton University Press.

Roefs, Marlene, Bert Klandermans, and Johan Olivier. 1998. Protest intentions on the eve of South Africa's first nonracial elections: Optimists look beyond injustice. *Mobilization* 3 (1): 51–68.

Roper, Steven D., and Florin Fesnic. 2003. Historical legacies and their impact on post-communist voting behavior. *Europe-Asia Studies* 55 (1): 119–31.

Rose, Richard. 2000. How floating parties frustrate democratic accountability: A supply-side view of Russia's elections. *East European Constitutional Review* 9(1/2).

Rose, Richard, Neil Munro, and Stephen White. 2001. Voting in a floating party system: The 1999 Duma election. *Europe-Asia Studies* 53 (3): 419–43.

Rose, Richard, Evgeny Tikhomorov, and William Mishler. 1997. Understanding multiparty choice: The 1995 Duma election. *Europe-Asia Studies* 49 (5): 799–823.

Rosenberg, William G. 1969. The Russian municipal Duma elections of 1917: A preliminary computation of returns. *Soviet Studies* 21 (2): 131–63.

Rosenstone, Steven J. 1982. Economic adversity and voter turnout. *American Journal of Political Science* 26 (1): 25–46.

Rosenstone, Steven J., and Raymond E. Wolfinger. 1978. The effect of registration laws on voter turnout. *American Political Science Review* 72 (1): 22–45.

Rutland, Peter. 1994. Democracy and nationalism in Armenia. *Europe-Asia Studies* 46 (5): 839–61.

Sakwa, Richard. 1995. The Russian elections of December 1993. *Europe-Asia Studies* 47 (2): 195–227.

Sartori, Giovanni. 1976. *Parties and party systems: A framework for analysis.* Cambridge: Cambridge University Press.

Scarrow, Susan E. 2001. Direct democracy and institutional change: A comparative investigation. *Comparative Political Studies* 34 (6): 651–65.

Schapiro, Leonard. 1977. *Government and politics of the Soviet Union.* London: Hutchinson.

Schattschneider, E. E. 1942. *Party government.* New York: Farrar and Rinehart.

Schedler, Andreas. 2002. The menu of manipulation. *Journal of Democracy* 13 (2): 36–50.

Schlesinger, Joseph A. 1991. *Political parties and the winning of office.* Ann Arbor: University of Michigan Press.

Schmitter, Philippe, and Terry L. Karl. 1994. The conceptual travels of transitologists and consolidologists: How far east should they attempt to go? *Slavic Review* 53 (1): 173–85.

———. 1995. From an Iron Curtain to a paper curtain: Grounding transitologists or students of postcommunism? *Slavic Review* 54 (4): 965–78.

Schmitter, Philippe C., and Terry L. Karl. 1991. What democracy is . . . and is not. *Journal of Democracy* 2 (3): 75–88.

Schumpeter, Joseph A. 1942. *Capitalism, socialism, and democracy*. New York: Harper and Brothers.

Setala, Maija. 2006. National referendums in European democracies: Recent developments. *Representation* 42 (1): 13–23.

Sheynis, Viktor. 1999. *Za chestnye vybory*. Moscow: Center of Economic and Political Research.

Shugart, Matthew S. 1992. Guerrillas and elections: An institutionalist perspective on the costs of conflict and cooperation. *International Studies Quarterly* 36:121–52.

———. 2005. Comparative electoral systems research: The maturation of a field and new challenges ahead. In *The politics of electoral systems*, ed. Michael Gallagher and Paul Mitchell. Oxford: Oxford University Press.

Shugart, Matthew S., and John M. Carey. 1992. *Presidents and assemblies: Constitutional design and electoral dynamics*. Cambridge: Cambridge University Press.

Shugart, Matthew S., and Martin Wattenberg. 2001. *Mixed-member electoral systems: The best of both worlds?* Oxford: Oxford University Press.

Shveda, Yuriy. 2001. Ukraina i maibutne gromadyanskogo suspil'stvo. Paper presented at the Building a Vital US-Ukrainian Partnership Conference, Lawrence, KS, April 2001.

Sigelman, Lee, and William D. Berry. 1982. Cost and the calculus of voting. *Political Behavior* 4 (4): 419–28.

Silver, Brian D., Barbara A. Anderson, and Paul R. Abramson. 1986. Who overreports voting? *American Political Science Review* 80 (2): 613–24.

Slider, Darrell. 1992. The October 1992 elections in Georgia. Paper Presented at the National Convention of the American Association for the Advancement of Slavic Studies.

Smith, Gordon. 1976. The functional properties of the referendum. *European Journal of Political Research* 4 (1): 31–45.

Smith, Steven S., and Thomas F. Remington. 2001. *The politics of institutional choice: The formation of the Russian state Duma*. Princeton, NJ: Princeton University Press.

Smithey, Shannon I., and John Ishiyama. 2000. Judicious choices: Designing courts in post-communist politics. *Communist and Post-Communist Studies* 33:163–82.

Sobyanin, A. A. and V. G. Sukhovolskiy. 1995. *Demokratiya, ogranichennaya falsifikatsiyami: Vybory i referendumy v rossii v 1991–1993 gg*. Moscow: Project Group for Human Rights.

Stokes, Susan C. 1999. Political parties and democracy. *Annual Review of Political Science* 2:243–67.

Suksi, Markku. 1993. *Bringing in the people: A comparison of constitutional forms and practices of the referendum*. Boston: Martinus Nijhoff Publishers.

Sutter, Daniel. 2003. Detecting and correcting election fraud. *Eastern Economic Journal* 29 (3): 433–51.

Swearer, Howard R. 1961. The functions of Soviet elections. *Midwest Journal of Political Science* 5 (2): 129–49.

Szczerbiak, Aleks, and Paul Taggart. 2005. The politics of European referendum outcomes and turnout: Two models. In *EU enlargement and referendums*, ed. Aleks Szczerbiak and Paul Taggart. London: Routledge.

Taagepera, Rein, and Matthew S. Shugart. 1989. *Seats and votes: The effects and determinants of electoral systems*. New Haven, CT: Yale University Press.

Tavits, Margit. 2005. The development of stable party support: Electoral dynamics in post-communist Europe. *American Journal of Political Science* 49 (2): 283–98.

Teper, Lazare. 1932. Elections in Soviet Russia. *American Political Science Review* 26 (5): 926–31.

Thames, Frank. 2007. Searching for the electoral connection: Party switching in the Ukrainian Rada. *Legislative Studies Quarterly* 32 (2): 223–46.

Thomassen, Jacques. 1976. Party identification as a cross-national concept: Its meaning in the Netherlands. In *Party identification and beyond: Representations of voting and party competition*, ed. Ian Budge, Ivor Crewe, and David Farlie. New York: Wiley.

Tomz, Michael, Joshua A. Tucker, and Jason Wittenberg. 2002. An easy and accurate regression model for multiparty electoral data. *Political Analysis* 10:66–83.

Tsebelis, George. 1990. *Nested games: Rational choice in comparative politics*. Berkeley: University of California Press.

———. 2002. *Veto players: How political institutions work*. Princeton, NJ: Princeton University Press.

Tucker, Joshua A. 2002. The first decade of post-communist elections and voting: What have we studied and how have we studied it? *Annual Review of Political Science* 5:271–304.

———. 2007. Enough! Electoral fraud, collective action problems, and post-communist colored revolutions. *Perspectives on Politics* 5 (3): 535–51.

Walker, Mark C. 2003. *The strategic use of referendums: Power, legitimacy, and democracy*. New York: Palgrave.

Wand, Jonathan N., Kenneth W. Shotts, Jasjeet S. Sekhon, Walter R. Mebane, Michael C. Herron, and Henry E. Brady. 2001. The butterfly did it: The aberrant vote for Buchanan in Palm Beach County, Florida. *American Political Science Review* 95 (4): 793–810.

Wantchekon, Leonard. 1999. On the nature of first democratic elections. *Journal of Conflict Resolution* 43 (2): 245–58.

White, Stephen. 1990. The elections to the USSR Congress of People's Deputies March 1989. *Electoral Studies* 9 (1): 59–66.

White, Stephen, and Ian McAllister. 2003. Putin and his supporters. *Europe-Asia Studies* 55 (3): 383–99.

White, Stephen, Ian McAllister, and Olga Kryshtanovskaya. 1994. El'tsin and his voters: Popular support in the 1991 Russian presidential election and after. *Europe-Asia Studies* 46 (2): 285–303.

White, Stephen, Richard Rose, and Ian McAllister. 1997. *How Russia votes*. Chatham: Chatham House Publishers.

White, Stephen, Matthew Wyman, and Sarah Oates. 1997. Parties and voters in the 1995 Russian Duma elections. *Europe-Asia Studies* 49 (5): 767–98.

Whitmore, Sarah. 2004. *State building in Ukraine: The Ukrainian parliament, 1990–2003*. London: Routledge Curzon.

Wilkinson, Steven I. 2004. *Voters and violence: Electoral competition and ethnic riots in India*. Cambridge: Cambridge University Press.

Wolfinger, Raymond E., and Steven J. Rosenstone. 1980. *Who votes?* New Haven, CT: Yale University Press.

Wright Jr., Theodore P. 1961. The origins of the free elections dispute in the Cold War. *Western Political Quarterly* 14 (4): 850–64.

Zakaria, Fareed. 2003. *The future of freedom: Illiberal democracy at home and abroad*. New York: W. W. Norton.

Zaslavsky, Victor, and Robert J. Brym. 1978. The functions of elections in the USSR. *Soviet Studies* 30 (3): 362–71.

REPORTS AND DOCUMENTS

Chupryna, Iryna. 2008. Not quite a color revolution in Armenia. http://democratiza
tionpolicy.org/wp-content/uploads/2008/03/dpc-analyst-no-1-25-mar-2008
.pdf (accessed May 15, 2008).

Commission on Security and Cooperation in Europe. 1994. *Report on elections in Kazakhstan, March 7, 1994.* Mimeo.

Federal Election Commission. 1990. *1990 U.S. election study tour of the Central Electoral Commission of the U.S.S.R.* Washington, DC: FEC.

Independent Assistance, and Consulting Center For the Sake of Civil Society. 2005. *Final report on parliamentary elections held in [sic] November 6, 2005.* Baku.

Materialy Vstesoyuznoi Konferentsii KPSS. 1988. Moscow: Izdatel'stvo Polit Literatury.

OSCE. 1996a. *Armenian presidential elections, September 24, 1996, final report.* Warsaw: OSCE.

———. 1996b. *Final report, presidential elections in the Republic of Moldova, November 17 and December 1, 1996.* Warsaw: OSCE.

———. 1996c. *International Observer Mission, election of President of the Russian Federation, 16th June 1996 and 3rd July 1996.* Warsaw: OSCE.

———. 1996d. *Parliamentary elections, Republic of Lithuania, October 20 and November 10, 1996.* Warsaw: OSCE.

———. 1998a. *Presidential election in the Republic of Azerbaijan, October 11, 1998.* Warsaw: OSCE.

———. 1998b. *Republic of Armenia, presidential election, March 16 and 30, 1998, final report.* Warsaw: OSCE.

———. 1998c. *Republic of Moldova, parliamentary elections, March 22, 1998.* Warsaw: OSCE.

———. 1998d. *Republic of Ukraine, parliamentary elections, March 29, 1998.* Warsaw: OSCE.

———. 1999a. *Republic of Armenia, parliamentary election, May 30, 1999, Final Report.* Warsaw: OSCE.

———. 1999b. *Republic of Estonia, parliamentary elections, March 7, 1999.* Warsaw: OSCE.

———. 1999c. *The Republic of Kazakhstan, presidential election, January 10, 1999.* Warsaw: OSCE.

———. 2000a. *Georgia, parliamentary election, 31 October & November 14, 1999.* Warsaw: OSCE.

———. 2000b. *Kyrgyz Republic, parliamentary elections, 20 February & March 12, 2000.* Warsaw: OSCE.

———. 2000c. *Republic of Georgia, presidential election, April 9, 2000.* Warsaw: OSCE.

———. 2000d. *Republic of Kazakhstan, parliamentary elections, 10 and October 24, 1999.* Warsaw: OSCE.

———. 2000e. *The Republic of Tajikistan elections to the parliament, February 27, 2000.* Warsaw: ODIHR.

———. 2000f. *Republic of Uzbekistan, election of deputies to the Oliy Majlis (Parliament), 5 & December 19, 1999.* Warsaw: OSCE.

———. 2000g. *Russian Federation, elections to the state Duma, December 19, 1999.* Warsaw: OSCE.

———. 2000h. *Russian Federation, presidential election, March 26, 2000.* Warsaw: OSCE.

———. 2000i. *Ukraine presidential elections, 31 October and November 14, 1999.* Warsaw: OSCE.

———. 2001a. *Belarus, parliamentary elections, 15 and October 29, 2000, Technical Assessment Mission.* Warsaw: OSCE.

———. 2001b. *Kyrgyz Republic, presidential elections, October 29, 2000.* Warsaw: OSCE.

———. 2001c. *Republic of Azerbaijan, parliamentary elections, November 5, 2000 & January 7, 2001.* Warsaw: OSCE.

———. 2001d. *Republic of Belarus, presidential election, September 9, 2001.* Warsaw: OSCE.

———. 2001e. *Republic of Moldova, parliamentary elections, 25 February, 2001.* Warsaw: OSCE.

———. 2002a. *Republic of Latvia, Saeima elections, October 5, 2002.* Warsaw: OSCE.

———. 2002b. *Ukraine, parliamentary elections, March 31, 2002.* Warsaw: OSCE.

———. 2003a. *Georgia, parliamentary elections, November 2, 2003.* Warsaw: OSCE.

———. 2003b. *Republic of Armenia, parliamentary elections, May 25, 2003.* Warsaw: OSCE.

———. 2003c. *Republic of Armenia, presidential election, 19 February and March 5, 2003.* Warsaw: OSCE.

———. 2003d. *Republic of Azerbaijan, presidential election, October 15, 2003.* Warsaw: OSCE.

———. 2004a. *Georgia, extraordinary presidential election, January 3, 2004.* Warsaw: OSCE.

———. 2004b. *Georgia, parliamentary elections, November 2, 2003.* Warsaw: OSCE.

———. 2004c. *Georgia, partial repeat parliamentary elections, March 28, 2004.* Warsaw: OSCE.

———. 2004d. *Republic of Belarus, parliamentary elections, October 17, 2004.* Warsaw: OSCE.

———. 2004e. *Russian Federation, elections to the state Duma, December 7, 2003.* Warsaw: OSCE.

———. 2004f. *Russian Federation, presidential election, March 14, 2004.* Warsaw: OSCE.

———. 2005a. *The Kyrgyz Republic, parliamentary elections, 27 February and March 13, 2005.* Warsaw: OSCE.

———. 2005b. *Kyrgyz Republic, presidential election, July 10, 2005.* Warsaw: OSCE.

———. 2005c. *Republic of Kazakhstan, parliamentary elections, 19 September and October 3, 2004.* Warsaw: OSCE.

———. 2005d. *Republic of Moldova, parliamentary elections, March 6, 2005.* Warsaw: OSCE.

———. 2005e. *Republic of Tajikistan, parliamentary elections, 27 February and March 13, 2005.* Warsaw: OSCE.

———. 2005f. *Republic of Uzbekistan, parliamentary elections, December 26, 2004.* Warsaw: OSCE.

———. 2005g. *Ukraine, presidential election, 31 October, 21 November and December 26, 2004.* Warsaw: OSCE.

———. 2006a. *Republic of Azerbaijan, parliamentary elections, November 6, 2005.* Warsaw: OSCE.

———. 2006b. *Republic of Belarus, presidential election, March 19, 2006.* Warsaw: OSCE.

———. 2006c. *Republic of Kazakhstan, presidential elections, December 4, 2005.* Warsaw: OSCE.

————. 2006d. *Ukraine, parliamentary elections, March 26, 2006.* Warsaw: OSCE.

————. 2007a. *Republic of Armenia, parliamentary elections, May 12, 2007.* Warsaw: OSCE.

————. 2007b. *Republic of Kazakhstan, parliamentary elections, August 18, 2007.* Warsaw: OSCE.

————. 2007c. *Republic of Latvia, parliamentary elections, October 7, 2006.* Warsaw: OSCE.

————. 2007d. *Republic of Tajikistan, presidential election, November 6, 2006.* Warsaw: OSCE.

————. 2007e. *Ukraine, preterm parliamentary elections, September 30, 2007.* Warsaw: OSCE.

————. 2008a. *Georgia, extraordinary presidential election, January 5, 2008.* Warsaw: OSCE.

————. 2008b. *Kyrgyz Republic, preterm parliamentary elections, December 16, 2007.* Warsaw: OSCE.

————. 2008c. *Republic of Armenia, presidential election, February 19, 2008.* Warsaw: OSCE.

OSCE, and UN. 1996. *Report of the OSCE/UN Joint Electoral Observation Mission in Azerbaijan on Azerbaijan's November 12, 1995, parliamentary election and constitutional reform.* Warsaw: OSCE.

Venice Commission. 2000. *Constitutional referendum in Ukraine.* Venice: Venice Commission.

Verkhovna Rada. 2001. Zasidannya dvadtsyat' pershe: Sesiyniy zal verkhovnoi rady Ukrainy, 22 bereznya 2001 roku.

MEDIA AND ELECTRONIC SOURCES

Abbasov, Shahin, and Khadija Ismailova. 2005. Reports: Opposition, police clash on Azerbaijan campaign trail. http://www.eurasianet.org/departments/insight/articles/eav080405.shtml (accessed April 20, 2008).

Abrahamyan, Gayane. 2008. The Armenian Revolutionary Federation: An "alternative" to politics as usual? http://www.eurasianet.org/armenia08/news/021308.shtml (accessed June 1, 2008).

ACE Project. 2008. "Direct democracy." http://aceproject.org/epic-en/dd (accessed June 3, 2008).

ADEPT. 2007. "Political parties of the Republic of Moldova." http://www.parties.e-democracy.md/en/parties (accessed December 11, 2007).

Agence France Presse. 2006. Opposition protests in Belarus since 1996—A chronology. March 25, 2006, Lexis-Nexis.

Associated Press. 1999. Court opposition to run in election, but party sees it as trap. March 1, 2006, Lexis-Nexis. October 21, 1999, Lexis-Nexis.

————. 2005. Kazakh opposition party vows to continue activity despite closure. January 10, 2005, Lexis-Nexis.

————. 2006a. Belarus' opposition candidate warns of protests in case of vote fraud. February 22, 2006, Lexis-Nexis.

————. 2006b. Belarus security services say opposition plans attempt to seize power. March 1, 2006, Lexis-Nexis.

————. 2006c. Belarusian court sentences independent election monitors to jail terms. August 4, 2006, Lexis-Nexis.

———. 2006d. Belarusian court upholds prison sentence for opposition presidential candidate. September 19, 2006, Lexis-Nexis.

———. 2006e. Court sentences Belarusian activist to 2 years in prison for insulting president. October 23, 2006, Lexis-Nexis.

———. 2007. Latvian referendum on national security short of necessary votes. July 7, 2007, Lexis-Nexis.

Association of Central and Eastern European Election Officials. n.d. International election standards. http://www.aceeeo.org/projects/standards.html.

Azerbaijan International. 1997. Major Issues: A presidential perspective. http://azer .com/aiweb/categories/magazine/53_folder/53_articles/53_majorissue.html (accessed October 20, 2007).

Baltic News Service. 1994. President will probably boycott 27th August referendum. August 16, 1994, Lexis-Nexis.

———. 2002a. Estonian Supreme Court not a tool for parties—Chair. July 22, 2002, Lexis-Nexis.

———. 2002b. Latvian PM calls for election law changes after lost case at human rights court. April 10, 2002, Lexis-Nexis.

———. 2006. Latvian Supreme Court finds results of Parlt [*sic*] elections valid. November 3, 2006, Lexis-Nexis.

BBC. 1992a. Deputy on failure of "right-wing plot." May 26, 1992, Lexis-Nexis.

———. 1992b. Estonian congress meeting adopts resolution on "colonists." May 25, 1992, Lexis-Nexis.

———. 1992c. Landsbergis warns of "creeping coup d'etat" from left wing. May 26, 1992, Lexis-Nexis.

———. 1992d. Russian defence committee chairman says referendum will complicate relations. June 15, 1992, Lexis-Nexis.

———. 1992e. Sajudis rally in Vilnius against left-wing majority in parliament. May 17, 1992, Lexis-Nexis.

———. 1994. Kyrgyz constitutional session to be formed. October 27, 1994, Lexis-Nexis.

———. 1995. Belarussian opposition asserts referendum undoubtedly falsified. May 17, 1995, Lexis-Nexis.

———. 1996a. Council of Europe official says Belarusian referendum was illegal. November 27, 1996, Lexis-Nexis.

———. 1996b. President Lukashenka revokes constitutional court referendum decision. November 8, 1996, Lexis-Nexis.

———. 1996c. Referendum results are not binding, says constitutional court chairman. November 27, 1996, Lexis-Nexis.

———. 1999a. Electoral commission accuses courts of hampering municipal elections. October 8, 1999, Lexis-Nexis.

———. 1999b. Parties call for rejection of referendum proposal for bicameral parliament. September 21, 1999, Lexis-Nexis.

———. 1999c. Tajik president, parliament speaker and premier vote in referendum. September 26, 1999, Lexis-Nexis.

———. 1999d. Tajikistan: Referendum held to amend constitution. September 26, 1999, Lexis-Nexis.

———. 2000a. Azeri opposition says courts not independent after election ban ruling. October 13, 2000, Lexis-Nexis.

———. 2000b. Some 3,000 leftists in Luhansk rally to abolish presidency, ignore referendum. March 18, 2000, Lexis-Nexis.

————. 2000c. Some 6,000 leftists protest against referendum in Kharkiv, Mykolayiv. March 17, 2000, Lexis-Nexis.

————. 2000d. Ukraine: Council of Europe warns Ukraine not to hold referendum. March 10, 2000, Lexis-Nexis.

————. 2002a. Paper reports vote-rigging in constitutional referendum in Azeri capital. August 25, 2002, Lexis-Nexis.

————. 2002b. Referendum 'totally falsified' in Azeri districts—paper. August 25, 2002, Lexis-Nexis.

————. 2002c. US Embassy calls for postponement of Azeri referendum. July 19, 2002, Lexis-Nexis.

————. 2003a. Armenian opposition official says constitutional court decision "political." April 18, 2003, Lexis-Nexis.

————. 2003b. Armenian opposition party files lawsuit on constitutional referendum. May 7, 2007, Lexis-Nexis.

————. 2003c. Council of Europe official against Armenian referendum proposal. April 25, 2003, Lexis-Nexis.

————. 2003d. Courts receive appeals from over 10,000 disenfranchised Armenians. February 19, 2003, Lexis-Nexis.

————. 2003e. Guide to Armenian parliamentary elections, May 2003. May 9, 2003, Lexis-Nexis.

————. 2003f. Kyrgyz opposition set to boycott constitutional referendum. January 15, 2003, Lexis-Nexis.

————. 2003g. Kyrgyzstan heading for further instability, Kazakh paper predicts. January 17, 2003, Lexis-Nexis.

————. 2003h. OSCE position not grounds for changing referendum date—Kyrgyz ministry. January 30, 2003, Lexis-Nexis.

————. 2005a. Armenian opposition leaders see revolution as way out of critical situation. November 27, 2005, Lexis-Nexis.

————. 2005b. Armenian speaker condemns ballot rigging at November constitutional referendum. December 5, 2005, Lexis-Nexis.

————. 2005c. Azeri opposition bloc denies revolution plans. October 25, 2005, Lexis-Nexis.

————. 2005d. European Commission supports constitutional reforms in Armenia. October 21, 2005, Lexis-Nexis.

————. 2006a. Belarus TV says opposition planning to rig election poll. February 27, 2006, Lexis-Nexis.

————. 2006b. Belarusian Supreme Court refuses to consider complaints by opposition candidates. April 5, 2006, Lexis-Nexis.

————. 2007a. Backgrounder: Kyrgyzstan moves to defuse constitutional crisis by referendum. October 12, 2007, Lexis-Nexis.

————. 2007b. Georgia crackdown "went too far." http://news.bbc.co.uk/2/hi/europe/7153561.stm (accessed December 20, 2007).

————. 2007c. Kazakh polls in compliance with "all democratic norms"—Austrian observer. August 19, 2007, Lexis-Nexis.

————. 2007d. Shanghai group observers say Kazakh election "legitimate." August 19, 2007, Lexis-Nexis.

————. 2007e. US observers say Kazakh president's popularity behind ruling party's poll win. August 19, 2007, Lexis-Nexis.

————. 2008. Armenian court throws out opposition presidential candidate's suit. February 12, 2008, Lexis-Nexis.

Bendersky, Yevgeny. 2005. Democracy in the former Soviet Union: 1991–2004. *Eurasia Net*. http://www.eurasianet.org/departments/insight/articles/pp010305 .shtml (accessed September 15, 2007).

Beshimov, Erdin. 2004. Akayev: We do democracy the Kyrgyz way. http://www .eurasianet.org/departments/insight/articles/eav101504.shtml (accessed October 20, 2007).

Bivens, Matt. 1994. Lithuanians to vote in honey-pot referendum. *Moscow Times*, December 15, 2007, Lexis-Nexis.

Brady, Henry E. 2000. What happened in Palm Beach? http://socrates.berkeley .edu/~ucdtpums/palm2.pdf (accessed June 1, 2002).

CBS News. 2004. Turkmenbashi everywhere. http://www.cbsnews.com/stories/ 2003/12/31/60minutes/main590913.shtml (accessed October 21, 2007).

Central Electoral Commission of Azerbaijan. 2007. "Elections and Referendums." http://www.cec.gov.az/en/common/election-referendum/2002.htm (accessed November 17, 2007).

Central Electoral Commission of the Republic of Kazakhstan. 2008. http://election .kz/portal/page?_pageid=73,473388&_dad=portal&_schema=PORTAL (accessed March 10, 2008).

Central Electoral Commission of Ukraine. 2002. http://195.230.157.53/pls/ vd2002/webproc0v (accessed July 11, 2002).

Charter, David. 2004. Votes in invisible ink just vanish in ballot. http://www .timesonline.co.uk/tol/news/world/article395198.ece (accessed June 4, 2008).

Chivers, C. J. 2007. Russia working to limit election observers. http://www.nytimes .com/2007/10/25/world/europe/25russia.html (accessed October 28, 2007).

Cohen, Ariel. 2007. Kazakh vote: A step forward. *Washington Times*, August 21, 2007, Lexis-Nexis.

Cutler, Robert M. 2004. Kazakhstan holds elections for a new parliament. *Central Asia-Caucasus Analyst*, http://www.cacianalyst.org/?q=node/2483 (accessed December 6, 2007).

de Pourbaix-Lundlin, Marrietta, and Matyas Eorsi. 2008. Election secrets revealed. *Transitions Online*, http://www.tol.cz/look/TOL/article.tpl?IdLanguage=1&I dPublication=4&NrIssue=266&NrSection=2&NrArticle=19553 (accessed April 22, 2008).

Demourian, Avet. 2008. 8 dead in clashes in Armenia. *Associated Press*, September 26, 1996, Lexis-Nexis.

———. 1996. Armenia's president bans rallies after bloody clash; tanks in streets. *Associated Press*, March 2, 2008, Lexis-Nexis.

Deutsche Presse-Agentur. 1996a. Conservatives carry Lithuanian run-off election. November 10, 1996, Lexis-Nexis.

———. 1996b. Kyrgyz president Akayev wins referendum on extra powers. February 11, 1996, Lexis-Nexis.

———. 1996c. Lithuanians vote Sunday in general election and two referendums. October 19, 1996, Lexis-Nexis.

———. 1996d. New Belarus parliament ends proceedings against Lukashenko. November 26, 1996, Lexis-Nexis.

———. 1998a. Advocates of citizenship reform declare victory in referendum. October 4, 1998, Lexis-Nexis.

———. 1998b. Kyrgyz president wins constitutional changes. October 19, 1998, Lexis-Nexis.

———. 1998c. Latvian citizenship question at issue in referendum. October 3, 1998, Lexis-Nexis.

———. 1999a. 1st roundup: Latvian referendum on pension reform. November 13, 1999, Lexis-Nexis.

———. 1999b. Roundup: Turnout too low for Latvia's referendum to be valid. November 13, 1999, Lexis-Nexis.

———. 2006. Belarus KGB: Protestors "will be considered terrorists." March 16, 2006, Lexis-Nexis.

———. 2007a. Latvia's "referendum on nothing" heads for nothing result. July 7, 2007, Lexis-Nexis.

———. 2007b. Latvian voters force referendum on cancelled security laws. May 3, 2007, Lexis-Nexis.

Eurasia Insight. 2006. New constitution comes into force in Kyrgyzstan. http://www.eurasianet.org/departments/insight/articles/eav110906.shtml (accessed June 2, 2006).

Eurasianet. 2005. "Azerbaijan Elections 2005." http://www.eurasianet.org/azerbaijan/map/ (accessed October 20, 2007).

Fuller, Liz. 2005. Azerbaijan: From showmanship to brinksmanship. http://www.rferl.org/featuresarticle/2005/09/bc0cc2d5-0e73-45dd-9c5d-a4314ee66ed8.html (accessed April 20, 2008).

Gordon, Michael R. 1996. President of Belarus pushes referendum to expand power. *New York Times*, December 17, 2007, Lexis-Nexis.

Gurin, Charles. 2004. Borodin predicts a referendum to extend Putin's term http://www.jamestown.org/publications_details.php?volume_id=401&issue_id=3113&article_id=2368714 (accessed March 4, 2008).

Gurova, Tatyana, and Aleksandr Mekhanik. 2004. Tema nedeli. Politika posle Beslana. Za diktaturu demokratii. September 20, 2004, Eastview Publications.

Interfax. 2005. Azeri opposition rejects accusations of preparing coup. October 25, 2005, Lexis-Nexis.

———. 2007. Russian diplomat criticizes OSCE for double standards in election observation. March 3, 2007, Lexis-Nexis.

Interfax-Ukraine. 2004. Ukrainian election chief explains unusually slow vote count in presidential election. *Action Ukraine Report* Vol. 4, No. 207, listserv.

International IDEA. 2007. "Main Findings." http://www.idea.int/vt/findings.cfm (accessed Novermber 14, 2007.

Inter-Parliamentary Union. 1994. Declaration on criteria for free and fair elections. http://www.ipu.org/Cnl-e/154-free.htm (accessed September 15, 2007).

Ismayilov, Rovshan. 2005a. Azerbaijan opposition charges US with "double standards." http://www.eurasianet.org/departments/insight/articles/eav120705.shtml (accessed April 20, 2008).

———. 2005b. Azerbaijan: Two more officials sacked. http://www.eurasianet.org/departments/civilsociety/articles/eav102005.shtml (accessed April 20, 2008).

Ismayilova, Khadija. 2005. Vote count: Exit polls and official results slightly differ. http://www.eurasianet.org/azerbaijan/news/discrepancy_20051107.html (accessed April 20, 2008).

ITAR-TASS. 1995. New constitution adopted in nationwide referendum. FBIS-SOV-95-169, August 31, 1995, pg. 67.

Ivanov, Vitaliy. 2007. Putin i ego "referendum." *Izvestiya*, November 19, 2007, http://www.izvestia.ru/comment/article3110431/ (accessed January 27, 2008).

Ivanova, Olyessa. 2007. Exit polls: Kazakh president's party sweeps parliament election, opposition may be shut out. August 19, 2007, Lexis-Nexis.

Karmanau, Yuras. 2004. Belarusian high court orders opposition political party shut down. August 3, 2004, Lexis-Nexis.

Kashin, Vasiliy, Ekaterina Kudashkina, and Oksana Goncharova. 2006. Opposition split. March 27, 2006, Lexis-Nexis.

Kazakhstanskaya Pravda (Almaty). 1995. Commission establishes referendum ballot. *Kazakhstanskaya Pravda*, FBIS-SOV-95-072, April 14, 1995, pgs. 65–66.

Kramer, Andrew E., Anne Barnard, and C. J. Chivers. 2008. Georgia fight spreads, Moscow delivers ultimatum. August 11, 2008. http://www.nytimes.com/2008/08/12/world/europe/12georgia.html?hp (accessed August 11, 2008).

Kravchenko, Oleg. 2001. Osobennosti natsiolnal'noy politicheskoy kukhni. Polubol'shinstvo, poluoppozitsiya, poluvlast'. *Delovaya Ukraina*, March 23, 2001, Eastview Publications.

Kuzio, Taras. 2002. Is Kuchma genuine in his political reform? *RFE/RL Poland, Belarus and Ukraine Report*, September 3, 2002, listserv.

Lambroschini, Antoine. 2007. Kazakh leader celebrates total election sweep. August 20, 2007, Lexis-Nexis.

Levy, Clifford. 2007. Putin basks in election win despite broad criticism. *New York Times,* December 4, 2007, http://www.nytimes.com/2007/12/04/world/europe/04russia.html?scp=15&sq=russian+election (accessed December 17. 2007).

MacWilliam, Ian. 2005. Kazakhs "not ready for democracy." *BBC*, June 14, 2005, http://news.bbc.co.uk/2/hi/asia-pacific/4093890.stm (accessed October 21, 2007).

McFaul, Michael. 2000. Indifferent to democracy. *Washington Post*, March 3, 2000, http://www.cdi.org/russia/johnson/4146.html (accessed March 5, 2000).

Medetsky, Anatoly. 2005. Signs of a 3rd term campaign. *Moscow Times*, August 16, 2005, http://www.moscowtimes.ru/stories/2005/08/16/003.html (accessed September 25, 2007).

Melnichuk, Anna. 2004. Ukrainian government accused of interference in media coverage ahead of presidential vote by all media watchdogs and international observers. *Action Ukraine Report* Vol. 4, No.169, listserv.

Namatbayeva, Tolkun. 2007. Kyrgyz court throws poll results into doubt. December 18, 2007, Lexis-Nexis.

New York Times. 1993. Pressure grows on Azerbaijan leader to quit. June 23, 1993, http://query.nytimes.com/gst/fullpage.html?res=9F0CE6DB133DF930A15755C0A965958260 (accessed December 15, 2007).

———. 1994. Economic referendum in Lithuania fails. August 28, 1994, Lexis-Nexis.

Other Russia. 2007. Russians skeptical about "national leader." http://www.theotherrussia.org/2007/12/05/russians-skeptical-about-%E2%80%98national-leader%E2%80%99/ (accessed January 19. 2008).

Pannier, Bruce. 2006a. Kazakhstan: Zheltoqsan protest marked 20 years later. *RFE/RL*, December 14, 2006, http://www.rferl.org/featuresarticle/2006/12/1b31a151-3c74-413b-909c-876e8f3020a9.html (accessed April 15, 2008).

———. 2006b. Tajikistan: Experts say incumbent president will be easily reelected. RFE/RL, October 5, 2006, http://www.rferl.org/featuresarticle/2006/10/4cf5cde9-0d90-464d-ba17-4ed26a557165.html (accessed October 21, 2007).

Peach, Gary. 2007. Latvia's president ends 8 years in office by overseeing controversial referendum. *Associated Press*, July 7, 2007, Lexis-Nexis.

Peuch, Jean-Christophe. 2005. Armenia: Opposition claims fraud in contro-versial referendum. RFE/RL, November 27, 2005, http://www.rferl.org/featuresarticle/2005/11/24d61784-dfb4-4b04-a1b0-644e68723ca7.html (accessed December 14, 2007).

Ponomarev, Sergei. 2007. Putin says OSCE refusal to send election observers to Rus-sia directed by U.S. November 26, 2007, Lexis-Nexis.

RFE/RL. 1998. Yeltsin still wants to scrap proportional representation. Vol. 2, No. 38, Part I, listserv.

———. 2001. Ukrainian president vetoes proportional parliamentary election law. February 21, 2001, listserv.

———. 2005a. Armenia: 10 questions about the constitutional referendum. Novem-ber 21, 2005, http://www.rferl.org/featuresarticle/2005/11/069e36d4-46e4-40bd-b2fe-5ba74230a09e.html (accessed December 13, 2007).

———. 2005b. Uzbek president slams export of democracy. December 8, 2005, http://www.rferl.org/featuresarticle/2005/12/ae6a739b-a32a-4b6c-aa69-42-d08cd7b3ae.html (accessed October 21, 2007).

———. 2007a. Putin says West forcing will on world. February 10, 2007, http://www.rferl.org/featuresarticle/2007/02/a50c8a12-b6a8-44ad-92dd-58183e78a032.html (accessed October 20, 2007).

———. 2007b. Pro-Putin party wins landslide in Russian elections. December 3, 2007, http://www.rferl.org/featuresarticle/2007/12/DC8A62FC-A7A3-427C-8901-AEBE572D7AF7.html (accessed December 5, 2007).

———. 2007c. Turkmen leader says democracy cannot be imported. February 18, 2007, http://www.rferl.org/featuresarticle/2007/2/284B905D-0C9C-4F44-9A37-285290F680CF.html (accessed October 21, 2007).

———. 2007d. Ukrainian election watchdog registers opposition bloc's candidates. Vol. 11, No. 151, listserv.

———. 2007e. Ukrainian opposition bloc denied registration for parliamentary polls. Vol. 11, No. 148, listserv.

———. 2007f. Ukrainian opposition bloc pushes for registration of election candi-dates. Vol. 11, No. 149, listserv.

———. 2008a. Kazakhstan Elections. http://www.rferl.org/specials/kazakhelections/parties.asp (accessed January 3, 2008).

———. 2008b. "Results of Previous Elections and Referendums." http://www.rferl.org/specials/kyrgyzelections/pastelections.asp (accessed January 3, 2008).

RFE/RL Caucasus Report. 2003a. Chess, Poker, or Roulette? November 2003, listserv.

———. 2003b. Parliamentary ballot catalyzes shifts in Georgian political landscape. September 2003, listserv.

———. 2003c. Shevardnadze's resignation resolves constitutional deadlock. Novem-ber 2003, listserv.

———. 2003d. Voter-list chaos fuels fears. October 2003, listserv.

Reuters. 2007. Fraud and pressure marred Russia election: Observers. December 18, 2007, http://www.reuters.com/article/worldNews/idUSL188201320071218 (accessed December 19, 2007).

RIA Novosti. 2006. 600 people charged over Belarus election protest. April 5, 2006, Lexis-Nexis.

Rosbalt Information Agency. 2007. Gryzlov: Dekabrskiye vybory prevrashchayutsya v referendum po doveriyu prezidentu. October 16, 2007, http://www.rosbalt.ru/2008/2/18/422935.html (accessed February 27, 2008).

Rossiya. 1995. Political trends in Central Asia analyzed. FBIS-SOV-95-121, June 23, 1995, 1–3.

Saidazimova, Gulnoza. 2005a. Kyrgyz opposition holds protest ahead of first election results. *RFE/RL Central Asia Report*, Vol 5, No. 8, listserv.

———. 2005b. Kyrgyz youth leader speaks out about opposition organization's intentions. *RFE/RL Central Asia Report*, Vol. 5, No. 8, listserv.

———. 2005c. Kyrgyzstan's fragmented opposition ponders next move after election defeat. *RFE/RL Central Asia Report*, Vol. 5, No. 10, listserv.

Solovyov, Dmitry. 2007. Fraud and pressure marred Russian elections: Monitors. *Reuters*, December 18, 2007, http://www.reuters.com/article/worldNews/idUSL188201320071218 (accessed March 6, 2008).

Stern, David L. 2007. Kyrgyzstan parliament dissolved; fraud seen in constitution vote. *New York Times*, October 23, 2007, Lexis-Nexis.

Sultanova, Aida. 2005a. Azerbaijani TV broadcasts former high officials' confessions of funding opposition. *Associated Press*, November 1, 2005, Lexis-Nexis.

———. 2005b. Police clash with opposition protestors in Azerbaijani capital. *Associated Press*, November 26, 2005, Lexis-Nexis.

TASS. 2004. Some 12,184 Foreign observers to monitor Ukrainian [*sic*]. December 21, 2004, Lexis-Nexis.

———. 2007. CIS Observers satisfied with democratic polls in Kazakhstan. August 19, 2007, Lexis-Nexis.

Ukrainian News Agency. 2004. Yushchenko's HQ connects CEC's verification of 30% protocols on 132 constituencies out of 225 with falsification of Ukrainian presidential election. *Action Ukraine Report* Vol. 4, No. 210, listserv.

Vakhonicheva, Olga. 2007. Zloupotrebleniye administrativnym resursom pravyash-chaya partiya postavila vo glavu ugla. *Svobodanews*, November 29, 2007, http://www.svobodanews.ru/Article/2007/11/29/20071129095759020.html (accessed March 6, 2008).

van der Schriek, Dan. 2002. Azerbaijani president determined to press ahead with referendum. http://www.eurasianet.org/departments/insight/articles/eav072402a.shtml (accessed December 14, 2007).

Wall Street Journal. 1994. World Wire: Moldovans favor independence. March 8, 1994, Lexis-Nexis.

Yablokova, Oksana. 2004. Deputy stripped of Duma seat. *Moscow Times*, June 4, 2004, Lexis-Nexis.

Zaks, Dmitry. 1996. Belarus referendum triggers concerns on validity. *Moscow Times*, November 27, 1996, Lexis-Nexis.

Zviglianich, Volodymyr. 2000. The referendum and prospects for democracy in Ukraine. http://www.jamestown.org/publications_details.php?volume_id=7&issue_id=434&article_id=3743 (accessed September 24, 2007).

INDEX